Jacob Tonson, Kit-Cat Publisher

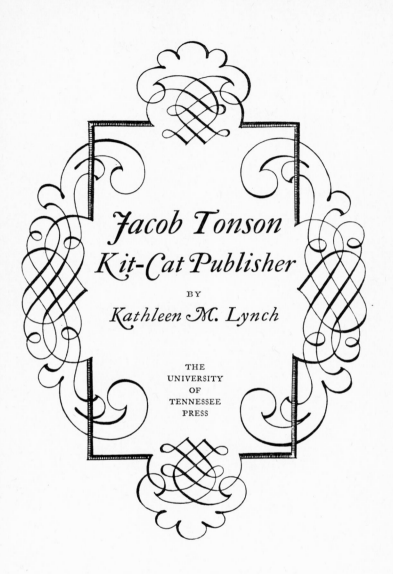

Jacob Tonson
Kit-Cat Publisher

BY

Kathleen M. Lynch

THE
UNIVERSITY
OF
TENNESSEE
PRESS

BOOKS BY
KATHLEEN M. LYNCH

.

The Social Mode of Restoration Comedy (1926)
A Congreve Gallery (1951)
Congreve's *The Way of the World.* Edited by (1965)
Roger Boyle, First Earl of Orrery (1965)
Jacob Tonson, Kit-Cat Publisher (1971)

LIBRARY OF CONGRESS CATALOG CARD NUMBER 77–111046
STANDARD BOOK NUMBER 87049–122–9
Copyright © 1971 by The University of Tennessee Press, Knoxville
Manufactured in the United States of America
First Edition

IN MEMORY OF

John C. Hodges

Preface

In books on the history of publishing, Jacob Tonson has been generally recognized as the greatest of English publishers. Nevertheless, in the centuries since his death, he has had no share of the precise attention which scholarly critics have accorded the famous men for whom he published. Until very recently, he has been permitted to slumber, except in Sarah Lewis Carol Clapp's delightful little book, *Jacob Tonson in Ten Letters by and about Him* (1948) and in a number of unpublished doctoral dissertations. While he has been thus neglected, large quantities of Tonson material have disappeared, and the Tonson manuscripts long preserved by the descendants of Jacob Tonson junior at Bayfordbury have been widely dispersed (1924–1945) or destroyed.

The doctoral dissertations of G. F. Papali, Hale Sturges, and Lawrence Edwards have revealed the possibilities and the difficulties that confront the biographer of Tonson. Papali's *Jacob Tonson, Publisher. His Life and Work, 1656–1736* (1968) is not substantially altered from the author's Ph.D. thesis, accepted by the University of London in 1933. The lists of Tonson's publications compiled by Papali and Sturges present an impressive total. For 1678 to 1720 Papali lists over seven hundred and twenty-five items. Sturges raises the approximate number to seven hundred and fifty. Logan O. Cowgill of Washington, D. C., a Tonson collector, estimates the total number as approximately eight hundred and twenty-five to eight hundred and fifty. A descriptive Tonson bibliography of larger scope would be valuable and would require a full-length volume.

The most recent publication on Tonson is Harry M. Geduld's *Prince of Publishers. A Study of the Work and Career of Jacob Tonson* (1969), which provides a detailed and useful account of publishing conditions in England from the Restoration onward and Tonson's adaptation to them. Placing his emphasis almost exclusively on Tonson as a publisher, Geduld comments that "the first full-length biography" of Tonson "has yet to be written." In the present volume, which was already in manuscript when *Prince of Publishers* appeared, I have undertaken a biographical review, as fully documented as possible, of Tonson's many-faceted career.

In the preparation of this book I have been assisted by a grant from the American Philosophical Society and a fellowship from the Folger Shakespeare Library. For kind and varied services I am indebted to many persons, including the staffs of the British Museum, the Bodleian Library, and the Folger Shakespeare Library. I wish especially to thank Mr. Richard Ormond, Assistant Keeper of the National Portrait Gallery in London, for arranging for my use of the Tonson MSS deposited there. The chart of the Tonson Pedigree was prepared from my notes by Miss Priscilla Randolph of the Folger Shakespeare Library.

Kathleen M. Lynch

Funchal, Madeira

Contents

List of Plates

Jacob Tonson, Kit-Cat Publisher

Heritage

y the compelling force of his character Jacob Tonson overcame what might have been serious handicaps. Although a "prince of publishers," he was unattractive in appearance, unrefined in manners. He was heavy-jowled, corpulent, slovenly, "left-legged" and awkward in gait, loud-voiced and blustering. He would flatter no one. Yet he was accepted on his own hearty terms by the members of the exclusive Kit-Cat Club, the most famous of all literary clubs, which he founded and presided over. The noblemen and gentlemen of the club, many of whom regarded literary pursuits as a diverting pastime, found Tonson a comical dog, delightful in his cups and capable of matching wits with the wittiest. They not only loved Jacob; they respected him. A self-educated man, Tonson was a mine of general knowledge, a lively walking dictionary, a court of appeal in matters of literary taste. He was separated from his convivial aristocratic friends by his tireless, enlightened industry, befitting a tradesman, which enabled him to become England's first professional publisher.

Of the many Jacobs in the history of his family, Jacob Tonson the Elder, as he is usually called, was the most distinguished. The names Jacob and Richard were perennial favorites with the Tonsons and appear in successive generations with consistent and symmetrical regularity. In the case of Jacob Tonson, the good Old Testament name of Jacob lent itself to such a satirical variation as "Bocai" or the affectionate one of "Cob." More significantly, "Printed for Jacob Tonson" on the title page of a book could be regarded as a guarantee of the value of the contents.

The pedigree of the Tonsons cannot be traced farther back than Richard Tonson, grandfather of Jacob the Elder. From the parish registers of St. Andrew, Holborn, in London, which was his parish church, we learn that "Richard Tonnson Shoemaker died in his house agt. Middle Roe" on November 19, 1643, and was buried three days later.[1] Middle Row was a block of houses in High Holborn, then a suburb of London, extending northwest out of the Old Bailey at Fleet Lane to Snow Hill in Farringdon Ward. Perhaps the most conspicuous building on Middle Row was the Quest House, which in 1590, and probably later, had a bootmaker's shop at the eastern end. In the Quest Room, with the sheriff of Middlesex presiding, inquests were held for some years into disorders which occurred in the county.[2]

Jacob's grandfather made his will on October 9, 1641, two years before his death. The brief document provides the few details from which a limited appraisal of his life and character may be attempted. Although he was probably still in early middle age, Richard Tonson was able to make comfortable provision for his family. His bequests reflect his interest in his nephews and nieces. To his nephew, Nicholas Soame, he left twenty pounds, and to his niece Margaret, sister of Nicholas, ten pounds; and if they should die, these legacies were to be divided equally among the children of his brother John. The legacies were to be paid out of money owing to Tonson from Sir Eastwill Brome, agent of Charles I. Tonson's "loving wife Margrett" was to have "one full moitie" of his estate for her own use, the other half to be divided equally between their two sons, Jacob and Richard. Margaret was to be sole executrix, with Tonson's brother John and his brother-in-law, Christopher Nicholson, assisting as supervisors of the estate. If his children should die, their legacies should go to the children of John Tonson.[3] Richard Tonson's death occurred in a period of political crisis, and his will was not proved until after Margaret Tonson's death, twelve years later. On December 12, 1655, letters of administration were issued to her "sorrowful Sonne," Jacob Tonson,[4] father of Jacob the Elder.

At the death of Richard Tonson, his eldest son Jacob was twenty-three years of age. He had been baptized at St. Andrew, Holborn, in November, 1620. His brother Richard was baptized in December of the following year.[5] On the completion of his apprenticeship to John Johnson on December 18, 1646, Jacob was admitted a freeman of the Barber Surgeons' Company.[6]

As the son of a tradesman it had been necessary for him to join a Livery Company in order to become a freeman of the City, that is, a member of the Corporation of the City of London, with all the rights and privileges involved. Only by becoming a freeman could one exercise a trade and vote both for members of Parliament for the City and for the Council of Aldermen and Councilmen which governed the Corporation. One became a "freeman by apprenticeship" by being bound to a freeman and serving him as an apprentice for not less than seven years. The fact that Jacob Tonson became a freeman of the Barber Surgeons' Company did not restrict his choice of a trade,[7] and he chose his father's.

By 1650 Jacob had married Elizabeth Walbancke, eleven years his junior, daughter of Matthew Walbancke, stationer, and his wife Elizabeth, of "Baldwin's Garden in Gray's Inn Lane."[8] As near neighbors the Tonson and Walbancke families may have been long acquainted.

Although Jacob the Elder never knew his paternal grandfather, Richard Tonson, in early childhood he must have been impressed by the vigorous personality of his mother's father. Matthew Walbancke (c.1595–c.1661) was a native of Egginton, Derbyshire, son of John Walbancke, yeoman.[9] After completing an apprenticeship to Robert Wilson, a Holborn bookseller, also a native of Egginton, Walbancke conducted a successful bookselling and publishing business for over forty years. His shops at both gates of Gray's Inn were conveniently located to meet the needs of Gray's Inn barristers. But although he specialized in law books, his interests were varied.

From a literary point of view, perhaps Walbancke's most attractive publication was *Annalia Dubrensia, Upon the yeerly celebration of Mr. Robert Dovers Olimpick Games upon Cotswold-Hills*, published in 1636. Robert Dover's grandson, a London barrister, had interested Walbancke in this memorial volume, celebrating the rustic games which for forty years Dover had directed and managed, to the delight of the neighboring gentry, on Cotswold Hills in Gloucestershire. A frontispiece depicted the games, and Michael Drayton, Ben Jonson, Thomas Heywood, and other less distinguished poets, thirty-two in all, contributed complimentary verses. As his grandson Jacob was to do on occasion later on, Walbancke supplied a prefatory note, which he addressed to his "worthy friend," Dover's grandson. "If amongst so many noble Poetts," he wrote somewhat grandiloquently, "I presume to play the Orator, blame me not, the incitements prompting mee thereto, in any competent and indifferent judgments being excusable."[10]

A few years later, Walbancke tried his hand at journalism, adding one more weekly newsbook to nearly a score which flourished between 1643 and 1646 and which represented royalist and parliamentary interests when the Civil War was at its height. Walbancke's newsbook appeared as *A Diary, or an Exact Journal Faithfully communicating the most remarkable proceedings in both Houses of Parliament.* Enough numbers have survived to illustrate Walbancke's emphatic sympathies with the parliamentary forces, to which "we owe not only our safety but subsistence," his spirited reporting of events, and his healthy quarrel with the editor of the rival royalist paper, *Mercurius Aulicus,* who had vomited lies upon the *Diary,* but "It is beneath my nature and complexion to be scurrilous."[11]

On March 18, 1667, after Matthew Walbancke's death, Elizabeth Walbancke, his widow, assigned the shop and rooms under the old gatehouse near Gray's Inn Lane and the shop and rooms under the new gatehouse which were her late husband's,[12] granted to her "last" February 5, to Jacob Tonson, her son-in-law, citizen and barber surgeon of London, and her daughter Elizabeth.[13] Eventually the bookshop at the gatehouse near Gray's Inn Lane, with which they must have been familiar in childhood, was to serve Walbancke's grandsons for the same purpose.

A lawsuit throws some light on family affairs of the Tonsons and indicates that Matthew Walbancke's son-in-law Jacob was a shrewd man of business. A family relationship did not deter him from acquiring the property of his aunt, who in her ignorance had signed over to him her legal right to it. John Tonson, a shoemaker like his younger brother Richard, left his property in the parish of St. Botolph without Aldgate, where he lived,[14] to his wife, Anne Griffin Tonson. In 1656, after John Tonson's death, his widow signed an agreement, drawn up by Matthew Walbancke, with Jacob Tonson her nephew, giving her nephew, in return for the payment of her debts, control of her properties, with the stipulation that they should remain in the name of the Tonsons. Two years later, Jacob Tonson paid what Anne Tonson's son Richard still owed for his mother's living expenses, Richard having renounced any claim to the properties which had been his father's. In February, 1666, however, this "ancient widow," who, as Tonson noted, was "seventy years of age or thereabout," contemplated marriage with Geoffrey Trotter, a shipwright, whom she had led to believe, for she was "an illiterate woman, not understanding such matters," that by paying her debts he could enjoy her property for his life. Jacob Tonson nipped the budding romance and won the lawsuit of *Tonson vs. Tonson*.[15]

A successful tradesman and a man of property, Jacob Tonson could provide well for a young family of five children. The fourth child and second son of Jacob and Elizabeth Tonson was Jacob the Elder, who was baptized at St. Andrew, Holborn, on November 12, 1655. The boy's eldest sister Elizabeth was then a child of four, his brother Richard was two, and his sister Rose was a year old. Tabitha, the youngest child, was born ten years later. In St. Andrew's register of baptisms, the address of the Tonsons, at the date of Tabitha's birth, is given precisely as "in Holborn, above Gray's Inn Lane End."[16] Of the lives of Jacob the Elder's three sisters very little is known.[17] His brother Richard was to become a reputable bookseller and publisher, and Jacob himself was to become the most famous of the Tonsons.

As a shoemaker or cordwainer[18] Jacob's father made boots and shoes of imported calf hide, as well as other leather goods. He lived over his shop with his wife, family, apprentices, and servants. The Civil War brought cordwainers large orders for boots for the army in Ireland, and the Dutch War brought similar orders for shoes for the navy. All of the Livery Companies were heavily taxed to support the parliamentary forces, and the taxes levied on them frequently forced them to borrow money to pay interest on the debts which they incurred. In the winter of 1648–1649 a thousand parliamentary soldiers under Colonel John Hewson, a former cordwainer, were quartered on the City, and the halls of the Livery Companies were used as barracks. In 1657 Hewson was banqueted at Cordwainers' Hall, the feast consisting of "a Lomber Pye, Lobsters, Choyne of Salmon, and Wine Extraordinary."[19]

Immersed though he undoubtedly was in the conduct of his business in difficult times, Jacob the Elder's father considered the education of his sons a matter of major importance. Perhaps it was hoped that the two boys might succeed Matthew Walbancke in his well-established publishing business. As a first step toward such a future, young Jacob may have been sent at about the age of five to a "petty-school" to learn reading, writing, and arithmetic. Two of his great-nephews were to attend Eton College, but the educational opportunities of Jacob the Elder were more modest. At about seven, he probably became a pupil at a good grammar school or a small boarding school. There he would have had strict discipline in the study of Latin, classical literature, and grammar until apprenticeship put an end to his formal education.

It is at least a tempting conjecture that Jacob might have been a private pupil at Charterhouse School. Many years later, in a letter to his nephew, he commended the practice which used to be followed at the Charterhouse of having a boy in the upper end of the school assist a young pupil in his studies.[20] Nor is it beyond the realm of possibility that young Jacob might have spent some months as a boarder at the school which Edward Cocker conducted near St. Paul's in 1664. Cocker collected a large library of rare manuscripts and printed books on science in various languages. Pepys, who knew him, described this gifted schoolmaster as "a great admirer and well read in all our English poets and undertakes to judge of them all, and that not impertinently."[21]

The even tenor of Jacob's school days was disrupted by two national crises, London's Great Plague of 1665 and Great Fire of 1666. An impressionable boy of nine, with a tenacious memory, Jacob would have been acutely sensitive to the grim terrors of the Plague Year, which brought the apprehension or reality of death to every Londoner's home. The fatal disease had already invaded his own parish when Jacob's youngest sister Tabitha was baptized at St. Andrew, Holborn, on April 2, 1665. Beginning in the western suburbs of London, for some months the Plague was peculiarly severe in the parishes of St. Giles-in-the-Fields, St. Andrew, Holborn, and adjacent parishes. In a single week in July one hundred houses were shut up in the parish of St. Andrew, Holborn, alone. Trading was at a standstill, and not one merchant in a hundred remained in the city.

But if Jacob's father was still a constable of High Holborn, as he had been in 1664,[22] he would have been obliged to stay in London to perform the dangerous duties of entering and shutting up infected houses and placing watchmen at their doors. Young Jacob undoubtedly listened to his father's accounts of the plight of neighbors. He would have walked at times in the middle of deserted streets, heard the cries of distress from casements suddenly flung wide, and been impressed by the melancholy aspect of long rows of empty

6

houses, their open windows "shattering with the wind."[23] At night the peremptory call of the bellman, "Bring out your dead," would be heard as the dead-cart passed by to pick up corpses for burial.

The weekly Bills of Mortality, which the boy's elders scrutinized with consternation, recorded from the appalling scourge an incomplete death toll of 97,306. When the Plague finally abated in October, shopkeepers and merchants were the first to venture back to London. There is no evidence that the Tonson family had ever left the city.

In September the following year London suffered a second crippling calamity in the Great Fire, when in four days and nights an area of the city a mile and a half long and half a mile wide was completely destroyed—five-sixths of London within the walls. Only a few (St. Andrew, Holborn, was one) of the numerous churches which had made London a city of bell towers and spires survived. Forty-four Companies' Halls were burned. The medieval walls of the Guildhall withstood the flames, and its documents, including 4,000 citizens' wills, were preserved in the vaults.[24] No such miracle spared the great stores of stationers' books which had been placed hurriedly for safety in the crypt of St. Faith's, beneath the choir of St. Paul's. When the flaming roof of the cathedral broke through the sealed vault where the books were stored, "they were all consumed, burning for a week following."[25] The stationers suffered losses from the Fire estimated at £200,000. Although Holborn escaped this second disaster, tradesmen in that part of the city must have found it difficult to obtain needed supplies and carry on business as usual.

Perhaps exhausted by the overwhelming events which had occurred during his mature years, young Jacob's father died in early middle age. His will, which he made on July 10, 1668, is an interesting document. He left his property to his wife Elizabeth, unless she should remarry, in which case it was to be divided equally among his five children, or the survivors among them. He directed his wife to invest "to the best advantage" within six months of his decease £500 and to pay £100, with the interest, to each of his children at the age of twenty-one, or, in the case of his daughters, when they married. His wife was to apprentice his sons to the trades of their choice, to provide for them, "and send them to school as she thinks fit," and to bring up his daughters "according to her discretion." He made his wife sole executrix, "not doubting of her performance hereof according to my trust in her resolves." His brother Richard and William Jolly were to be supervisors of his will and assist his wife in managing her affairs.[26] A few months after making his will, Jacob Tonson died. He was buried on October 16 in the church of St. Andrew, Holborn.[27]

The reference to his brother Richard in Jacob Tonson's will raises a vexatious question regarding the apparent disappearance of Jacob the Elder's uncle from the Tonson family circle in Holborn. Uncle Richard appears to have been the Richard Tonson who served as one of the officers, a captain in 1653, a major in 1656,[28] in Colonel Richard Lawrence's regiment in Ireland during the Civil War, and who received a grant of land in county Cork from Charles II for services in Ireland shortly before the Restoration. Major Richard Tonson died at Spanish Island, county Cork, in 1693.[29] Years later, Jacob Tonson junior, nephew of Jacob the Elder, was corresponding[30] with his cousin in Ireland, Richard Tonson of Spanish Island and Dunkettle, who was Major Richard's grandson. This Richard Tonson was a member of the Irish House of Commons and a man of great wealth. After Richard's death, his cousin (?), Colonel William Hull, took the name of Tonson and was created Baron Riversdale of Rathcormac, county Cork.[31] It is evident that the English Tonsons valued their connection with their prominent Anglo-Irish relatives.

Left at her husband's death with five young children to care for, and with her husband's only brother inconveniently distant in Ireland, Elizabeth Tonson must have welcomed the apprenticeship of her eldest son Richard to his grandmother. Elizabeth Walbancke was now conducting, apparently on a reduced scale, the publishing business of her deceased husband. It was not unusual for a bookseller's widow to carry on his trade, at least temporarily.

Mrs. Walbancke shared certain copyrights with Samuel Heyrick. By 1663 Heyrick was located in Matthew Walbancke's old bookshop under the Holborn gateway of Gray's Inn. In that year, as indicated on its title page, a fourth edition of Nicholas Collyn's *A Brief Summary of the Laws and Statutes of England* was "Printed by T. M. for Elizabeth Walbancke at Grayes-Inn-Gate in Grayes-Inn-Lane, and Samuel Heyrick at Grayes-Inn-Gate in Holborne." Although Elizabeth Walbancke sold all or parts of copyrights of some of her husband's books,[32] she published a number under her own name. In 1674 she reprinted, as "enlarged with useful Additions,"[33] a law book evidently much in demand, John March's *Actions for Slander*, first published by her husband in 1647. Richard Tonson began his apprenticeship to "Elizabeth Walbanck Widdowe" on April 7, 1668,[34] and was admitted a freeman of the Stationers' Company on September 4, 1676.[35] His grandmother probably retired at about the date when he ended his apprenticeship.

Elizabeth Tonson's younger son Jacob soon followed in the footsteps of his brother and became a bookseller's apprentice. On June 6, 1670, a few months before his fifteenth birthday, Jacob was apprenticed to Thomas Basset, a well-known publisher at the George, near St. Dunstan's Church in Fleet Street.[36] Jacob became a member of his master's household, sharing the life of the family with two or three other apprentices. His master provided lodging, board, and clothing. The eight years of his apprenticeship were formative years in Jacob's life, for during them he was receiving the best possible training for his future career. He had numerous opportunities to increase his knowledge of books and widen his circle of acquaintances among booksellers and publishers.

The life of a young apprentice was strenuous but could be exhilarating. At six o'clock in the morning Jacob would have opened the shutters of his master's shop. He was required to clean the shop, wait on customers, collect books from other booksellers and from printers, deliver books to customers and call on them for the settlement of accounts, and pack books for the country trade. He may have had some practice in bookbinding.[37] His only free days were Sundays and holidays. The bookshop was a sociable place. By paying a small subscription, one might read there the most recent publication; and if one did not finish at a single sitting, one might leave a marker to keep the place and return another day. Some booksellers permitted their apprentices to be seen absorbed in reading a book, so that a customer might be tempted to inquire about it.[38] Whether or not Thomas Basset favored this kind of indulgence, there can be no doubt that in one way or another Jacob Tonson managed to read many of the books in his master's shop. This being the case, it is of considerable interest to note what books Thomas Basset was publishing while Jacob was his apprentice.

We can only surmise what books published by Basset were most useful to Jacob Tonson in the program of self-education on which he most certainly embarked. He might have tested the validity of the assurance that Edward Cocker's *The Compleat Writing Master* (1670) offered "such plain and easie Directions for young learners, that they may in a short time (without the help of a teacher) fit themselves for any Trade or Imployment whatsoever." Jacob's interest in history, which was to continue throughout his life, may have been stimulated by Peter Heylyn's *A Help to English History*, "with the Coats of Arms of the Nobility blazoned" (1671), published by Thomas Basset and Christopher Wilkinson. Just before and early in Jacob's apprenticeship, Basset published several other works by this eminent historian and theologian.

Without the substantial knowledge of Latin and French which he had acquired, Jacob Tonson would have been on less easy terms with the distinguished scholars who were to become his friends. Basset, and some of the publishers who shared copyrights with him, specialized in English-Latin and English-French dictionaries, which came out regularly during Jacob's apprenticeship. The most ambitious of these was the English-Latin *A Copious Dictionary* (third edition, 1673), edited by Francis Gouldman and printed by six publishers, including Basset. Jacob also would have had access to Latin texts of Ovid and Virgil reprinted by Basset and other publishers. It is probable that he was personally acquainted with John Davies, a writer for whom Basset frequently published. Davies had spent several years in France and returned to England to become "the most active translator from the French in his age."[39]

A work by John Davies that must have attracted Jacob Tonson's attention was *Epictetus Junior* (1670), a translation, with some additions, of La Rochefoucauld's *Maximes*. "Maxims of modern morality" would have been very much to the taste of such an enterprising young man as Jacob Tonson. He was no doubt prepared to stake his whole future on the conviction: "to hearken attentively, and to answer pertinently, is one of the greatest perfections a man can be Master of."[40] And he would readily have agreed: "Nothing is impossible; there are certain ways conducing to the accomplishment of all things, and if we had Will enough, we should never be destitute of the means."[41] Since Jacob was interested in book illustration, the "sculptures" of another book by John Davies, *The History of Barbados . . . and the rest of the Caribby Islands* (second edition, 1669), would have particularly appealed to him. Tropical trees, plants, beasts, reptiles, birds, and fish are all elaborately illustrated in this curious work, which includes "A Caribbian Vocabulary" extensive enough for the more modest needs of a visitor.

The acquiring of copyrights of important works and reprinting them was one of the functions of an industrious publisher. Jacob Tonson, who was to profit by judicious efforts of this sort in his own publishing career, may well have been impressed by his master's success in such ventures. One notable achievement was John Ogilby's *The Fables of Aesop, Paraphrased in Verse, adorned with 160 copper Sculptures, and illustrated with Annotations* (third edition in two volumes, 1674). Robert Clavell and Richard Chiswell shared the copyright with Thomas Basset. In 1675 Basset and Chiswell undertook a formidable task, which justified a lengthy advertisement "to all Noblemen, Gentlemen, and Others" to the effect that the publishers had purchased the copyright of John Speed's "laborious and most exact Geography of the Kingdoms of *England, Scotland,* and *Ireland,*" which had been seven years out of print, "the greatest part of an Impression, then newly Printed, being destroyed by the late dreadful Fire, 1666." They were reprinting this work, "with a fair Character upon Royal Paper, with divers Amendments and Additional Illustrations," and hoped to publish the volume by next Midsummer Term.[42] Two years later, the book appeared as *Theatre of the Empire of Great Britain,* with engraved maps for each description, "the whole Impression . . . done upon Royal Paper and some of them upon Dutch Royal, for such as are curious."[43]

Some of the editions of other publishers would also have attracted the attention of Basset's eager young apprentice. The eight years of Jacob's apprenticeship were fruitful years in the publishing trade. During that period Henry Herringman published eight plays by Dryden, two by Wycherley, Etherege's *The Man of Mode,* and the works of Cowley, D'Avenant, and Suckling. There were two editions in English of Juvenal, one of Horace, and one of Caesar. George Sawbridge reprinted Baker's *A Chronicle of the Kings of England* (1670, 1674). William Cademan published Settle's *The Empress of Morocco With Sculptures. The Like never done before*

(1673). John Starkey published Milton's *Paradise Regained* and *Samson Agonistes* (1674). Wycherley's third and fourth plays and five plays by Aphra Behn were printed by other publishers.[44]

Since Thomas Basset published at times with twenty or more others, with whom he shared copyrights, Jacob Tonson probably had a fairly wide acquaintance among these men. Outstanding among them were George Sawbridge, Richard Chiswell, and Robert Clavell. John Dunton remarked of Chiswell: "His Name at the bottom of a Title-Page does sufficiently recommend the Book. He has not been known to print either a bad Book, or a bad Paper. He is admirably qualified for his business, and knows how to value a Copy according to its worth."[45] Chiswell was to participate in the fourth folio edition of Shakespeare's *Works* (1685). Robert Clavell, in partnership with John Starkey, founded the periodical bibliography, *Mercurius Librarius* (1668), which was to be succeeded by the *Term Catalogues*. George Sawbridge was the most distinguished publisher of the three. He was treasurer of the Stationers' Company for many years, master of the company in 1675, and sheriff of London, and amassed a fortune. He was highly respected by Jacob Tonson, who paid him the sort of homage which Tonson was ever ready to accord to eminent men.

While he was still an apprentice, Jacob learned from George Sawbridge how a publisher should react to just criticism, and he never forgot the lesson. In his old age Tonson reminisced on the subject in a letter to his nephew. Sawbridge negotiated with Thomas Blount for a new and enlarged edition of Baker's *Chronicle*,[46] which was a history in vogue; but to save money he decided to employ another editor (Edward Phillips). Blount, "nettled," published a small octavo showing "several palpable errours" in this edition. "Sawbridge like a wise man (and he was one) took noe notice of Blount's book but to have the matter carefully examined & corrected his next Edition by Blount."[47] Blount had attacked the "continuator" as a person "of incompetent parts for so great an undertaking" and had accused the printer of "supine negligence" and "a grosse number of Errata's."[48] In the course of his publishing career, there must have been various occasions when Jacob Tonson curbed his resentment and discreetly followed Sawbridge's example.

Although during his apprenticeship Jacob undoubtedly had many good friends among his contemporaries, we know definitely of only one of them. This friend was William D'Avenant, slightly younger than Jacob, the second surviving son of Sir William D'Avenant, the dramatist, by his third wife. A few details of this friendship emerge from an undated letter Tonson wrote to his nephew many years later, in which he vividly recalled a certain Sunday afternoon excursion when he was a young apprentice:

> I was very intimately acquainted when young with one Mr William Davenant 2d Son to Sr William ye Poet, this Gentleman was after of Magdalen Hal in Oxford & published a Book printed there being a translation relating to old Authors in 8°. He was after unfortunately drowned in france as he was Swimming. This Mr Davenant told me that Mr Milton helped him in his study of ye lattin & Greeke Authors, to whom he used to goe in order to his Learning—That when his father was in the tower he was very much assisted by Mr Milton in his gaining his Liberty, & if I am not very much mistaken he at the same time told me his father in return upon ye restoration was very helpfull to Milton, & Milton was very acknowledging for it & uppon that score offered his willingness in doing any thing that shoud be gratefull to Sr William—It was a little after Miltons death he told me this, I had a mind to have seen Miltons Books & Mr Davenant went with me in order to it; I was then in my prentiship & coud not goe except on a Holyday or Sunday, soe ye next Sunday we went. Mr Milton was some time before then removed from Jewin Street to Moorfields near ye Artillery ground & it being in ye afternoon about Sermon time, there was noe body at home, & soe we returned home. I have often since when at Moorfields cast a look towards that street, & the houses were then thought Such as any substantial trader or merchant might dwel in.[49]

Tonson attempted to call on Milton probably in 1673, toward the end of Milton's life, when Milton "contracted his Library"[50] and was selling a portion of it. Jacob failed in his immediate objective, the acquisition of something of Milton's; but his tenacity of purpose, one of his dominant traits, served him well. The prize he was to seek and which he was subsequently to gain, the copyright of *Paradise Lost*, was to lay the foundation of his wealth.

Before his very early death in 1681, William D'Avenant had published a translation, adding "something of my own," of a French text, *Notitia Historicorum Selectorum; or Animadversions upon the Antient and famous Greek and Latin Historians* (1678). If we may judge by the preface to this work, Jacob's friend was a learned and perceptive young man. "If it be true, as *Clemens Alexandrinus* asserts," D'Avenant reflected earnestly, "that our Souls are of the nature of Wells, from whence we must alwaies draw something, to make their waters more wholesome and pure: I do not repent of a trouble which has been so profitable to me, and which at least has kept my better part from corruption for want of exercise."[51]

Jacob was admitted to the freedom of the Stationers' Company on January 7, 1678,[52] and at once began publishing at the Judge's Head in Chancery Lane. His father's legacy of £100, with the addition of ten years' interest, afforded only a limited capital with which to set up a business. However, Jacob was familiar with the essentials of his trade; he had connections among booksellers; and he was not lacking in confidence. Moreover, he could count on the support of his brother Richard.

Richard Tonson was already a successful publisher at Gray's Inn Gate in Gray's Inn Lane, in the shop that had been Matthew Walbancke's. It seemed desirable at the outset to both Tonsons to publish plays as a means of extending their contacts with dramatists and with patrons of the theater, and this proved to be a fortunate procedure. Richard Tonson's first important publications were in the field of dramatic literature.

In 1676–1679 Richard published ten plays, two of them with his brother.[53] Young Thomas Otway, later to achieve fame with *The Orphan* (1680) and *Venice Preserved* (1682), was the author of four of these plays: *Don Carlos* (1676), adapted from a French romance; *Titus and Berenice* (1677), adapted from Racine; *The Cheats of Scapin* (1677), adapted from Molière; and *Friendship in Fashion* (1678), an original comedy. Two of the plays were very well liked. *Don Carlos*, admirably acted, "got more money than any preceding modern Tragedy"[54] and was reprinted by Richard Tonson in 1678; and *The Cheats of Scapin* held the stage for many years. Otway was a youthful protégé of Aphra Behn, who may have introduced him to Richard Tonson. Richard also printed Sir Charles Sedley's mediocre tragedy *Antony and Cleopatra* (1677) and the songs in Charles D'Avenant's *Circe*, shortly followed by the play itself (1677). *Circe*, which its author had written at the age of nineteen, although a poor play, had three editions. Charles

D'Avenant was the older brother of William D'Avenant and was probably a friend of both Tonsons. Other early ventures by Richard in dramatic publications were *The Siege of Babylon* (1678), by Samuel Pordage, and *Edgar, The English Monarch* (1678), by Thomas Rymer.

Thomas Rymer, a young barrister of Gray's Inn, was more interested in literature than in the law. Richard Tonson published a learned but pedantic treatise by Rymer, in which Rymer advocated strictly classical standards of dramatic criticism, *The Tragedies of the Last Age consider'd and examin'd by the Practice of the Ancients, and by the Common Sense of All Ages* (1678). Rymer sent Dryden a copy of this work, on the blank leaves of which Dryden wrote detailed observations, with the conclusion: "My judgment on this piece is this; that it is extremely learned; but that the author of it is better read in the Greek than in the English poets."[55] *Edgar, The English Monarch*, written to illustrate Rymer's theories, proved to be too frigid a piece for the stage and was never acted. After 1679 Richard Tonson restricted his publications almost entirely to law books, leaving the field of polite literature to his brother.

Jacob Tonson found it expedient to publish at first with other publishers.[56] He shared the copyright of a longwinded romance in three volumes with James Magnes and Richard Bentley of the Post House in Russell Street, Covent Garden, who specialized in romances and plays. This work was *The Heroine Musqueteer, or The Female Warrior* (1678), a translation of a French romance, followed in the same year by *The Second Part of the Heroine Musqueteer* and *The Third and Fourth Parts of the Heroine Musqueteer*.

Jacob made better choices in sharing with his brother Richard the copyrights of two plays by Aphra Behn, *Sir Patient Fancy* (1678) and *The Feign'd Courtezans* (1679). The former play, one of Mrs. Behn's best, was based chiefly on Molière's *Le Malade Imaginaire*. Aphra Behn was the prolific and usually impoverished author of witty and lubricious plays, which were popular on the stage and which sold well. Jacob Tonson was to continue to publish for her and was to write a complimentary poem in her honor. The women of his own family had been heads of households, and Jacob respected Mrs. Behn's valiant struggle to support herself by her pen.

Also, like her many other admirers, he appreciated her charm. He would not have thought worse of her for her bold and spirited defense of female writers in the Epilogue to *Sir Patient Fancy*.

Jacob published alone *Brutus of Alba, or The Enchanted Lovers* (1678), a tragedy by Nahum Tate, and *The Counterfeits* (1679), a comedy attributed to John Leanerd, based on a romance, *The Trepanner Trepann'd*, which John Davies, author of *Epictetus Junior*, had translated from a Spanish source. Tate's play was dedicated to his kind patron, Lord Dorset, who perhaps recommended him to Jacob Tonson. We may assume that by this date, if not earlier, Dorset and Tonson had become congenial friends.

The year 1679 marked the beginning of Jacob's career as Dryden's publisher. In this year Tonson published with Abel Swalle of the Unicorn in St. Paul's Churchyard *Troilus and Cressida*, Dryden's "corrected" version of Shakespeare's play. On the understanding that he would share in the profits, Swalle is said to have advanced the purchase money, £20, for the copyright of *Troilus and Cressida*.[57] No doubt it was much to Jacob's satisfaction that after this date he was under no financial obligation to share the copyrights of Dryden's plays with any other publisher.

It is not known when Jacob Tonson first met Dryden. The great man held a kind of literary court in two places, at the shop of his publisher, Henry Herringman, at the Blue Anchor in the Lower Walk of the New Exchange, and at Will's Coffee-House. Did Jacob, like young Francis Lockier, afterward Dean of Peterborough, "thrust" himself into the exhilarating company at Will's, where Dryden so courteously received younger men?[58] Tonson must have admired Herringman's exclusive control of Dryden's literary work. Accustomed to making hopeful plans long before their chance of fruition, Jacob may have resolved, even in his apprenticeship, that he would publish for Dryden at the earliest opportunity. It was a stroke of singular good fortune for a young man of twenty-four to attain such a goal. The association with Dryden was to be a long one and was the bedrock of Tonson's publishing career.

Dryden and Tonson

or twenty years, until Dryden's death, Jacob Tonson was to remain the poet's publisher. Those who have made much of their quarrels might instead have reflected on the mutual respect and loyalty which preserved for so long a period the friendship of two such positive men. They held radically different views on issues of major importance to them both, yet their relationship, if at times acrimonious, was strong enough to endure divergences of aims and opinions on which many less solid alliances have foundered.

The publication of *Troilus and Cressida* opened the way for a method of collaboration between Dryden and Tonson which, although useful to Dryden, was especially so to the young publisher. It was Dryden who introduced Tonson to various "eminent hands" and to others who aspired to eminence, for whom, as for Dryden, Tonson was to publish during the ensuing years. At Will's Coffee-House Dryden met regularly men of wit and learning who were his admirers. Moreover, as Johnson was to remark, "His reputation . . . was such that his name was thought necessary to the success of every poetical or literary performance, and therefore he was engaged to contribute something, whatever it might be, to many publications."[1]

Dryden initiated his significant service to his new publisher with *Ovid's Epistles, Translated by Several Hands*, which Tonson published in 1680. The twenty-three epistles were translated by eighteen authors, including Dryden, Nahum Tate, Aphra Behn, Thomas Rymer, Elkanah Settle, and Thomas Otway. The anonymous versions of two epistles, Epistle 5, "Ariadne to Theseus," and Epistle 19, "Dido to Aeneas," a second translation of the text "by another hand," have been attributed to John Somers, with whom Tonson must have been acquainted by this date. Dryden contributed Epistle 2, "Canace to Macareus," and Epistle 18, "Dido to Aeneas," and with John Sheffield, Earl of Mulgrave, Epistle 13, "Helen to Paris."

Dryden wrote the preface to this volume, in which, with his usual critical acumen, he appraised the genius of Ovid, especially the "prodigality" of his wit, and expressed the opinion that Ovid's *Epistles* are "his most perfect piece." The translations, commented Dryden, represented in general a mean between a literal translation and imitation, a version in which the dress of the author might be varied but the substance was preserved. He explained that one of the contributors (Mrs. Behn) "who is of the Fair Sex, understood not Latine. But if she does not, I am afraid she has given us occasion to be asham'd who do." And he paid his customary generous tribute to the "Excellencies" of his fellow translators which would make "ample Satisfaction for my Errours."[2]

The *Epistles* proved to be so popular that Tonson published four more editions during Dryden's lifetime and three after his death.[3] The 1681 edition included another version of "Oenone to Paris" by John Cooper, in compensation for Mrs. Behn's want of Latin, although her own version was retained.

Following the appearance of the first edition, another publisher, obviously trying to capitalize on its success, printed in the same year *The Wits Paraphras'd*, a burlesque of the *Epistles*. Tonson immediately responded with Alexander Radcliffe's *Ovid Travestie*, in which the paraphraser is advised to follow an employment "more agreeable with his Genius (if he have any) than that of Poetry."[4]

In 1681 Jacob Tonson published with his brother Richard *The Spanish Fryar*, Dryden's most successful play. Excellently acted, *The Spanish Fryar* brought "vast Profit"[5] to the Duke's Theatre. As a Protestant play, satirizing the lustful and greedy Friar Dominic, it had great popular appeal because of the current alarm over the alleged Popish Plot. A few years later, when James II was on the throne, he prohibited the acting of this play until after certain offensive passages had been removed in the second edition of 1686. Dryden himself at that date entertained very different religious sentiments from those he had previously expressed.

Immediate success greeted another 1681 publication, a fine folio edition of Dryden's satiric poem, *Absalom and Achitophel*, which had been written at the request of Charles II. Tonson published this volume alone. Narcissus Luttrell marked his copy as a gift from his friend Jacob Tonson, received on November 17, "An excellent poem agt ye Duke of Monmouth, Earl of Shaftesbury & that party & in vindication of the King and his friends."[6] The Earl of Shaftesbury, arrested for treason, had been committed in July to the Tower, where he remained for over four months; and the poem appeared anonymously about November 9, a few days before the Earl was brought before a grand jury and tried but acquitted. If the poem failed to prejudice the trial, its timeliness nevertheless procured it a most extraordinary sale. The first edition was sold in about a month, and six more editions were published in 1681 and the following year. Dr. Johnson said that his father, a bookseller, told him that the sale of the poem was so large that "he had not known it equalled but by Sacheverell's trial."[7] Tonson must have rejoiced in his profits, although his sympathy may have been limited for a king who did not respect his parliaments.

Dryden was confident enough of his powers as a satirist to believe that his poem could "force its own reception," even with the King's enemies. "For there's a sweetness in good Verse, which Tickles even while it Hurts: And no man can be heartily angry with him, who pleases him against his will." Dryden had the additional problem of not offending the sensibilities of the King. Since the conflict between the King (David) and his son Monmouth (Absalom), artfully instigated by Shaftesbury (Achitophel), had not been resolved, Dryden was unable, as well as unwilling, to give the poem a definite conclusion. Well aware of the King's affection for his wayward son, he "could not obtain from myself to shew Absalom unfortunate." The reconciliation of Absalom and David might still come to pass. As for Achitophel, Dryden was not without hope "that the Devil himself may, at last, be sav'd."[8] The structural defect of the poem did not obscure the constellation of graces which inspired Johnson's fine tribute: "acrimony of censure, elegance of praise, art of delineation of characters, variety and vigour of sentiment, happy turns of language, and pleasing harmony of numbers."[9]

Dryden had discovered that political satire was a happy medium for his poetical talents. After Shaftesbury had been released on bail, a medal was struck in his honor to celebrate his acquittal. Dryden's services were again required by the King, who suggested the plan for another satire, *The Medall*, and gave Dryden "a present of a hundred broadpieces for it."[10] The poem was published by Tonson in March, 1682. Prefixed to the satire was an "Epistle to the

Whigs" in which Dryden ironically dedicated to that party a work which represented "your own Heroe. tis the Picture which you admire and prize so much in little."[11] The vehemence of this second attack on Shaftesbury provoked a scurrilous attack on Dryden, *The Medal of John Bayes* (1682), attributed to Thomas Shadwell.

Tonson may have proposed[12] *The Second Part of Absalom and Achitophel,* which he published in the same year. This sequel was mainly the work of Nahum Tate, although Dryden contributed two hundred lines, including those demolishing Settle and Shadwell (Og and Doeg). Dryden reserved his full-length attack on Shadwell for *MacFlecknoe,* printed in an unauthorized text by D. Green.[13] In 1684 Tonson published the authorized text in *Miscellany Poems.*

Tonson, like Dryden himself, was aware that brief occasional poems complimenting members of the royal family were always in demand. As poet laureate Dryden was expected to produce such pieces and did so frequently and easily. In the midst of larger projects, he found time to write his *Prologue to the Duke* and *Prologue to the Duchess,* which Tonson published in attractive folio editions. The former was spoken at a revival of Otway's *Venice Preserved* which James attended.

Also in that busy year of 1682 Tonson published Dryden's *Religio Laici,* which he reprinted the next year. Here Dryden turned aside from political issues to defend, but with reservations, the Anglican faith he was later to renounce. In collaboration with Nathaniel Lee, Dryden next produced a tragedy, *The Duke of Guise,* which was printed by Lee's publisher, Richard Bentley, and Tonson. This controversial play, licensed only after a delay of two months, was defended in *The Vindication,* published by Tonson alone, a prose tract in which Dryden denied having insinuated parallels between the entry of Guise into Paris and Monmouth's return to England against the King's command.

Meanwhile Dryden had become involved in an important venture, embarked on by Tonson, a translation of *Plutarchs Lives* from the Greek text. The lives were the work of forty-one scholars, chiefly Oxford and Cambridge men, selected by Tonson, no doubt in consultation with Dryden. Somers again chose to be anonymous in his life of "Alciabiades."[14] Dryden wrote "The Life of Plutarch" for Volume I (1683) and probably supplied for Tonson the note from "The Publisher to the Reader," assuring readers that the

translation added "a farther Lustre, even to Plutarch himself."
Dryden included a puff for Tonson, affirming, "Now as to the
Bookseller's Part. . . . It is impossible, but a Book that comes into
the World with so many circumstances of Dignity, usefulness, and
esteem, must turn to account."[15] Tonson's gratification at the reception of Volume I encouraged him to proceed as rapidly as possible with the remaining volumes, as he indicated in a note "To the
Reader," signed by "Your Servant / J. Tonson," in *The Second
Volume of Plutarchs Lives* (1684). Volume III was published in
the same year, Volume IV in 1685, and Volume V in 1686. Tonson
printed later editions in 1702–1711 and 1716.

His duties as royal historiographer obliged Dryden to undertake,
at the King's command, the translation of a long history by Louis
Maimbourg, *The History of the League*, which Tonson published
in 1684. The book was dedicated to the King and had a frontispiece
representing Charles seated on his throne. The parallel between
forces opposed to the monarchy in France and the enemies of the
King's government in England could not be mistaken. In a letter to
Tonson, Dryden commented that Tonson's report that "the History
of the League is commended" had given him "great satisfaction."
Dryden added: "Take it all together, & I dare say without vanity
'tis the best translation of any history in English, though I cannot
say 'tis the best History; but that is no fault of mine."[16]

In spite of his services to his royal patron, Dryden's pension was in
arrears, as the King's benefactions usually were. In need of money,
Dryden welcomed, and may have suggested, Tonson's ambitious
scheme for the publication of an annual miscellany of poems by
talented writers, in which Dryden's own contributions would have
a conspicuous place. Tonson did not originate but he did popularize
this type of literary entertainment; and although his Miscellanies
appeared irregularly and were less successful after Dryden's death,
and although their method of publication led to the inclusion of
some dross amongst the gold, they proved to be the best of their
kind. Besides giving the reading public in a convenient form old and
new works by well-known writers, the Miscellanies "'discovered"
the gifts of younger men of letters and saved from oblivion some
pieces which otherwise would have been lost.

Four volumes of Tonson's Miscellanies were published in Dryden's lifetime. They are often referred to as Dryden's Miscellanies,

and indeed, according to the title page of the 1704 edition, the first four volumes were "Publish'd by Mr. Dryden." But, as has been remarked, claiming Dryden as the publisher of these volumes was "something of a publisher's flourish."[17] Dryden apparently proposed certain appropriate selections for the Miscellanies and discussed with Tonson much of the material submitted. But Tonson advertised for all gentlemen who were interested to send their poems to him and assembled and arranged their contributions.

The first volume of the Miscellanies was published by Tonson without dedication or preface in 1684. It was entitled: *Miscellany Poems, Containing a New Translation of Virgil's Eclogues, Ovid's Love Elegies, Odes of Horace, And Other Authors; With Several Original Poems by the Most Eminent Hands.* The first one hundred pages of this volume were devoted to previously printed longer poems by Dryden: "MacFlecknoe" (Dryden's authorized text), "Absalom and Achitophel," and "The Medall," all published without Dryden's name. Interspersed among the other contributions are several of Dryden's translations: an elegy from Ovid's *Amores*, an idyll of Theocritus, and Virgil's fourth and ninth eclogues. A large number of Dryden's prologues and epilogues are included. Among other contributors were Thomas Creech, Sir Charles Sedley, Thomas Rymer, George Stepney, Nahum Tate, the Earl of Roscommon, Richard Duke, Thomas Otway, and Knightley Chetwood. Prominence is given to Virgil's very popular eclogues. From Dryden's astringent satires, with which the volume begins, the casual reader could proceed at his chosen pace to Virgil's "Last Eclogue," sounding that note of nostalgia so much admired and so often sounded in pseudo-classical poetry:

> Amongst the Vines the Willows and the Springs,
> *Phillis* makes Garlands and *Amintas* sings.[18]

No sooner had the First Miscellany been published than Tonson and Dryden began planning a second. Dryden proposed including in this volume the *Religio Laici,* but he deferred to Tonson in excluding it in favor of new pieces, adding, however, the word of caution that "since we are to have nothing but new, I am resolved we will have nothing but good, whomever we disoblige." Dryden promised to supply "four Odes of Horace, forty lines of Lucretius, the whole of Nisus and Eurialus, both in the fifth and the ninth of Virgil's

Eneids; . . . there will be forty lines more of Virgil in another place, to answer those of Lucretius; I meane those very lines which Montaign has compar'd in those two poets; & Homer shall sleep on for me: I will not now meddle with him."[19]

Sylvae: or, The Second Part of Poetical Miscellanies was published by Tonson in May, 1685. Dryden wrote a preface in which he confessed that he had recently been affected by "the disease (as I may call it) of Translation." Although he had intended to translate only a few of the pastorals of Theocritus and odes of Horace, these efforts had spurred him on to renew his acquaintance with Lucretius and Virgil. After some remarks on the essential qualifications of a translator, he concluded: "I hope it will not be expected from me, that I shou'd say any thing of my fellow undertakers in this Miscellany. Some of them are too nearly related to me, to be commended without suspicion of partiality: Others I am sure need it not, and the rest I have not perus'd."[20]

Nearly a third of the contents of *Sylvae* was the work of Dryden. His contributions, published for the first time, were: three passages from Virgil's *Aeneid*; parts of Book I, II, III, IV, and V of Lucretius; three idylls of Theocritus; three odes and an epode of Horace; and two songs. Among anonymous contributions were a part of Virgil's "Fourth Georgic" and various offerings from Horace, Theocritus, and Ovid. Tonson himself contributed anonymously "On the Death of Mr. Oldham," paying tribute to Dryden as mighty Pan:

> He that now rules with undisputed sway,
> Guide of our Pens, Crowned with eternal Bays.[21]

The alteration of the political scene with the death of Charles II in February, 1685, spelled ultimate disaster for Dryden. Temporarily, his circumstances improved. A month after the King's death, Tonson published Dryden's *Threnodia Augustalis*, a "funeral-pindarique" poem in memory of the King. A second edition followed in the same year. In paying sincere, if extravagant, tribute to a king whom he had served so faithfully, Dryden took pains to dilute the rhapsody of grief with an ardent eulogy of the King's brother, "a Monarch ripen'd for a Throne,"[22] for whom he predicted a far brighter future than was to be James's fate.

Dryden's opera, *Albion and Albanius*, designed to celebrate

Charles's triumph over the Whigs, had been rehearsed several times before the King and praised by him; but Charles died while it was being prepared for the stage. Revised by Dryden, the play was lavishly produced in June, 1685, and had run for six nights at Dorset Garden when a performance is said to have been interrupted by the news that Monmouth had landed in Dorset and was leading an invasion. Within a month Monmouth was captured; he was sent to the Tower and was executed on July 15. Although not acted again, the opera was published at the time of its short and expensive stage history. Dryden had some satisfaction in adding a postscript to his preface, in which he stated that the death of Charles had necessitated the addition of only twenty or thirty lines. The change to a new monarch had been made "without the least confusion or disturbance: And those very causes which seem'd to threaten us with troubles, conspir'd to produce our lasting Happiness."[23]

Dryden's longest poem, *The Hind and the Panther*, was written in defense of the new king's arbitrary and deeply resented policy of dispensing with the Test Act for the benefit of the Roman Catholics. Tonson published the poem in 1687. It attracted widespread attention, was promoted by James II, and was twice reprinted by Tonson before the end of the year. Shortly before James's accession, Dryden had been converted to the Roman Catholic religion. This was a genuine conversion, offering Dryden a solution to his need, which he had already expressed, for an "omniscient church"; but his enemies, as might have been expected, accused him of seeking to curry favor with a Roman Catholic king who had renewed his official appointments. In a short preface to the first edition, Dryden explained that he had made use of the conventional medium of the beast fable, which is "as old, to my knowledge, as the Times of Boccace and Chawcer on the one side, and as those of the Reformation on the other."[24] He chose an argumentative milk-white Hind (the Roman Catholic Church) to defend her religion against an equally argumentative companion, a beautiful but spotted Panther (the Church of England).

As Dr. Johnson objected: "A fable which exhibits two beasts talking Theology appears at once full of absurdity."[25] So thought two young men, Charles Montague and Matthew Prior, who lost no time in attacking Dryden's poem in a witty and very popular satire, *The Hind and the Panther Transvers'd To the Story of The Country-Mouse and the City-Mouse,* published by W. Davis. The anonymous poets inquired in their preface with assumed gravity:

> Is it not as easie to imagine two Mice bilking Coachmen, and supping at the Devil; as to suppose a Hind entertaining the Panther at a Hermits Cell, discussing the greatest mysteries of Religion? ... If it is absurd in Comedies to make a Peasant talk in the strain of a Hero, or a Country Wench use the language of the Court; how monstrous is it to make a Priest of a Hind, and Parson of a Panther? To bring 'em in disputing with all the Formalities and Terms of the School? Though as to the Arguments themselves, these, we confess, are suited to the Capacity of the Beasts, and if we would suppose a Hind expressing herself about these Matters, she would talk at that rate.[26]

The legend has been denied that Dryden was reduced to tears by the levity of "two young fellows that I have always been very civil to."[27] According to another legend, Lord Dorset, when presenting Montague to King William, said: "I have brought a *Mouse* to wait on your Majesty." "I will make a man of him," replied the King and settled £500 on Montague.[28] At any rate, Montague's political career seems to have been promoted by his share (probably less than Prior's) in the burlesque. Montague was to be created Baron Halifax and was appointed First Lord of the Treasury.

The birth of a son, James Francis Edward Stuart, to James II was very promptly welcomed by James's poet laureate in *Britannia Rediviva,* published by Tonson in June, 1688, twelve days after the birth of the Prince. Dryden summoned all of his eloquence to honor an event which served only to hasten the downfall of the misguided king. We may detect that Dryden sensed approaching disaster, even while he implored:

> A Harvest ripening for another Reign,
> Of which this Royal Babe may reap the Grain.[29]

Dryden's desire to serve his new religion and the King also found expression at this time in his translation of Dominique Bouhours's *The Life of St. Francis Xavier,* published by Tonson in 1688 and dedicated to Queen Mary.

In this same year, Tonson published his illustrated edition of *Paradise Lost.* We may suppose that it was at Tonson's request that

Dryden supplied the epigram on Milton which was placed under the portrait of the poet in the frontispiece of this volume. Tonson's desire to create a larger reading public for Milton must have been shared by Dryden, who did not hesitate to rank Milton with Homer and Virgil. Dryden's lines were reprinted as "Upon Milton's Paradise Lost," with Dryden's name attached, in Tonson's 1716 edition of his Miscellanies.

Before the infant Prince, for whom Dryden had in vain hoped a serene future, had reached the age of seven months, the bloodless Revolution of 1688 had been completed. William's invasion had been successful, James had abandoned his throne, and William and Mary had been accepted as joint monarchs. In consequence of these events, Dryden was deprived of his two official posts and lost whatever political influence he had possessed. He did not renounce the religion he had adopted, and he refused to support the new government in any way; but he never again engaged in political controversy. His Whig friends did not desert him. Dorset, acting as Lord Chamberlain, was obliged to remove Dryden from the laureateship, which he gave to Shadwell. Nevertheless, Dorset continued to befriend Dryden, who acknowledged, among Dorset's other favors, "a most bountiful Present, which, at that time, when I was most in want of it, came most seasonably and unexpectedly to my Relief."[30] His now greatly restricted income compelled Dryden to return to the writing of plays and of more extensive translations of classical authors.

Financial difficulties may have led Dryden to choose another publisher, Joseph Hindmarsh, to publish his modified heroic play, *Don Sebastian* (1690). Hindmarsh probably offered him more money for the copyright than Tonson was willing to give; but a few months later, with *Amphitryon*, Dryden returned to Tonson, who was to remain his regular publisher. The purchase of the copyright of *Amphitryon* was apparently negotiated jointly by Jacob and Richard Tonson shortly before Richard's death, which occurred in September, 1690.[31]

The popularity of *The Spanish Fryar* may have induced the two brothers to engage in this final act of their intermittent partnership. Their business and domestic interests had been diverging. Jacob remained a bachelor. Richard had married in 1679 Mary Draper of

Wandsworth, Surrey, by whom he had a daughter Elizabeth, born in 1680, and a son Jacob, born in 1682.[32] Jacob junior, as he was called, was probably named for his uncle. He was educated for the publishing business and on reaching maturity was to become his uncle's invaluable partner. At Richard's death, his widow acquired his copyrights and took over his publishing business. *Amphitryon* appeared at the end of October, 1690, as "Printed for J. Tonson, at the Judge's Head in Chancery-lane near Fleet-street, and M. Tonson at Gray's-Inn-Gate in Gray's-Inn-Lane." Jacob Tonson published the music of the songs separately.

Dryden's "Epistle Dedicatory" to *Amphitryon* reflects his anxious concern to retain the good will of those "who have been pleas'd to own me in this Ruin of my small Fortune; who, though they are of a contrary Opinion themselves, yet blame me not for adhering to a lost Cause; and judging for my self, what I cannot chuse but judge; so long as I am a patient Sufferer, and no disturber of the Government."[33] *Amphitryon* was popular on the stage and was reprinted by Jacob Tonson in 1694 and 1706.

At a time when party feeling produced the bitterest animosities, Tonson's loyalty to a great poet, who, however distinguished, was a proudly professed Tory and Jacobite, cannot be regarded as otherwise than generous, and so Dryden must have considered it. Founder of the most famous club of his day, the Whig Kit-Cat Club, and an uncommonly active supporter of "the immortal King William," Tonson made allowance for a gulf between his political principles and Dryden's which could not possibly be bridged.

In 1691 Tonson published *King Arthur*, which Dryden originally intended to mark the triumph of Charles II over the difficulties which had beset his reign. In his "Epistle Dedicatory" to Lord Halifax, Dryden noted regretfully the changes which he had been obliged to make in his original design, in order "not to offend the present Times, nor a Government which has hitherto protected me."[34] Tonson may have recommended the conciliatory dedication to Halifax and also the deletion from the first edition of a parenthetical passage that might have been embarrassing to a government which "by a particular Favour," wrote Dryden, "wou'd have continued me what I was, if I could have comply'd with the Termes which were offered me."[35] Dryden's "best patroness," the Duchess of Monmouth, had persuaded Queen Mary to read the play, and the Queen had given it her royal approbation. In short, all steps had been taken to secure for the opera, aided by Purcell's music, a favorable reception. *King Arthur* was to be Dryden's most frequently revived play.

Dryden's interest in writing plays waned with *Cleomenes* (1692), completed by Thomas Shadwell, and a final tragicomedy, *Love Triumphant* (1694). Tonson had become Dryden's publisher too late to print the heroic plays at the height of their popularity, the masterpiece of *All for Love*, and several lighter plays where Dryden's wit burned brightest. But copyrights of the older plays were eventually obtained by Tonson. In 1695 he published a collected issue of current editions of Dryden's *Works* in four volumes.

Translation offered Dryden a better financial prospect than his now less popular heroic plays. He began the long labor of translating and editing Juvenal, a task which he interrupted briefly to write a panegyric in memory of the Countess of Abington, published by Tonson in 1692. The following year Tonson published in a folio edition *The Satires of Decimus Junius Juvenalis: Translated into English Verse . . . Together with the Satires of Aulus Persius Flaccus*. Besides editing this volume, Dryden contributed the greater part of it: five satires of Juvenal; the six satires of Persius; and in the "Dedication" to Dorset, one of his liveliest and best essays, his "Discourse concerning the Original and Progress of Satire." Juvenal's other satires Dryden distributed among a number of co-translators. He may have chosen to translate all of Persius himself because his assistants found Juvenal more congenial or less exacting.

That Tonson, "with mercantile ruggedness,"[36] made an exact count of Dryden's lines and paid him accordingly is evident from a letter he wrote to Dryden, probably in November, 1692, with reference to a new miscellany which was being prepared for publication. Tonson had agreed to pay the poet fifty guineas for a portion of Ovid's *Metamorphoses* to be included in the Third Miscellany and had actually made the payment. However, after receiving the translation, "wch I read wth a great deal of pleasure, & think nothing can be more entertaining,"[37] Tonson counted the lines and considered himself cheated, for Dryden had submitted only 1,146 lines, and Tonson found that he was paying more in proportion than the sum (twenty guineas) which Dryden had asked for 556 lines from "a strange bookseller" (Peter Motteux), who had refused the offer. Tonson ended his letter with hopeful courtesy:

> I own yt if you dont think fit to ad something more, I must submit: 'tis wholy at yor choice, for I left it intirely to you: but I believe you cannot imagine I expected soe little; for you were pleased to use me much kindlyer in Juvenall [2,280 lines] wch is not reckond soe easy to translate as Ovid. Sr, I humbly beg yor pardon for this long letter, & upon my word I had rather have yr good will than any mans alive; & whatever you are pleased to doe will alway acknowledge my self Sr Yor most obliged humble Servt, / J Tonson[38]

Accepting the rebuke, Dryden produced enough additional lines to satisfy Tonson's sense of business rectitude but decided that in the future he would make contracts for his translations in advance.

In June, 1693, Tonson published *Examen Poeticum: Being the Third Part of Miscellany Poems*. In the "Dedication" for this Miscellany, Dryden attacked Rymer, recently appointed historiographer royal, who had written slightingly of Dryden in *A Short View of Tragedy*, published the previous year. Of the fifteen contributions of Dryden, ten were printed for the first time: the first book of Ovid's *Metamorphoses*, and episodes from the ninth and thirteenth books; the last parting of Hector and Andromache from the sixth book of Homer's *Iliad*; and a few other pieces. The first ninety-eight pages were devoted to Dryden's selections from Ovid. Among other translations were passages from Homer and Horace by Congreve and from Ovid's *Love Elegies* by Henry Cromwell. Congreve and Prior were among the contributors of lyrics, and Addison, a student at Magdalen College, Oxford, contributed complimentary verses "To Mr. Dryden." The volume ends with "A Poetical History of the French Disease" (syphilis), translated by Tate from the text of Frascatorius.

The Annual Miscellany For the Year 1694 was printed a year later. It was published with a frontispiece but without a preface. Dryden, who had already begun work on his translation of the whole of Virgil, contributed only the third book of Virgil's *Georgics* and "To Sir G. Kneller." Addison contributed a translation of nearly all of the "Fourth Georgic," an episode from Ovid, "A Song for St. Cecilia's Day," and "An Account of the Greatest English Poets." Congreve and Prior were again represented, as well as less distinguished writers.

Dryden's work on Virgil was now sufficiently advanced for arrangements to be made for publishing the volume. On June 15, 1694, Dryden and Tonson signed a legal contract for a subscription edition, Congreve acting as a witness. Dryden agreed to translate Virgil's *Eclogues*, *Georgics*, and *Aeneid* "with all convenient speed," meanwhile engaging in only a few minor literary labors. Tonson was to pay Dryden in installments: £50 for the *Eclogues* and *Georgics*; £50 when the first four books of the *Aeneid* were completed; £50 at the end of the eighth book; and £50 at the end of the twelfth. Tonson was to provide one hundred plates, previously used in Ogilby's *Virgil*, and was to solicit one hundred subscribers, at five guineas each, three guineas to be paid in advance and two on delivery of the book, and was to supply at his charge the titles and coats of arms of the subscribers. Dryden was to receive any subscription payment in excess of five guineas and might order as many books as he wished, paying the difference between the price of the large paper for subscribers and the common paper. When the sixth book of the *Aeneid* had been finished, Dryden was to give notice that only those who subscribed to the volume could have the large paper.[39]

The terms of payment for the subscribers to the second printing were subsequently arranged between Dryden and Tonson. The price paid was to be two guineas, of which one guinea was to be paid to Francis Atterbury, who was to collect for Dryden at the time of subscription, and the second guinea to Tonson on receipt of the book. The books for these subscribers were to have as fine paper, print, and engravings as those for the first subscribers, but were not to include the coats of arms.[40] Dryden's profits for the translation, which have been variously estimated, were probably about £1,400.[41]

The letters of Dryden to Tonson, while the monumental task was progressing, reveal the intermittent turbulence which affected their relations at that time. Dryden was old, in failing health, by preference indolent, and resentful of pressure to get on with his work. Moreover, he was irked by having his gifts always shrewdly estimated as a business proposition. In one letter he wrote that it was "high time" to conclude the agreement for the second subscriptions, and this must be done at once. The bargain made between them, Dryden noted, was "much to my loss," although his only regret now was that Tonson might lose his profit "by your too good opinion of my Abilities." Congreve would meet with them (to witness the second agreement) "as a Common friend; for as you know him for yours, I make not the least doubt, but he is much more mine."[42] Dryden reminded Tonson that the payment for the four middle books of the *Aeneid* must be made in "good silver," not in the coins in current circulation but of inferior value which he had been receiving. Author and publisher argued over Dryden's share in the second subscriptions. Dryden had told Congreve "that I knew you too well to believe you meant me any kindness, & he promised me to believe accordingly of you, if you did not. But this is past, & you shall have your bargain if I live, and have my health."[43]

In another letter Dryden wrote to Tonson of a fresh grievance, the publisher's refusal to pay any additional sum for the notes which Dryden was to supply; yet making them short would save half a year's labor. "Upon triall," declared Dryden, "I find all of your trade are Sharpers & you not more than others; therefore I have not wholly left you"; and he signed this letter: "not your Enemy, & may be your friend / John Dryden."[44] At a later date, Dryden admitted: "What I wrote yesterday was too sharp; but I doubt it is all true. Your Boys comeing upon so unseasonable a visit, as if you were frighted for your self, discomposed me."[45]

Legends of the feuds between Dryden and Tonson were current in their day and persisted long after their deaths. Undoubtedly exaggerated, they nonetheless reflect something of the quick tempers and acid wit of the two men. Dr. Johnson reported that Lord Bolingbroke told Dr. William King of Oxford that one day in his youth, when he visited Dryden and was talking with him, they heard another person enter the house. "This," said Dryden, "is Tonson. You will take care not to depart before he goes away; for I have not completed the sheet which I promised him; and if you leave me unprotected, I must suffer all the rudeness to which his resentment can prompt his tongue."[46] Edmund Malone in his account of Dryden's life relates an anecdote of one skirmish between author and publisher from which the poet emerged triumphant. Once, when Tonson refused to advance Dryden a certain sum of money, Dryden sent a second messenger with a satirical triplet, adding, "Tell the dog, that he who wrote these lines, can write more." The verses "had the desired effect." As later incorporated in William Shippen's satire, *Faction Display'd* (1704), these were the lines in which angry Dryden painted Jacob's portrait:

> *With leering Looks, Bullfac'd and Freckled fair,*
> *With two left Legs, and Judas-coloured Hair,*
> *With Frowzy Pores, that taint the ambient Air.*[47]

Yet the tone of Dryden's letters to Tonson is, on the whole, friendly. He had occasion to thank Tonson for gifts of melons and sherry, for collecting his Northamptonshire rents, for the pleasure of his company in the country, for advancing money for two watches to be sent to his sons in Italy, and for forwarding letters (which did not always reach them) to his sons. In one of his more relaxed moods, Dryden expressed to Tonson the hope that he would never lose Congreve's affection, "Nor yours Sir; as being Your most Faithful & much obligd Servant / John Dryden."[48] Sir Walter Scott judiciously appraised the long relationship: "But whatever occasional subjects of dissention arose between Dryden and his bookseller, mutual interest, the strongest of ties, appears always to have brought them together, after the first ebullition of displeasure had subsided."[49]

Dryden chose his long-time publisher to launch *The Husband His Own Cuckold* (1696), a comedy which John Dryden, Jr., had composed in Italy. The proud father took time off from his work on Virgil to write a preface and epilogue for his son's play. The preface concludes with Dryden's disarming defense of the young writer: "Farewell, Reader, if you are a Father you will forgive me, if not, you will when you are a father."[50]

Dryden's friends gave him all possible assistance in his burdensome project as the translator of Virgil. Gilbert Dolben loaned him editions of Virgil in Latin and commentaries on them. Knightley Chetwood contributed a "Life of Virgil" and the preface to the "Pastorals," and Addison wrote the preface to the "Georgics" and the prose synopses for the twelve books of the "Aeneis." To that "Excellent Young Man," Congreve, Dryden was indebted for comparing Dryden's version of the "Aeneis" with the original and showing Dryden many faults which he endeavored to correct.[51] The scope of his immense task Dryden found disheartening "in the wretched remainder of a sickly Age, worn out with Study, and oppress'd by Fortune."[52] On the major portion of the translation, the "Aeneis," to which Virgil had devoted eleven years, Dryden spent only three. Although he longed for more time to correct his errors, "some of my Subscribers grew so clamorous, that I cou'd no longer deferr the Publication."[53] At last, in August, 1697, Tonson published *The Works of Virgil*. Dryden dedicated the three divisions of his book to Lord Clifford, to the Earl of Chesterfield, and to the Marquis of Normanby, including in the third dedication a leisurely essay on epic poetry.

Dryden wrote to his sons that Tonson "missed of his design in the Dedication: though He had prepared the Book for it; for in every figure of Aeneas, he has caused him to be drawn like K. William, with a hooked Nose."[54] Tonson had obviously urged Dryden to dedicate his translation to the King, but Dryden had resisted such a concession to the Whigs. Tonson had been obliged to content himself with his publisher's prerogative: giving Virgil's hero, in slightly altered plates which were Tonson's own property, a nose unmistakably like the King's.

Alexander's Feast: or The Power of Musique, Dryden's second ode in honor of St. Cecilia's Day, was first presented, with great success, with music by Jeremiah Clarke, at Stationers' Hall in November, 1697. Tonson published the poem in December. Dryden directed Tonson to correct what seems to have been the poet's "small mistake," the writing of "Lais" for "Thais" in a copy which the author had submitted to the publisher.[55] Gratified by the reception of his ode, Dryden wrote to Tonson: "I am glad to hear from all Hands that my Ode is esteemed the best of all my poetry, by all the Town: I thought so my self when I writ it but being old, I mistrusted my own Judgment. I hope it has done you service, and will do more."[56] The popularity of the poem was enhanced by Handel's music in 1736, and ten editions appeared in a period of twenty years.

Dryden's last work, his *Fables, Ancient and Modern*, was published by Tonson in March, 1700, less than two months before Dryden's death. The *Fables* consists of nineteen paraphrases or translations, and three of Dryden's original poems, including a reprint of *Alexander's Feast*, with the Middle English text of Chaucer's poems in an appendix. The longest selections were from Chaucer and Ovid.[57] The three tales from Boccaccio, whom Dryden considered inferior to Chaucer, seem to have been intended as

fillers. It was a satisfaction to Dryden to offer his readers his translation of Book I of Homer's *Iliad*, for he found Homer's fire more
congenial than Virgil's sedateness; and if he lived long enough and
had "moderate health," he proposed to translate all of Homer.

The delightful preface to the *Fables* shows no diminution of
Dryden's powers, nor did he feel any. "What Judgment I had,"
wrote Dryden, "increases rather than diminishes; and Thoughts,
such as they are, come crowding in so fast upon me, that my only
Difficulty is to chuse or to reject; to run them into Verse, or to give
them the other Harmony of Prose."[58] With his usual perceptive-
ness, he discusses the four authors—Homer, Ovid, Boccaccio, and
Chaucer—whom he has freely paraphrased.

Dryden's modernization in the *Fables* of some of Chaucer's
Canterbury Tales was an experiment, now regarded as unfortunate, which he defended on the score that the greater part of his
countrymen could not understand the original text, and his only
desire was to "perpetuate" or at least "refresh" Chaucer's memory.
The paraphrases were obviously undertaken *con amore*. Dryden's
heartfelt praise of Chaucer gives the modern reader more pleasure
than Dryden's paraphrases and remains one of the finest pieces of
Chaucerian criticism. To Dryden, Chaucer "is a perpetual fountain
of good sense."

> Chaucer follow'd Nature every where; but was never so bold to go
> beyond her. . . . He must have been a Man of a most wonderful com-
> prehensive Nature, because, as it has been truly observ'd of him, he
> has taken into the Compass of his *Canterbury Tales* the various Man-
> ners and Humours (as we now call them) of the whole *English*
> Nation, in his Age. Not a single Character has escap'd him. . . .
> There is such a Variety of Game springing up before me, that I am
> distracted in my Choice, and know not which to follow. 'Tis suffi-
> cient to say according to the Proverb, that here is God's Plenty. We
> have our Forefathers and Great Grand-dames all before us, as they
> were in *Chaucer's* Days; their general Characters are still remaining
> in Mankind, and even in *England*, though they are call'd by other
> Names than those of *Moncks*, and *Fryars*, and *Chanons*, and *Lady
> Abbesses*, and *Nuns*: for Mankind is ever the same, and nothing lost
> out of Nature, though every thing is alter'd.[59]

It has been suggested that because of "miscellaneousness"[60] the
Fables did not prove popular enough for a second edition to be re-

quired before 1713. Tonson paid Dryden three hundred guineas for 10,000 lines, and Dryden's estate received an additional payment when the second edition was printed.[61]

Dryden died on May 1, 1700. The year after his death, Tonson, with Thomas Bennet and Richard Wellington, who held some of the copyrights, published a large folio edition in two volumes of *The Comedies, Tragedies, and Operas written by John Dryden, Esq. Now first collected, and corrected from the originals*. The publication was hastened as much as possible in accordance with Tonson's firm conviction that a famous man's works should be reprinted as soon as possible after his death. Kneller's fine portrait of Dryden, which Tonson owned,[62] was engraved as a frontispiece for the first volume of the plays. In *Poetical Miscellanies: The Fifth Part* (1704) Tonson printed ten pieces by Dryden not previously published, including two excerpts from Ovid's *The Art of Love*; and he printed in an edition of *The Art of Love* (1709) all of Dryden's translation of Book I.[63] When he reprinted *The Works of Beaumont and Fletcher* (1711) Tonson took pains to have inserted in the preface "just as he left them,"[64] the notes Dryden had written on blank leaves in his copy of Rymer's *The Tragedies of the Last Age*. In fairness to Tonson, it must be borne in mind that although the pecuniary advantages of these professional attentions to Dryden's memory weighed heavily with him, Tonson wished also the involvement in shading the great poet's laurels which friendship dictated. We have the testimony of Lockier that Tonson had "a good key" to Buckingham's popular satire on Dryden, *The Rehearsal*, "but refused to publish it because he had been so much obliged to Dryden."[65]

Seventeen years after Dryden's death, Tonson published in six volumes *The Dramatick Works of John Dryden, Esq.*, edited, with a critical preface, by their mutual friend, William Congreve, who thus fulfilled Dryden's request to "be kind to my Remains."[66] With quiet eloquence, Congreve paid homage to Dryden which has endeared both Dryden and Congreve to generations of Dryden's admirers. "He was of a Nature," wrote Congreve, "exceedingly Humane and Compassionate; easily forgiving Injuries, and capable of a prompt and sincere Reconciliation with them who had offended him. . . . To the best of my Knowledge and Observation, he was, of all the Men that ever I knew, one of the most Modest."[67] Congreve's preface might well have impressed Tonson, as it subsequently did

Samuel Johnson, as a tribute to Dryden to which "nothing can be objected but the fondness of friendship; and to have excited that fondness in such a mind is no small degree of praise."[68]

No such perfection of friendship existed between Dryden and Tonson. Their relationship was frequently marred by friction. Nevertheless, they were indispensable to each other. The aging poet, harassed by ill health, political disfavor, and poverty, required his loyal publisher's spur to unrelaxing literary exertion. Tonson needed the prestige of publishing for "Mr. Dryden" and the guidance of a man who was singularly qualified for that service.

*Among the
Kit-Cats*

he members of Jacob
Tonson's Kit-Cat Club
were eulogized by Horace
Walpole as "in reality the patriots that saved Britain."[1] This emphatic tribute, voicing, of course, a Whiggish sentiment, requires
some qualification. The Kit-Cat Club was composed of many, but
not all, of the leaders of the Whig political party in the reigns of
William and Mary, and Anne. These men were indeed patriots who
worked unceasingly, whether in or out of power, and with ultimate
success, for the clear-cut objectives of the Whig party: a limited
monarchy, with a strong Parliament; resistance to French aggres-
sion; the union of England and Scotland; and the succession of the
Protestant House of Hanover.

The rival Tory party, on the other hand, was divided into factions.
The more moderate Tories gave William some support in his war
policies but were unhappy under a king who was a foreigner, and
more so over the prospect of a German ruler. They rejoiced in
Queen Anne as a Stuart and in her unwavering support of the
Church of England. In Anne's reign they favored ending the conflict with France by limited concessions to Louis XIV. The most
extreme Tories, the Jacobites, intrigued to restore the Pretender, the
son of the abdicated James II, as James III of England. Because of
their divided aims, the Tories had no such solidarity as the Whigs
and could not produce a union of patriots comparable in influence to
the Kit-Cats.

If the Kit-Cat Club began as a sort of informal political forum,
it soon took on social and literary characteristics which likewise contributed to its fame. It occurred to Jacob Tonson that the pleasures
of eating, drinking, and sociability might well be encouraged by
regular weekly meetings of noblemen and gentlemen of similar
tastes. As a shrewd man of business, it also occurred to him that if he
himself offered weekly feasts, he might secure on favorable terms

the services of "eminent" men of letters among the club members and the patronage and financial support of the others. The club was called the Kit-Cat Club, apparently by way of compliment to Christopher (or Kit) Cat, the popular keeper of the tavern where the members met; and Tonson, by common consent, received the title of permanent secretary. An exclusive club, never exceeding thirtynine members at any one time, the Kit-Cats had the longest, most distinguished history of any of the numerous clubs of the period.[2] Even the acid pens of their Tory critics bear testimony to the fame of the Kit-Cats, extending "to the utmost limits of our learned Metropolis."[3]

The date of the founding of this celebrated club cannot be definitely determined. The most plausible reference to its origin is that of the Whig historian, John Oldmixon:

> This Club grew up from a private Meeting of Mr. Somers, afterwards Lord Chancellor, and another Lawyer, now in a very high Station in the Law, and Mr. Tonson, sen. the Bookseller, who before the Revolution, met frequently in the Evening at a Tavern, near Temple-Bar, to unbend themselves after Business, and have a little free and chearful Conversation in those dangerous Times. Their Supper was a Mutton Pye a piece, made by a Pastry-Cook in that Neighbourhood, who became famous for his Excellence in that Way. Other Gentlemen of the same good English Principles, joining themselves afterwards to this original Society, it became the most Noble One, and the most Pleasant, that perhaps ever was in the World.[4]

From another source we learn that the Earl of Dorset was "one of the first Founders of the Kit-Cat Club." The same writer remarks:

> This Club can have but thirty-nine Members, who are all Men of the first Rank, for Quality, or Learning; and most of them have been employed in the greatest Offices of State, and in the Army; and none but are Gentlemen of the greatest Distinction in some way or other. All their Pictures are drawn by that Great Master Sir Godfrey Kneller,[5] and kept in Commemoration of that August Assembly, by their ingenious Secretary, Mr. Tonson.[6]

The liveliest account of the early history of the club is provided by Edward Ward in *The Secret History of Clubs* (1709). Ward bestows on Bocai (Jacob), the founder of the club, the epithet of "an Amphibeous Mortal,[7] Chief Merchant to the Muses." Bocai's

neighbor, a tavern keeper at the end of Bell Court in Gray's Inn
Lane, had found the "knack" of humoring Bocai's palate; and
through Bocai's assistance he had moved from Gray's Inn Lane to
keep a pudding shop near the Fountain Tavern in the Strand, assured
"that Bocai and his Friends would come every week to Storm the
Crusty Walls of his Mutton-Pies, and make a Consumption of his
Custards." Bocai, "who had always a sharp Eye towards his own
Interest," became acquainted with "a parcel of Poetical young
Sprigs" fresh from the university, who had made themselves "Fa-
vourites of the late bountiful *Mecaenas*" (Dorset) and who, having
more wit than experience, "put but a slender value . . . upon their
Maiden Performances." To ingratiate himself with his guests, Bocai
invited them to "a collation of Oven-Trumpery" at the pastry shop.

> *Bocai* wisely observing the good effects of this Paistry [*sic*] Enter-
> tainment; and finding that Pies to Poets were as agreeable Food, as
> *Ambrosia* to the Gods, very cunningly propos'd their Weekly Meeting
> at the same Place; and that himself would be oblig'd to continue
> the like Feast every Club-Day, provided they would do him the
> Honour to let him have the Refusal of all their Juvenile Products,
> which generous proposal was very readily agreed to by the whole
> Poetick Clan: And the Cook's name being *Christopher*, for brevity
> call'd *Kit*, and his Sign being the Cat and Fiddle, they very merrily
> deriv'd a quaint Denomination from Puss and her Master, and from
> thence call'd themselves *The Kit-Cat Club*; and *Bocai*, in respect that
> he was Donor of the Feast, and promoter of this New Pudding Pye
> Establishment, had the Honour to be chosen Chair-Man of the So-
> ciety; to which presiding Authority, as most believe, he owes the
> Stateliness of his Brow, and the Haughtiness of his Temper.

Bocai always came to the meetings with some project to propose for
his own profit, and every week the listening town was charmed with
some "wonderful Off-Spring" of the Kit-Cats' "Teeming-
Noddles." Men of quality were glad enough to join so reputable a
club. Ward includes in his satire a mouth-watering account of the
luscious cheese-cakes, "shoals of Custards," pigeon pies, rose-water
codlin tarts, and jellies which provided a meal "fit for Gods or
Poets." Bocai's own choice was a well-seasoned mutton pie. As they
chew, the members reflect on various matters. One (Prior) thinks
of his "dear Cloe."[8]
Other details of the club are supplied in Sir Richard Blackmore's

The Kit-Cats. A Poem (1708). This Tory satirist credits Bocai with giving the Muses "tender Care" in William's "Military Reign," when they had little share of the royal favor. The Kit-Cats met on the "fair Strand," between the Courts, in a house which had for its sign "A Fountain red with ever-flowing Wine." "Hampstead's airy Head" provided another meeting place. "One night in Sev'n" Bocai

> assembled his poetic Tribe
> Past Labours to reward, and new prescribe:
> Hence did the Assembly's Title first arise,
> And *Kit-Cat* Wits sprung first from *Kit-Cat's* Pies.

As the "cheerful Bards" rehearse their weekly assignments, Bocai nods approval.

> Now Crowds to Founder Bocai did resort,
> And for his Favour humbly made their Court.
> The little Wits attended at his Gate,
> And Men of title did his Levee wait;
> For he, as Sovereign by Prerogative,
> Old Members did exclude, and new receive.
> He judg'd who most were for the Order fit,
> And Chapters held to make new Knights of Wit.[9]

In *Faction Display'd* William Shippen attacks the Kit-Cats in his account of "a fierce caball" that met "at dead of night" in "Faction's Court," where the members employ "their anxious Thoughts t'embroil the State." Various speakers take part in the midnight Satanic conclave, with Bibliopolo (Tonson) making the final address:

> Now the Assembly to adjourn prepar'd,
> When *Bibliopolo* from behind appear'd,
> As well describ'd by th' old Satyrick Bard [Dryden];
> *With leering Looks, Bull-fac'd, and Freckled fair,*
> *With two left Legs;*[10] *and Judas-coloured Hair,*
> *With Frowzy Pores, that taint the ambient Air.*[11]
> Sweating and Puffing for a while he stood,
> And then broke forth in this insulting Mood:
> I am the Touchstone of all Modern Wit,
> Without my Stamp in vain your Poets write.
> Those only purchase everlasting Fame,
> That in my Miscellany plant their Name.

Nor therefore think that I can bring no Aid,
Because I follow a Mechanick Trade,
I'll print your Pamphlets and your Rumours spread.
I am the founder of your lov'd Kit-Cat,
A Club that gave direction to the State.
'Twas there we first instructed all our Youth,
To talk Profane, and Laugh at Sacred Truth;
We taught them how to Tost, and Rhime, and Bite,
To Sleep away the Day, and drink away the Night.—
Some this Fantastick Speech approv'd, some Sneer'd,—
The wight grew Cholerick, and disappear'd.[12]

If the above descriptions of the Kit-Kat Club and its members seem a little fanciful, they are mainly supported by more sober evidence. Addison, one of the members, observed: "The Kit-Kat it self is said to have taken its Original from a Mutton-Pie."[13] A brief biography of Christopher Cat appeared in *The Dictionary of National Biography*. He was a Quaker, probably originally of Norwich, one of whose letters (of May 9, 1711), signed "Ch. Catt," has been preserved and reflects "an educated and a thoughtful mind." His portrait by Kneller was in the Exhibition of National Portraits at Kensington in 1867, as was a painting ascribed to Kneller of members of the Kit-Cat Club at tea in Christopher Cat's house in Chelsea Walk in 1716, when presumably Cat had retired on the ample proceeds of his tavern-keeping.[14] Cat apparently relished a joke as much as any of the Kit-Cats, if we are to believe a legend that they once requested him to bake some mutton pies with Thomas D'Urfey's works under them. When his patrons complained that the pies were not baked enough, Cat explained that the works were so cold that the dough couldn't bake.[15]

A valuable little document in the National Portrait Gallery is a list of subscribers to a meeting place for the Kit-Cat Society on Hampstead Heath. In Jacob's handwriting is the statement, dated May 15, 1702, that the new quarters are "to be finished by the following spring." Ten guineas each were contributed by thirteen donors, who signed the paper: Carlisle, Manchester, Essex, Cornwallis, J. Dormer, A. Stanyan, Grantham,[16] Hartington, S. Compton, Kingston, Mohun, Grafton, and S. Garth.[17] This summer retreat was the Upper Flask Inn on the eastern side of Hampstead High Street, on the edge of the Heath, where the members may have assembled under an old mulberry tree beyond a pool in the garden.

By the end of 1703, the Kit-Cats were having frequent meetings at Tonson's house at Barn Elms in a room which he had fitted up for them and their portraits. In June of that year, when Tonson was in Holland, Vanbrugh wrote to him: "the Kit-Cat wants you, much more than you ever can do them. Those who remain in towne, are in great desire of waiting on you at Barne-Elmes; not that they have finished their pictures neither; tho' to excuse them (as well as myself), Sir Godfrey has been most in fault. The fool has got a country house near Hampton Court, and is so busy about fitting it up (to receive nobody), that there is no getting him to work."[18] The Duke of Somerset had presented Tonson with his portrait, and the other club members followed his example.[19]

Two lists of the club members by contemporary historians are at variance. Boyer's list (1722)[20] of thirty names of those who "at first" were members includes names of twelve persons not represented among the Kit-Cat engravings (1735) of John Faber.[21] Of these it is known that Prior and Norton[22] were expelled from the club, and Topham[23] was still a member in 1708. Data are lacking as to the membership of nine others claimed by Boyer: Henry Boyle (later Lord Carleton), Charles Boyle (later Earl of Orrery), Wortley Montagu, John Smith, Henley, Colonel Farrington, Dr. Hans Sloane, John Harrison, and Dr. Merry. Oldmixon's more reliable list (1735)[24] of forty-six members parallels Faber's Kit-Cat portraits, except for Oldmixon's exclusion of Marlborough, and the sixth Earl of Dorset, also excluded by Boyer, who had died in 1706. Both Oldmixon and Faber regarded Kneller (who apparently was so considered only by courtesy) as a member. Compton, Congreve, Cornwallis, Dartiquenave, Garth, Kingston, Shannon, Somers, Stanhope, Stanyan, Stepney, Temple, Tonson, and Vanbrugh are represented as members in all three works.

The year 1702 is a convenient date to select for a review of the probable membership of the club at the beginning of the reign of Queen Anne. The first in rank among the older members was then Charles Sackville, sixth Earl of Dorset, K. G., considered the Augustan Horace of his day. "Hardly a first or second-rate author failed to enjoy Dorset's patronage."[25] Walpole epitomized Dorset as "the finest gentleman in the voluptuous court of Charles the Sec-

ond, and in the gloomy one of king William."[26] The uncle of Lady
Dorset, Henry Compton, Bishop of London, had signed on June 30,
1688, the secret invitation to Prince William of Orange to come
over to England. After William's arrival, when Princess Anne and
Lady Churchill secretly left the Court, they went first, about midnight, to the Earl of Dorset's, carrying nothing with them, and
Lady Dorset "furnished them with everything."[27] Dorset assisted
in the management of public affairs during the interval before the
Crown was offered to William and Mary in February, 1689, and
became Lord Chamberlain and a member of the Privy Council immediately after their accession to the throne. He was a Fellow of the
Royal Society. His satiric lyrics can still be valued, in Dr. Johnson's
words, as "what they pretend to be, the effusions of a man of wit,
gay, vigorous, and airy."[28]

Other senior members of the club in 1702 were Carbery, Somers,
Tidcomb, Wharton, Halifax, Garth, Tonson, and Dunch. Tonson,
the club's secretary, though a bookseller among lords, was already
"a lord among booksellers."[29] John Vaughan, third Earl of Carbery,
had served as a Lord of the Admiralty and was a former president
of the Royal Society. John Tidcomb was a soldier, colonel of a regiment of Foot. Edmund Dunch, Wharton's nephew, had supported
the Revolution and had begun a long career in the House of Commons. Dr. Samuel Garth was a Fellow of the College of Physicians.
Known as "the Kit-Cat Poet," he was the author of the popular
poem, *The Dispensary* (1699).

Wharton, Somers, and Halifax were the three Kit-Cats among
the five members of the highly influential Whig Junto.[30] Thomas
Wharton, fifth Baron Wharton, later first Marquess of Wharton,
had immense influence among the Whigs, which has been attributed
to the part which he played in the Revolution, his staunch loyalty to
its principles, his success in electioneering, and his long and brilliant
career in Parliament. "The discipline of the Whig party," it has
been claimed, "owed more to him than to any other single man."[31]
He declared that he whistled King James out of three kingdoms
with his ballad of "Lilliburlero," which had an extraordinary vogue;
and he was one of the first to declare for William, whom he joined
at Exeter in November, 1688. His blunt advice to William, after the
latter's accession, was: "Wee have made you king, . . . and if you
intend to governe like an honest man, what occasion can you have for

knaves [Tories] to serve you?"[32] Wharton has been described as "not merely the most colourful personality among the five lords of the junto but in many ways the most vivid character of his age."[33]

John Somers, Baron Somers of Evesham, an eminent barrister before he was thirty, had served as junior counsel for the Seven Bishops who in 1688 had thwarted James II's attempt to impeach them for treason. Somers had been Solicitor General, Attorney General, Lord Keeper of the Great Seal, Speaker of the House of Lords, and Lord Chancellor. A victim of Tory jealousy, he was compelled to resign his offices and was impeached by the House of Commons in 1701 for his assumed share in the Partition treaties,[34] but the charge against him was dismissed. For five years he was president of the Royal Society.

Charles Montague, Baron Halifax, later first Earl of Halifax, K. G., succeeded Dorset as a patron of men of letters. He had held the posts of Chancellor of the Exchequer, First Lord of the Treasury, and Auditor of the Exchequer. Like Somers, and for the same reason, he lost his offices and was impeached in 1701 but was acquitted. He had preceded Somers as president of the Royal Society.

Kit-Cats between the ages of thirty and forty in 1702 were Somerset, Manchester, Stepney, Walsh, Prior, Dartiquenave, Vanbrugh, Kingston, Mainwaring, Stanyan, Carlisle, Dormer, Congreve, Steele, and Addison. Charles Seymour, sixth Duke of Somerset, K. G., known as "the proud Duke," had been Gentleman of the Bedchamber to Charles II and James II. He was in arms with William at the Revolution, became Chancellor of the University of Cambridge, Speaker of the House of Lords, and Lord President of the Council. In July, 1702, he was sworn Master of the Horse to the Queen; and he was to keep that post for ten years, due largely to Queen Anne's regard for his Duchess.[35] Somerset's formidable pride was easily offended, and Swift not unjustly complained of his "indigested Schemes."[36] The Whigs discovered that he could be "very troublesom" if kept out of their secrets "& more so if he be let into 'em."[37] If unpredictable, on the whole Somerset was useful to the party; and he certainly took pride in his role as generous patron of Tonson and the club.

Manchester, Stanyan, Stepney, and Prior were diplomats. Charles Montagu, fourth Earl and later first Duke of Manchester, supported the Revolution, had been Ambassador Extraordinary to Venice and to Paris, and was principal Secretary of State at Anne's accession, from which office she at once removed him. In 1702 Abraham Stanyan was at the beginning of his diplomatic career and was secretary to Manchester in Paris. George Stepney, who had been envoy to several foreign countries, was sent to Vienna in 1702. Although his efforts in verse are negligible, he was a capable diplomat. "No *Englishman*," it was said, "ever understood the Affairs of *Germany* so well, and few *Germans* better."[38] Much of the time, during his relatively short life, he was out of England, and he missed his English friends. From Vienna, Stepney wrote to Tonson: "My hearty affections to the Kit-Cat. I often wish it were my fortune to make one with you at 3 in ye morning."[39] Matthew Prior, later to be expelled from the club, had antagonized its members by voting for the impeachment of the Whig ministers. He had been an under-secretary at The Hague and in Paris and had been appointed a commissioner of trade. He was already famous as the co-author with Charles Montague of *The Hind and the Panther Transvers'd To the Story of The Country-Mouse and the City-Mouse* and was the most popular poet among the Kit-Cats.

Charles Howard, third Earl of Carlisle, had served William in all of his campaigns. He held the offices of Gentleman of the Bedchamber, Deputy Earl Marshal, and First Lord of the Treasury. Evelyn Pierrepont, Earl and later first Duke of Kingston-upon-Hull, K. G., was a conspicuous figure in fashionable society. Charles Dartiquenave was celebrated for his epicurean tastes and his skill as a punster. John Dormer,[40] country squire of Rousham, near Oxford, was a Deputy Lieutenant of Oxfordshire in 1701.

Mainwaring, Walsh, Congreve, Vanbrugh, Steele, and Addison were all men of letters. In his own age William Walsh was esteemed as a critic and poet, and both Walsh and Arthur Mainwaring, a successful journalist, employed fluent pens in the service of the Kit-Cats. William Congreve had succeeded Dryden as the leading dramatist of the age. John Vanbrugh had produced two excellent plays and had begun work for Carlisle as architect of Castle Howard. Richard Steele was a captain in a regiment of Foot and author of a solemn moral treatise and a lively comedy. Joseph Addison, soon to win fame as the poet of Blenheim, had not yet returned from his European tour.

A third of the members of the club were in their twenties in

1702. These men were socially prominent, and many of them had military and political careers. Charles Lennox, first Duke of Richmond and Lennox, K. G., was A. D. C. to William for nine years and Lord High Admiral. Algernon Capell, second Earl of Essex; William Cavendish, Marquess of Hartington, later second Duke of Devonshire, K. G.; Richard Boyle, second Viscount Shannon; Charles Cornwallis, fourth Baron Cornwallis; and James Stanhope, later first Earl Stanhope, had all served in William's campaigns. Essex, a Gentleman of the Bedchamber to William, was to become a lieutenant general and commander in chief of the English forces in Spain. Sir Richard Temple, later first Viscount Cobham, and Charles Mohun, fourth Baron Mohun, were colonels of regiments of Foot, and both became lieutenant generals. Mohun, a boisterous rake and the least admirable member of the Kit-Cats, had three charges of murder brought against him and was to die in a duel with the Duke of Hamilton. Young James Berkeley, later third Earl of Berkeley, K. G., became an able naval commander and First Lord of the Admiralty. Stanhope and Robert Walpole, later first Earl of Orford, K. G., were already launched on their long and effective parliamentary careers. At the weekly meetings of the Kit-Cat Club, Walpole, who was to be the leader of the younger Whigs and whose activities in Parliament were to extend over forty years, received early and valuable instruction in "the arts of convivial politics."[41] Hartington, Cornwallis, Temple, Berkeley, Spencer Compton, later Earl of Wilmington, K. G., and Francis Godolphin, later second Earl of Godolphin, were also members of Parliament.

The youngest Kit-Cats in 1702 were Charles Fitzroy, second Duke of Grafton, K. G., and William Pulteney, later Earl of Bath, both under twenty. When Pulteney was a boy of seventeen, Congreve had submitted to him the manuscript of *The Way of the World* for his criticism.[42]

The dates of other admissions to the Kit-Cats are largely a matter of speculation. We do know that Thomas Hopkins was admitted to the club in June, 1708. Hopkins was a financier and man of great wealth who loaned money at good rates to the nobility and gentry. In Anne's reign the Whigs secured his appointment as Commissioner of the Salt Duties. At his first meeting with the Kit-Cats, Hopkins was reportedly "turned out of doors" for taking seriously Tonson's jest about the legality of his admission.[43] He became, however, an active member of the club. The portrait of Edward Hopkins[44] was not in Tonson's collection but was engraved by Faber for his volume of Kit-Cat engravings.

In December, 1709, the Duke of Marlborough was "admitted extraordinary of the Kitcat Club, and Jacob Tonson order'd to dedicate Caesar's Commentaries to him and not to the Duke of Ormond as he had promised, and six of the members are to write the epistle to him."[45] The Kit-Cats admired the victories of Queen Anne's great general and heartily supported the war with France, but Marlborough's election as an honorary member of the club was perhaps a political expedient, for he was a belated and reluctant Whig, and his Jacobite leanings were well known. In May, 1714, Vanbrugh wrote to Marlborough that he was "troubled" by "an odd report" that it was strongly suspected that the Duke was "wholy embark'd in the pretenders interest" and was to bring him over.[46]

Henry Fiennes Clinton, seventh Earl of Lincoln, K. G., was in active opposition to the Tory ministry in the last four years of Anne's reign. With nothing but a pension to depend on, he resisted the overtures of Robert Harley and proved himself an incorruptible Whig. Other Kit-Cats whose dates of admission to the club are not known were Lionel Cranfield Sackville, seventh Earl and first Duke of Dorset, K. G.; Richard Lumley, afterward second Earl of Scarborough, K. G.; John Montagu, second Duke of Montagu, K. G.; Richard Boyle, third Earl of Burlington, K. G.; Thomas Pelham-Holles, who became Earl of Clare and Duke of Newcastle-upon-Tyne, K. G.; and Theophilus Hastings, ninth Earl of Huntingdon. The youthful Duke of Newcastle, whose political career chiefly post-dates the Kit-Cat Club, was a warm patron of the club in the final years of its history.

Jacob Tonson had his favorites among the club members. It is doubtful how much credit should be attached to the rather unflattering picture of Tonson's friendship with Congreve in Nicholas Rowe's "The Reconcilement," published in *The Muses Mercury* in March, 1707, and curiously described in that journal as "a Paper of Verses . . . far from being satyrical." The poem is in the form of a debate between Tonson and Congreve. Tonson laments the passing of those merry days at his house in Fleet Street when the two friends shared wine, wit, and mirth and Tonson considered himself "the happiest creature on God's yearth." Congreve regrets the alteration in Jacob's cheerful, honest ways since he took to drinking with noble lords and toasting their ladies. Tonson concedes that he now "dotes" on Captain Vanbrugh, "A most sweet-natur'd gentleman, and pleasant." And Congreve, for his part, confesses that his affections have been transferred to Temple and Delavall.[47] However, when Tonson inquires if Congreve might be persuaded to leave his new friends and let Tonson "warm my bunnions at your fire," Congreve agrees that he *would* forsake for Tonson "the gay sailor and the gentle knight,"

> Though civil persons they, you ruder were
> And had more humours than a dancing bear.[48]

Jesting aside, Tonson told Pope that Garth, Vanbrugh, and Congreve were "the three most honest-hearted, real good men" of the poetical members of the Kit-Cat Club.[49] Tonson both loved Congreve and profoundly admired his genius, and Vanbrugh was probably Tonson's most intimate and congenial friend. The company of doctors, particularly of witty ones, always delighted Tonson. No man would have relished more keenly Garth's rejoinder to Steele, when Steele rebuked the doctor for lingering over his wine at the club and neglecting his patients. "Nay, nay, Dick," said Garth, pulling out his consulting list, "it is no urgent matter after all, for nine of them have such bad constitutions that not all the physicians in the world could save them; and the other six have such good constitutions that all the physicians in the world could not kill them."[50]

According to Pope, Tonson declared that the club would be "ruined" the day Lord Mohun and James Berkeley entered it. When Mohun broke down the gilded emblem on the top of Tonson's chair, Jacob complained to his friends "that a man who would do that would cut a man's throat." Tonson "had the good and the forms of the society much at heart."[51] Nevertheless, Tonson's own manners, in his more relaxed hours at the club, were not above reproach. At one Kit-Cat meeting which "caused much diversion," Jacob "in his cups," sitting between Dormer and Walpole, "told them that he sat between the honestest man in the world and the greatest villain; and explained himself that by the honest man he meant Dormer, the other was a villain for forsaking his patrons and benefactors the juncto,[52] for which poor Jacob was severely bastinadoed."[53] In "Jinny the Just" Prior hinted at Tonson's exuberant unrestraint

> When J—— bawls out to the Club for a toast.[54]

The connection between the Knights of the Toast or Toasters and the Kit-Cat Club is shrouded in impenetrable mystery. Both clubs sat as midnight judges of wine, beauty, and wit, but perhaps the Knights of the Toast limited themselves to that function. The Toasters may have been the earlier club and may not have survived the first years of the eighteenth century. According to Blackmore, the Kit-Cats eclipsed "the fading Toast."[55] Some of the Kit-Cats may have belonged to both clubs. It is not clear whether Henry Heveningham refers to the Toasters or to the Kit-Cats in "An Epistle from Henry He[ve]ningham in Londn to the Duke of Somerset at Newmarket," beginning:

> The Knights look dull, the Toasts grow scurvy
> And ev'ry Thing's turn'd topsy turvy
> The President whome You've seen so jolly
> Gives up himself to Melancholy.[56]

These verses and another (lost) satire by Heveningham were answered in "A Letter from I. Bickerstaff to H. Heveningham occasioned by his 2 last Letters," in which "Harry" is reproached for ridiculing "the Toast" and exposing "our President" in rude rhymes.[57] Pope assumed that "our President" signified "Ja. Tonson."[58] Heveningham is mentioned in "A Ballad to the tune of Packington's Pound," in which fashionable ladies are accused of spending their time in church ogling "the Knights of the Toast."[59]

Although their toasting habits were similar,[60] the two clubs had a separate existence. They occupied opposite sides of the theater in a revival of Betterton's *The Humours of Sir John Falstaff* in 1701.[61] On the day of Dryden's funeral, when Dorset Garden had been let out for a bear baiting, butchers and bakers filled the boxes

> Where Kit-Cats sate and Toasters would be seen,
> These swoln with Wit, and those with Letch'ry lean.[62]

In a certain Kit-Cat "Ballad" in praise of "My Strawberie" the separate identity of the clubs is again recognized:

> The Kitt Katts and the Toasters
> Did never care a fig

For any other Beautie
Besides the little Whig.[63]

As practiced by the Kit-Cats, toasting was a fine art. After they had dined, their first business was toasting in succession the ladies whose names had been cut with a diamond on their toasting glasses, each name being followed by complimentary verses. In a letter to Lady Granby a certain John Charlton described the toasting at a meeting of the Kit-Cats on November 4, 1703. He observed: " 'tis proper to tell your Ladyship that a great number of glasses are chose and a set number of ladys names are writ on them, and as an addition some fine thing is to be said on every lady, and writ there to. . . . Above thirty glasses will have something of the kind I send your Ladyship, for which I ask your pardon if as I hear them I send them to you."[64]

The details of only one election, at that an irregular one, have been preserved. This election must have occurred about 1697, for Lady Mary Pierrepont, afterward Lady Mary Wortley Montagu, was less than eight years old when her father, the Earl of Kingston, proposed her to the club as a toast. Long afterward, Lady Louisa Stuart reported the incident as recalled by Lady Mary:

As a leader of the fashionable world and a strenuous Whig in party, he [Lord Kingston] of course belonged to the Kit-Cat Club. One day, at a meeting to choose toasts for the year, a whim seized him to nominate her [Lady Mary], then not eight years old, a candidate; alleging that she was far prettier than any lady on their list. The other members demurred, because the rules of the club forbade them to elect a beauty whom they had never seen. "Then you shall see her," cried he; and in the gaiety of the moment sent orders home to have her finely dressed and brought to him at the tavern, where she was received with acclamations, her claim unanimously allowed, her health drunk by every one present, and her name engraved in due form upon a drinking-glass. The company consisting of some of the most eminent men in England, she went from the lap of one poet, or patriot, or statesman, to the arms of another, was feasted with sweetmeats, overwhelmed with caresses, and, what perhaps already pleased her better than either, heard her wit and beauty extolled on every side. Pleasure, she said, was too poor a word to express her sensations; they amounted to ecstasy; never again, throughout her whole future life, did she pass so happy a day. . . . Her father carried on the frolic, and, as we may conclude, confirmed the taste, by having her picture painted for the club-room, that she might be enrolled a regular toast.[65]

Lists of the toasts for the years 1701, 1703, 1708, 1712, and 1714 have survived. The names of certain popular beauties recur, notably those of Lady Sunderland, Lady Carlisle, the Duchess of Bolton, Mrs. Dunch, and Lady Wharton.[66] The first three of these lists are included in a little manuscript volume in the British Museum, Add. MSS. 40,060, which supplies, if poorly, between the years 1687 and 1712, "the tragic absence of a minute-book"[67] of Kit-Cat meetings. The entries in this volume, in the same hand and usually dated, refer mainly to Kit-Cat activities.[68]

In 1701, with the War of the Spanish Succession in prospect, the motif for the toasts was "La Flote Triomphante," the ladies being represented as ships of war. Forty-three "ships" were designated, among them Lady Carlisle as "La Fière," Lady Wharton as "La Friponne," the Duchess of St. Albans as "La Conquerante," Lady Manchester as "L'Invincible," the Duchess of Bolton as "La Soleille," Lady Essex as "La Belle," Diana Kirke as "La Bijou," and Lady Mary Sackville as "L'Esperance."[69] The manuscript list is preceded by the lines:

> What can resist our two great Naveys joyn'd?
> With that we conquer'd France, with this Mankind.

Following the list is "The Oath of the Tost by Mr Congreve."

> By Bacchus and by Venus swear
> That you will only name the fair
> Whose Chains you at the present wear.
> And so lett witt with Wine go round
> And she you love prove kind and sound.[70]

In the 1716 edition of *The Fifth Part of Miscellany Poems* Tonson included "Verses Written for the Toasting-Glasses of the Kit-Cat Club in the Year 1703." Thirty-two ladies were toasted in that year, some by more than one member, with Garth, Halifax, Congreve, and Mainwaring writing the greatest number of signed toasts. Some Kit-Cats may have felt unequal to composing verses or hesitant to acknowledge their efforts. The verses are in similar, conventional vein, all of the ladies being heralded as goddesses whose charms are irresistible. Halifax celebrated Dorset's daughter, the fifteen-year-old Duchess of Beaufort,[71] as well as her parents, in the lines:

> Offspring of a Tuneful Sire,
> Blest with more than mortal Fire,
> Likeness of a Mother's Face,
> Blest with more than mortal Grace:
> You with double Charms suprize,
> With *His* Wit, and with *Her* Eyes.[72]

Congreve, who toasted four ladies, paid special tribute, in the graceful language which he could always command, to pretty Di Kirke:[73]

> Fair Written Name, but deeper in my Heart;
> A Diamond cannot cut like Cupid's Dart.
> Quickly the Cordial of her Health apply;
> For when I cease to toast bright Kirk, I die.[74]

The marriage of Diana Kirke to John Dormer, Congreve's fellow Kit-Cat, was to end in disaster. The tragedy of Diana Dormer had already been played out before Jacob Tonson published these toasts. The notorious publisher Edmund Curll added the Dormers to his profitable series of infamous cases of adultery and divorce.

No verses have been preserved for 1708, but the ladies were toasted in that year with such flattering epithets as: "The Desirable" (Lady Rialton), "The Miracle" (Lady Sunderland), "The Conquering" (Lady Monthermer), "The Careless" (Mrs. Dunch), "The Dejected" (Lady Scudamore), "The Belov'd" (the Duchess of Bolton).[75] Neatly printed lists of the toasts for 1712 and 1714 are among the Tonson MSS in the National Portrait Gallery in London. Each list has thirty-nine names, comprising a number of former toasts and many new ones. Both lists are headed by the Duchess of Bolton and include all four handsome daughters of the Duke of Marlborough. Jacob Tonson was an astute enough publisher to realize the advertising appeal of printed lists, and they may have been an annual publication. In January, 1716, Steele informed Leonard Welsted:

> I have writ three Couplets for the Toasts. They are to be printed under their Names for the Kitt Catt Club. These are the Verses:
>
> > Bright dames, when 1st we meet unheeded passe
> > We read frail charms on Monuments of Glasse.
> > In Joyless Streams the Purple Chrystal flows

Till each is nam'd for whom each Bosom glows.
Then Friendship Love and Wine unite their fires
Then all their Homage pay, where each admires.[76]

Having paid ceremonial court to the ladies, the Kit-Cats were free to direct against them some well-aimed barbs of witty raillery. The Punch Club, perhaps an appendage of the Kit-Cats, conducted mock trials against ladies who exacted from their admirers too severe a servitude. In a set of whimsical "Votes" (dated March, 1702) at the Punch Club is the item:

The Complaint of Edward Dunch Esq Member of this house shewing that Lady Eliz Cromwell[77] had by Litigious words affronted his person and endeavoured by severall Scandalous invectives to destroy his unblemisht reputation with the Ladies.
Ordered that the said Lady be brought to the Bar of the house, and she was accordingly brought, where she owned her offence and on her knees received a reprimand from Mr Speaker[78] but at the request of Mr Congreve was discharged without paying her fees.[79]

One of the amusements of the club was extemporaneous versifying in which the more nimble-witted members engaged. The Kit-Cat manuscript volume in the British Museum includes a dialogue (untitled, dated July, 1708), which may be a fairly faithful version of one such fencing match. The poem has been attributed to Arthur Mainwaring and is said to have been "either written at the Kit-Cat Club, or at their Request."[80] Marlborough's recent victory in the battle of Oudenarde had put the Kit-Cats in the highest spirits, and Jacob in the Chair began the meeting with a novel toast for the occasion.

Tonson   Since Cob gives the Feast
And Hoppy's deceas'd
     And the Club's at Service so hard
Wee think it our duty
To toast a New Beauty
     Call'd Mademoiselle Oudenard.

Thomas Hopkins at once protested at this fresh example of Tonson's erratic appraisal of beauties.

Hopkins   All joy to his Grace
For this Ninth of his Race

> She's as fair as most of the Former
> But where is that He
> Durst so impudent be
> To compare her with Lady Mounthermer.

Topham then entered the fray to attack Hokpins as a feeble rhymster.

Topham
> Was't his Zeal or his Drink
> Made Hoppy's grave Ink
> Flow as even his blood was grown Warmer
> Tho it cost him some pains
> From his Politick brains
> To squeeze out a Rhime to Mounthermer.

> He at last has thought fitt
> To shew that in Witt
> He's no more than in Judgment a Novice,
> And there's hopes that in time
> Memorials in Rhime
> Will be sung by the Clerks in his Office.

> Some may reckon such Ayres
> Too pert for Gray Hairs
> And that his years may his Fancy endanger.
> But dispair not Old Man
> Let thy gingle chime on
> For Cato learnt Greek at the same Age.

Hoppy's reply
> Such good Friends as wee
> Should better agree
> But since you are pleas'd to begin Sr
> My old foolish Muse
> Shall never refuse
> To engage with a wise man of Windsor.

At this juncture Halifax intervened to assail Topham.

Ld Halifax
> Tho your Worships Antique
> And vers'd in Old Greek,
> With moderns you never could pass
> Till the Chancellors Wine
> Did your Fancy refine
> And taught you Records thro' a Glass.

Topham's
Answer
[to Halifax]

You mistake the thing quite
I was sooner polite
  And have had from your Master a Summons
To see books and eat hard
When you were no Bard
  But an indigent Lawyer in Commons.

I owe nothing to Boyle
For his Wine or his Oyle
  To feed my Poetic Invention
Whilst Summons is made
Of your whole rhiming Trade
  To rig out one poor Jack French-man.

[to Hopkins]

Then rouse me no more
Thou Witt of threescore
  When time shall thy Poetry blast
Great Demosthenes
In my English shall please
  And my notes on Herodotus last.

After one more ambiguous sally, Hopkins made a final thrust:

[to Halifax]

Your Lordship is bitt
To strike Sallies on Witt
  For whatso'ere Lownds can say for 't
There's no fund or bottom
In Hopkins or Topham
  And you must be sure to pay for 't.[81]

Various poems and ballads were either composed at the club meetings or given their first airing there by their Kit-Cat authors. Prior's "Celia to Damon" (February, 1703), his delectable "An English Padlock" (January, 1705), and Vanbrugh's "To a Lady More Cruel than Fair" (November, 1703) were notable offerings of this sort.[82] At the Brothers' Club the club printer, John Barber, regularly appeared after dinner with pieces just off the press for the club members to discuss.[83] At the Kit-Cat Club it was not necessary to send for Tonson, who was on the spot, and who no doubt had come to the meetings well equipped with his recent publications.

Kit-Cat poets and dramatists put their pens at the service of their country, supporting, of course, Whig interests. Addison was the author of the most famous of the poems, *The Campaign* (1704), and the most famous play, *Cato* (1713), which the Tories also attempted to claim for their cause. Rowe's *Tamerlane* (1701), Joseph Trapp's *Abra-Mulé* (1704), and Dennis's *Liberty Asserted* (1704), the two former published by Tonson, are other examples of Whig propaganda which the Whigs helped to popularize.[84] Congreve wrote for Whig gatherings a lively Whiggish ballad, "The History and Fall of the Conformity Bill" (January, 1705),[85] and another ballad called "The Frenchman's Lamentation" (July, 1708) on King Louis' defeat at Oudenarde.[86] The Kit-Cat manuscript volume in the British Museum ends with "A New Protestant Litany" (February, 1712), a humorous attack on the Tory ministers, Harley and St. John, saved in the nick of time by the creation of "a dozen" new Tory peers.[87]

The Kit-Cats were well known for their patronage of dramatists and the theater. On May 14, 1700, Edward Hinton wrote to his cousin, John Cooper: "Dryden was buried by the Bishop of Rochester at the Abbey on Monday; the Kit-Cat Club were at the charge of his funeral. . . . Dr. Garth made a Latin speech, and threw away some words and a great deal of false Latin in praise of the poet."[88] Dryden's body, said to have been rescued by Garth from an ignoble burial, had lain in state for twelve days in the Hall of the College of Physicians. Garth had issued printed invitations,[89] no doubt supplied by Tonson, to the funeral service, and the Kit-Cats and many others followed the procession to Westminster Abbey, where Dryden was buried between the graves of Chaucer and Cowley. According to a contemporary satire, "Jacob [Tonson] the Muses Midwife" was a prominent figure among the mourners.[90]

Another occasion for manifesting Kit-Cat solidarity was the very popular revival in January, 1700, of Betterton's *The Humours of Sir John Falstaff* for Betterton's benefit, a production which must have been far from pleasing to Jeremy Collier and other critics of the theater. Prior, happy to be back in England, gave Abraham Stanyan a joyous account of the revival.

> To-morrow night Batterton [*sic*] acts Falstaff, and to encourage that poor house the Kit Katters have taken one sidebox, and the Knights of the Toast have taken the other. We have made up a Prologue for Sir John in favour of eating and drinking, and to rally your toasts, and I have on this occasion four lines upon Jacob. We will send you the whole Prologue when we have it together.
>
> N.B.—My Lord Dorset is at the head of us, and Lord Carbury

is general of the enemy's forces, and that we dine at my Lord Dorset's and go from thence in a body.[91]

The Prologue mentioned by Prior and spoken by Betterton as Falstaff was published that same year and perhaps includes two of Prior's lines, a possible reference to Tonson's corpulence:

> But here I see a side-Box better lin'd,
> Where old plump Jack in Miniature I find.[92]

The club members often attended the theater *en masse*. On these occasions Dorset could be recognized by his ribbon of the Garter, with D'Urfey "or some other Impertinent Poet" talking to him. Halifax sat "on the Kitcat side," with Jacob Tonson "standing Door-Keeper for him."[93] Dramatists found it worth while to solicit the support of the club. William Burnaby in the Prologue to his maiden effort, *The Reform'd Wife*, expressed the hope that the Kit-Cats could either enjoy his humble fare or seek better refreshment in Kit-Cat day dreams.

> Often for Change the meanest things are good,
> Thus tho' the Town all delicates afford,
> A Kit-cat is a Supper for a Lord.
> But if your Nicer taste resolves to day
> To have no relish for our Author's Play,
> Place some diverting Scene before your Mind,
> And think of that, to which you will be kind,
> So thus when heavily the moments pass,
> Toaster's to Circulate the lazy Glass
> By nameing some bright Nymph their draughts refine,
> And taste at once the joys of Love and Wine.[94]

Thomas D'Urfey dedicated his comic opera *Wonders in the Sun* (1706), published by Tonson, to "the Right Noble, Honourable and Ingenious Patrons of Poetry, Music, &c. The Celebrated Society of the Kit-Cat Club."[95]

To the building of the new Queen's Theatre in the Haymarket, which opened in 1705 with Vanbrugh and Congreve as joint managers, twenty-nine persons subscribed, including the following Kit-Cats: Somerset (heading the list), Richmond, Carlisle, Halifax, Essex, Manchester, Kingston, Grafton, Cornwallis, Dunch, Hartington, and Wharton. The subscribers, who were to have the privilege of seeing all plays and operas gratis, agreed to pay one hundred guineas in four equal installments: one, on the signing of the lease; the second, when the walls were twenty feet high; the third, when the walls had been carried up to the roof; and the fourth, when the building was covered.[96] Tonson evidently received the subscriptions, for according to a satiric advertisement, they were collected "at the Sign of the two left Legs near Gray's Inn Back-Gate."[97] A Jacobite journalist, Charles Leslie, described in scornful language the dedication of the theater:

> The Kit-Cat Club is now grown *Famous* and *Notorious*, all over the *Kingdom*. And they have Bulit [*sic*] a *Temple* for their *Dagon*, the new *Play-house* in the *Hay-Market*. The *Foundation* was laid with great *Solemnity*, by a Noble Babe of *Grace* [Lady Sunderland]. And over or under the *Foundation Stone* is a Plate of *Silver*, on which is Graven *Kit Cat* on the one side, and *Little Whigg* on the other. This is in *Futurum rei Memoriam*, that after *Ages* may know by what *Worthy Hands*, and for what good *Ends* this stately *Fabrik* was Erected. And there was such *Zeal* shew'd, and all *Purses* open to carry on this Work, that it was almost as soon *Finish'd* as *Begun*. While *Paul's* Work is become a Proverb.[98]

Subsequently, probably in 1707, the Kit-Cats were involved in a subscription of four hundred guineas "for the encouragement of good comedies" at the Haymarket Theatre. Pope once saw a paper (now lost) in the handwriting of Halifax to this effect.[99] For further details of the transaction we are indebted to Colley Cibber. "Three plays of the best Authors" were to be chosen, and each subscriber was to have three tickets for the first day of each play, for his single payment of three guineas. Halifax "so zealously encouraged" this subscription that it was soon completed. "The Plays were *Julius Caesar* of Shakespear; the *King and No King* of Fletcher; and the Comic Scenes of Dryden's *Marriage a la Mode* and of his *Maiden Queen* put together." The effort was so successful that both actors and managers profited, and several actors had their salaries "handsomely advanc'd."[100]

The Kit-Cats were much interested in architecture. Many of them had traveled extensively on the Continent and, impressed by what they had seen, had returned home to have their ancestral country houses enlarged or new mansions erected. Vanbrugh's services as an architect were much in demand. Among his architectural enterprises, in addition to Blenheim and the Haymarket Theatre, were Castle Howard for Carlisle; Kimbolton Castle for Manchester; Kneller Hall for Kneller; various small temples at Stowe for Cobham; Claremont, as well as alterations in Nottingham Castle, for Newcastle; and Grimsthorpe for the Duke of Ancaster. In 1705 a group of Kit-Cats made an unheralded visit to inspect progress on the works at Blenheim. Nicholas Hawksmoor, assistant surveyor at Blenheim, listed the visitors as Carlisle, Kingston, Granville, Wharton, Hartington, Godolphin, and "2 other gentlemen."[101] From a letter from Vanbrugh to Tonson, twenty years later, it appears that Vanbrugh and Tonson[102] were the two others who made that tour.

The reign of Queen Anne was the period of greatest political activity in the history of the Kit-Cats. During this period the Whigs were mainly in vigorous opposition to the government and, with very few exceptions, provided a united and effective front against the Tories. Kit-Cat deserters were expelled from the club, Prior being a conspicuous example. Prior's expulsion rankled with him, for he felt that his literary reputation had been impugned. In the sixth number of *The Examiner* Prior bitterly reproached his former allies:

> The *Collective* Body of the Whigs have already engross'd our Riches; and their *Representatives* the *Kit-Cat*, have pretended to make a Monopoly of our Sense. Thus it happens, that Mr. P———r, by being expell'd the Club, ceases to be a *Poet*; and Sir *Harry F*———*e* becomes one by being admitted into it. 'Tis here that Wit and Beauty are decided by plurality of Voices: The *Child's* Judgment shall make *H*———*y* pass for a Fool; and *Jacob's* Indulgence shall preserve Lady *H*———*t* from the Tallow Candle.[103]

On one occasion Richmond called a special meeting of the club to investigate the conduct of Somerset.[104] On April 7, 1710, James Brydges wrote to General Cadogan: "The Duke of Somerset (Thursday was sevennight) was expellet the Chit-cat [*sic*] by a vote brought in ready cut and dried by Ld. Wharton: the crime objected, the words of the vote say, was for being suspected to have held conferences with Robin the Trickster [Robert Harley]."[105] But Somerset soon returned to the Whigs and was readmitted to the club.

Both William and Anne preferred to keep a balance between the two political parties, although William's personal sympathies were with the Whigs and Anne's with the Tories. By dismissing his Whig ministers, near the end of his reign, William won Tory co-operation in two important Whig objectives: the Act of Settlement (1701), providing for the succession of the House of Hanover, and the Treaty of Grand Alliance (1701), bringing England the assistance of Austria and Holland in the war with France. On his deathbed William earnestly urged the union of England and Scotland. In the reign of Queen Anne the Whig opposition was able to implement the Act of Settlement with the Regency Act (1706), providing the machinery which was to lead to the quiet and orderly Hanoverian succession, and sponsored the Act of Union with Scotland (1707), which brought the Whigs the support of the Scottish Presbyterians. Indeed, the Whigs accomplished more in opposition than in their brief period of power (1708–1710), when Somers served as Lord President of the Council.

Marlborough's great victories (1704–1708) strengthened the Whigs and compelled Marlborough to form an alliance with them in order to obtain the financial assistance necessary for prosecuting the War of the Spanish Succession. In 1710 there were serious Whig reverses. Walpole was charged with corruption and spent some time in the Tower, waited upon by Whig friends and meditating revenge. Duchess Sarah and Marlborough were dismissed. The Peninsula campaign ended disastrously with the defeat and capture of Stanhope at Brihuega. One hopeful development for the Whigs was the appointment of the Duchess of Somerset to the post of Groom of the Stole (1710), for her influence more than balanced that of Abigail Masham, bedchamber woman to the queen. In fact, the Duchess of Somerset proved to be the best friend at Court that the Whigs ever had, and her influence exceeded that of any of the Whig statesmen. During the last years of Anne's reign, the Tory ministry seemed to be making progress in secret negotiations with Louis and with French Jacobite agents. But the death of Anne in the summer of 1714 effected an abrupt end to these maneuvers and ushered in a long period of Whig supremacy.

The known political activities of the Kit-Cats during Anne's reign may be regarded as the tip of an iceberg, with a much greater accumulation hidden beneath the exposed surface. Rumors abounded, encouraged by vindictive Tories. As early as 1703 a political mission was read into Tonson's journey to Holland in that year. Vanbrugh jestingly warned his Kit-Cat friend: "do you know that the Torys (even the wisest of 'em) have been very grave upon your going to Holland; . . . I could win a hundred pounds, if I were sure you had not made a trip to Hanover, which you may possibly hear sworn when you come home again; so I'd advise you to bring a very exact Journal, well attested."[106] It was insinuated that Tonson and Halifax weighed state affairs "in frequent close Debate."[107] It was reported that "some persons of distinction, in their secret conferences, which they held late at night" seriously considered parliamentary action to remove Mrs. Masham from the Queen's service, but abandoned the project when Somers, Wharton, and Halifax advised against it as an unconstitutional procedure.[108] In the anxious days of June, 1714, when the dangerous nature of the Queen's illness was recognized, the Kit-Cat Club was holding meetings "every evening" with the recently arrived "Dublin Plenipo's" at Jenny Man's Coffee House at Charing Cross.[109]

Even when the political activities of the Kit-Cats have sound historical confirmation, many details of them are still missing. Wharton suggested the outline of the Regency Act, which the ministry drew up with the legal help of Somers and which Wharton "piloted through" [110] the House of Lords. Halifax was subsequently sent to Hanover to present a copy of the act to the Elector. Somers drew up the proposal for the Act of Union with Scotland, "perhaps the best piece of service that he ever rendered to his country,"[111] and the Commissioners appointed to deal with the Scotch in this matter included Somerset, Somers, Wharton, Halifax, Carlisle, Kingston, and Hartington.[112]

Some of the Kit-Cat schemes backfired. Chief of these was the impeachment and trial (February, 1710) of Henry Sacheverell, an Anglican clergyman who had attacked the Revolution in a sermon preached at St. Paul's. On December 20, 1709, John Bridges (the younger) wrote to Sir William Trumbull: "The fate and impeachment of the poor Doctor [Sacheverell] was some time since fully concluded upon at the Kit-Cat Club, where my Lord Marlborough, they say, was present, assented to it, and has actually enrolled himself a member of that detestable society."[113] The Whigs unwisely made a *cause célèbre* of the trial. Although Sacheverell was voted guilty by a small majority, the sentence imposed on him was so mild as to be insignificant. He had defended himself with oratorical fervor and, with Tory pressure, became a popular idol. Dissenters' meeting houses were burned by a riotous mob, and the Queen's Horse Guards had to save the Bishop of Salisbury's house from a similar fate.[114] As a consequence of anti-Sacheverell zeal, the Whig ministry fell, and Tory dominance was assured by the Queen's creation of twelve Tory peers.

The Kit-Cats were thwarted in their attempt to stage a public demonstration against the Tory ministry's peace policy on November 17, 1711, the anniversary of Queen Elizabeth's birthday. They subscribed considerable sums, according to Swift a thousand pounds,[115] for elaborately dressed effigies of the Pope, the Devil, the Pretender, and various Jesuits, cardinals, and friars, which were to be carried in a torchlight procession and burned. It was alleged, but not verified, that they had distributed money for a popular riot to coincide with these ceremonies. The Tory ministers ordered the images seized and held in custody until the "danger" was over. Such excessive caution made the ministers look rather foolish, as Oldmixon took pleasure in noting in his account of the episode:

> the Earl of Dartmouth issued out his Warrant to her Majesty's Messengers, for the seizing and securing the said Paste-board Pictures; pursuant to which Warrant, from one of her Majesty's principal Secretaries of State, several of the Queen's Messengers, sustain'd by a Detachment of the Troops of the Household, march'd at 12 o'Clock at Night, November the 16th, to an empty House in Drury-Lane, where they found the Pictures aforesaid array'd in Taffety and Tinsel, and meeting with no Resistance from them, nor the empty House, they took hold of them, and carry'd them very manfully to the Earl of Dartmouth's Office: And the Truth is, these were the only Trophies the new Ministers had to brag of. . . . The train'd Bands of London and Westminster were immediately raised, notwithstanding the Enemies were Prisoners in the Secretary's Office, and kept three days together under Guard, to the great Diversion of the Whigs, and of such Tories whose Wits were not run away from them. The Earl of Wharton being ask'd by one of them, What was become of the Pictures of the Devil, the Pope, and the Pretender? Answer'd merrily. Their Disciples came by Night and stole them away.[116]

The Kit-Cats were as mystified as most of the nation by the secret peace negotiations with France which were carried on from 1711 to the death of the Queen. Prior's journey in disguise to Paris to convey a private message to Louis from the Tory ministers could not be kept a secret, for he was arrested in Dover on his return to England. Mainwaring in a ballad on "Mat's Peace," predicting the pillory for Prior, commented:

> The News from Abroad does a Secret reveal,
> Which has been confirm'd both at Dover and Deal,
> That one Mr. Mathews, once called plain Mat,
> Has been doing at Paris, the Lord knows what.[117]

As Prior continued to act as intermediary between the English ministers and the French government, it seemed increasingly probable that unless the Whigs took immediate precautions, the Pretender might be foisted upon England as Anne's successor.

In 1713, when Tonson went to the Continent on business connected with his trade, he was also entrusted with a political mission for the Kit-Cats. From Utrecht on September 29, 1713, John Drummond wrote to the Earl of Oxford: "A famous printer, commonly called secretary to the Kitcat Club, is on this side, doing his friends all the service he can."[118] By November, Tonson was in Paris, investigating Prior's apparent involvement in Jacobite plots. On May 2 of the following year, Nathaniel Hooke, an English Jacobite spy in the service of the French government, wrote to the Marquis d'Argenson that Tonson, *"créature du duc de Somerset, de Mylord Wharton, de l'évêque de Salisbury e des plus zélez Whigs et fort avant dans leurs secrets,"* had been in Paris for some time and was often at St. Germain. Hooke declared that Tonson's trade was only the pretext for his visit and that *"il est certainement employé pour observer M. Prior, et pour fournir . . . des armes à ses patrons contre lui et contre le service du Roy."*[119] The report came a little too late to be useful, for Tonson had returned to England in April.[120] In view of the usual tactics employed by both Jacobites and their adversaries in gaining information, Dottin must be considered unduly severe in his verdict that "Tonson's good character, already damaged by what we learn of his disputes with Dryden, is completely destroyed"[121] by Hooke's report.

Whatever his intentions may have been, Tonson returned to England and to the Kit-Cats empty-handed. Prior had nothing to tell him,[122] for the French agents, realizing that he was no Jacobite, had carefully excluded Prior from any knowledge of the actual steps being taken to bring James to the English throne.[123] Nor was Prior, humorous and perceptive, an unsuspecting victim of Jacob's probing. On November 23, 1713, Prior wrote to Bolingbroke: "Jacob Tonson is here, the dog is a kind of a convert; but can the leopard change his spots?"[124] In a later letter to Bolingbroke, Prior remarked that he and Tonson had been amicably searching for some books of travels that Bolingbroke wanted, but "neither I nor Jacob Tonson can find them."[125]

Steele was the best, as well as the most reckless, of the Whig journalists whose pens were at the disposal of the Kit-Cats. If "the Club" meant for Steele, as it did for Vanbrugh, the Kit-Cat Club, it was the Kit-Cats who raised a subscription for the publication of Steele's best and most controversial pamphlet, *The Crisis* (1713), in which Steele affirmed that the Protestant succession was in danger. In an undated note to his wife (October, 1713) Steele wrote:

> I have, on second thoughts, resolved to go to the Club and ask for a Subscription my self: And, with as gay an air as I can lay before them that I take it to be their Constitution to do it as I am labouring in the common Cause.
>
> P. S. It frets my proud heart to do this, but it must be.[126]

Steele's appeal was successful, and in a later note he was able to tell his wife: "I find what I desire is transacting and to be done by a General Subscription, for divulging the Crisis all over the Kingdom."[127] *The Crisis* did have a country-wide circulation, some forty thousand copies being sold; but the pamphlet was the chief cause of Steele's expulsion from the House of Commons, where his Kit-Cat friends vainly defended him. Within a month of the publication of *The Crisis*, Tory ministers were asking the Pretender to change his religion and were baffled by his refusal to do so. On June 24, 1714, Steele wrote to Mrs. Steele: "Lord Wharton, whom I met at the House, engaged me at the Kitt Katt at three of Clock,"[128] for a meeting at which further attacks on the ministry were very likely debated.

Although the Tory ministers had feared for some months that the Queen's illness might result in her death, they were unprepared for it when she suffered a stroke and died on August 1, 1714. The Whigs, on the contrary, were ready for the event. The quarrels of

Harley and Bolingbroke had precipitated the dismissal of the latter, and another Lord Treasurer had not been appointed. A contemporary historian commented: "measures were early concerted by the Kit-Cat Club with a Major-General [Cadogan] who had a considerable Post in the Foot-Guards, to seize the Tower, upon the first appearance of Danger, and to secure in it such Persons as were justly suspected to favour the Pretender."[129] Such action proved unnecessary. When the Queen lay dying at Kensington and the Privy Council was in session there, Somerset and Argyll,[130] who were members of the Council but had not been summoned to the meeting, informed Baron Bothmar, the Elector of Hanover's agent, of the Queen's relapse and rode hastily to the palace, where the Duke of Shrewsbury welcomed them at the Council. The dying Queen gave the Lord Treasurer's staff to Shrewsbury, a moderate Tory. At the Queen's death, the Duchess of Somerset handed over to the Council a sealed packet, thought to contain the Queen's wishes regarding the succession, but which the Queen had desired to be burned without being opened; and "after some debate," her wishes were carried out.[131] The steps arranged in the Regency Act for the Hanoverian succession were taken in due course without the slightest disorder, and George I ascended the throne of England.

In the reign of George I honors came swiftly to members of the Kit-Cat Club,[132] but the important days of the club had ended. A note on March 30, 1717, from Steele to his wife, supplies the last reference to a meeting of the club: "The omission of last post was occassioned by my attendance on the Duke of Newcastle, who was in the chair at the Kit-Cat."[133] As late as January 18, 1719, Dr. Abel Evans, an Oxford poet, submitted verses to Tonson to be returned in case "the Club do not like these verses & you do not think of printing 'em."[134] It is almost certain that Tonson's long absence in Paris (1718–1720) brought the club to an end. Long ago, Blackmore had queried:

> Who else has Shoulders equal to its weight? [135]

Jacob Tonson had indeed provided the unifying force of the Kit-Cat Club. When Tonson was in Holland, Vanbrugh had assured him: "the Kit Catt will never meet without you."[136] And Somerset had reported: "our club is dissolv'd till you revive it again which wee are impatient off."[137] After the club had ceased to exist, surviving members recalled with gratitude and nostalgia the genial warmth of Kit-Cat meetings, which they attributed in large part to the founding secretary who gave the feast. In reminiscent mood Grafton wrote to Tonson: "I wish it was in my power . . . to be able to contribute to our passing those agreeable Days and Nights again. Pray come to your Tenement. We will doe all in our power to make it Chearfull."[138] In the summer of 1725, when he spent a fortnight at Stowe, Vanbrugh paid Tonson a similar tribute: "our former Kit Cat days were remembered with pleasure. We were one night reckoning who was left,[139] and both Ld Carlisle and & Cobham exprest a great desire of having one meeting next Winter, if you come to Towne, not as a Club, but old Friends that have been of a Club, and the best Club, that ever met."[140]

Jacob's Ladder to Fame

onson had a gift for appraising the talents of budding authors. Moreover, he had surrounded himself with a group of excellent advisers. A youthful poet, Alexander Pope, was naturally elated when he received a letter from Tonson expressing an interest in his earliest literary achievement, his "Pastorals." On April 20, 1706, Tonson wrote to Pope:

Sr,

I have lately seen a pastoral of yours in mr Walsh & mr Congreves hands, which is extreamely ffine & is generally approv'd off by the best Judges in poetry.[1] I Remember I have formerly seen you at my Shop & am Sorry I did not Improve my Acquaintance with you. If you design your Poem for the Press no person shall be more Carefull in the printing of it, nor no one can give a greater Incouragemt to it; than Sr yor Most Obedient / Humble Servant / Jacob Tonson
Pray give me a line pr Post.[2]

The flattering inquiry led to the publication of the "Pastorals," together with Pope's paraphrase of Chaucer's "Merchant's Tale" as "January and May" and the "Episode of Sarpedon" from Homer's *Iliad*, in *Poetical Miscellanies: The Sixth Part* (1709). Pope received a total of thirteen guineas for these contributions.[3]

Wycherley, whom Pope was assisting with a revision of his poems, perceived that his young friend had taken an important step in the right direction. He assured Pope: "I approve of your making Tonson your Muse's Introductor into the World, or Master of the Ceremonies, who has been so long a Pimp, or Gentleman-Usher to the Muses."[4] As for Pope, he could not conceal his satisfaction that "beyond all my Expectations, & far above my Demerits," he had been "most mercifully repriev'd by the Sovereign Power of Jacob Tonson" from the hands of "those barbarous Executioners of the Muses," the critics.[5]

When the Sixth Miscellany came out, Wycherley was able to report to the young poet that "nothing has lately been better received by the Publick than your part of it."[6] With a becoming, if affected, modesty, Pope replied:

> This modern Custom of appearing in Miscellanies, is very useful to the Poets, who, like other Thieves, escape by getting into a Crowd, and herd together like *Banditti*, safe only in their multitude. . . . I can be content with a bare saving game, without being thought an Eminent hand (with which title *Jacob* has graciously dignify'd his Adventurers and voluntiers in Poetry.) *Jacob* creates Poets, as Kings sometimes do Knights, not for their honour, but for money. Certainly he ought to be esteem'd a worker of Miracles, who is grown rich by Poetry.[7]

The offensive implication of "a bare saving game" brought a vigorous protest from Wycherley: "The Salt of your Wit has been enough to give a relish to the whole insipid Hotch-Potch it is mingled with; and you will make *Jacob's Ladder* raise you to Immortality."[8]

It was Bernard Lintot, rather than Tonson, who published most of Pope's poems. The change of publisher may have been due to the fact that Tonson and Pope were too well matched in the art of driving shrewd bargains. Pope did contribute a paraphrase of Chaucer's "Wife of Bath's Prologue" to Steele's *Poetical Miscellanies* (1714) and the episode of "Dryope" to Garth's edition of *Ovid's Metamorphoses*, both published by Tonson. Jacob junior, Tonson's nephew, published Pope's *The Works of Shakespear* (1723–1725), no doubt because he held most of the copyright for Shakespeare's works. The relations between Pope and Jacob junior became tinged with acrimony, and their differences had not been settled at the latter's death. The younger publisher offended Pope by publishing, with others, Lewis Theobald's rival edition of *The Works of Shakespeare* (1733), and he may have refused to resign his rights to certain poems for a collected edition of Pope's works.

Tonson began publishing for William Congreve in 1693; and unlike Pope, Congreve never transferred his allegiance to another publisher. The swiftness of Congreve's rise to the top of Jacob's ladder must have been a source of extraordinary pleasure to the publisher, and Congreve's abandonment of his dramatic career in 1700 at the age of thirty must have been deplored by Jacob quite as much

as by Congreve's other friends. Congreve continued to be regarded
by Tonson, as well as by Pope, as "Ultimus Romanorum"[9] and provided a yardstick by which Tonson measured other contemporary
dramatists and found them wanting.

Congreve contributed to Charles Gildon's *Miscellany Poems
upon Several Occasions* (1692), published by Peter Buck, five
pieces: two paraphrases of odes by Horace; "Upon a Lady's Singing,
Pindarick Ode"; and two short lyrics. Buck also published Congreve's first play, *The Old Batchelour* (1693), to which Dryden,
much impressed by its merits, had added some finishing touches. It is
probable that Dryden introduced Congreve to Tonson; and Dryden
and Tonson lost no time in enlisting Congreve's services for Tonson's Third Miscellany. In this volume reappeared in a slightly revised version Congreve's "Upon a Lady's Singing," now entitled
"On Mrs. Arabella Hunt Singing"; Congreve's paraphrase of
Horace's "Ode 9, Book I," both already published in Gildon's
Miscellany Poems; and in addition Congreve's paraphrases of two
other odes by Horace and his translation of "Laments" for Hector
from Homer's *Iliad*.

In his Dedication for the Third Miscellany, Dryden publicly attached to Congreve's translation from Homer the seal of generous,
unqualified approval. Dryden professed himself unable to mention
Congreve "without the Honour which is due to his Excellent Parts,
and that entire Affection which I bear him." He was convinced that
"my Friend has added to the Tenderness which he found in the
Original; and without Flattery, surpass'd his Author"; and he
wished Congreve had the leisure to translate all of Homer "and the
World the good Nature and Justice to encourage him in that noble
Design of which he is more capable than any Man I know."[10] To
what more valuable introduction to the literary world than this could
any young writer aspire?

Congreve was invited to translate one of Juvenal's satires, the
"Eleventh," for Dryden's impressive translation of *Juvenal and
Persius*. To the satires of the latter were prefixed congratulatory
verses in which Congreve praised Dryden as "Thou great Revealer
of dark Poesie" and "Apollo's darling Priest." In language more
felicitous and very likely more heartfelt than adorns many of Congreve's compliments to his patrons, Congreve affirmed:

As Coin, which bears some awful Monarchs Face
For more than its Intrinsick Worth will pass:
So your bright Image, which we here behold,
Adds Worth to Worth, and dignifies the Gold.[11]

Tonson published four of Congreve's plays in fairly rapid succession: *The Double-Dealer* (1694), *Love for Love* (1695), *The
Mourning Bride* (1697), and *The Way of the World* (1700).
The Double-Dealer included Dryden's famous verses to Congreve,
on which Edmund Gosse so aptly commented: "Perhaps since the
beginning of literary history there is no other example of such fine
and generous praise of a young colleague by a great old poet."[12]
Tonson did not have occasion to reprint the play until 1706. *Love
for Love* was more popular and was reprinted in 1695, 1697, and
1704. *The Mourning Bride* was reprinted in 1697 and 1703 and
The Way of the World in 1706. Meanwhile, theatrical productions
of Congreve's plays by distinguished actors served to establish Congreve's reputation ever more firmly as the leading dramatist of his
age. Jeremy Collier's attack on Congreve in *A Short View of the
Immorality and Profaneness of the English Stage* (1698) did not
damage Congreve's fame, but Congreve added nothing to it by a
somewhat frivolous reply in *Amendments of Mr. Collier's False
and Imperfect Citations*, published by Tonson in the same year.

Congreve is represented in Tonson's Fourth Miscellany by his
"Prologue to the Queen Upon Her Majesty's coming to see the Old
Batchelour" and "To Cynthia Weeping and not Speaking." In "To
Mr. Congreve" in this volume Charles Hopkins expressed what
seems to have been the consensus of Congreve's friends: "Beyond
the Poet, we the Person love."[13] Tonson's Fifth Miscellany has a
dozen of Congreve's lyrics, among which are two of the finest, "A
Hue and Cry after Fair Amoret" and "Pious Selinda goes to
Pray'rs." In the 1716 edition of *The Sixth Part of Miscellany Poems*
Tonson printed Congreve's Kit-Cat poem, "A Ballad: On the Victory at Audenarde," with Joseph Keally's Latin translation of it. An
indication of the popularity of the "Ballad" is a comment which
Lady Cowper made to the Prince of Wales in 1714. She recorded
in her *Diary*: "I told the Prince of Wales that before his coming
hither [to England], I and my Children had constantly drunk his
Health by the Name of *Young Hanover Brave*, which was the title
Mr. Congreve had given him in a Ballad. This made him ask who

Mr. *Congreve* was, and so gave me an Opportunity of saying all the Good of Mr. *Congreve* which I think he truly deserves."[14]

It became increasingly difficult to secure Congreve as a contributor to miscellanies. The editors of *Luctus Britannici* (1700) regretted that "no Fav'rite Congreve shines"[15] in their volume. Steele's *Poetical Miscellanies*, published by Tonson as a continuation of the Tonson series, has no contribution by Congreve. Steele reprinted here, however, his verses, "To Mr. Congreve, occasion'd by his Comedy, called, *The Way of the World*,"[16] and in dedicating the *Miscellanies* to Congreve observed that "the Town's opinion of them will be raised, when it sees them address'd to Mr. Congreve."[17]

Congreve's elegiac and political poems resemble the similar effusions of less gifted contemporaries. Tonson printed them elegantly, with the title pages of the elegies black bordered. The poems have not worn well nor contributed to Congreve's permanent fame, although at the time of printing they were well received. Much to Dr. Johnson's disgust, Congreve was not to be outdone by any one in extravagant pastoral imagery. In *The Mourning Muse of Alexis* (1695), one of the innumerable elegies on the death of Queen Mary, all Nature is convulsed at the Queen's death: swans die at her tomb, Echo mourns, water gods fill their urns with their tears, fauns and nymphs rove the plain distractedly, satyrs wound themselves, Pan breaks his pipe and Cupid his bow. Tonson printed a second edition of the poem that same year. *The Tears of Amaryllis for Amyntas* (1703), on the death of the Marquess of Blandford, has similar artificial pastoralism but in a quieter, more tender vein.

Like other contemporary poets, Congreve celebrated outstanding political events of his time: the victory of Namur in *A Pindarique Ode, Humbly Offer'd to the King on His Taking Namure* (1695); the Peace of Ryswick in *The Birth of the Muse* (1698); the victory of Ramillies in *A Pindarique Ode, Humbly Offer'd to the Queen, On the Victorious Progress of Her Majesty's Arms, under the Conduct of the Duke of Marlborough* (1706). Congreve equally applauded William's "resistless way"[18] and Anne's serenity "amidst the Jars / and Tumults of a World in Wars."[19] In *The Birth of the Muse*, which Johnson with some justice considered "a miserable fiction,"[20] Jove is depicted as creating the Muse to sing heroic deeds, especially William's. The poem was eagerly anticipated. On October 5, 1697, Dr. J. Woodward wrote to John

Evelyn: "Mr. Congreve is, I hear, engaged in a poem on occasion of the peace, and all who are acquainted with the performance of this gentleman expect something very extraordinary."[21]

Congreve's love of music is evidenced in the masque of *The Judgment of Paris* (1701) and *A Hymn to Harmony* (1703). Four distinguished composers competed on different days for prizes to be awarded for the best music for the masque. Congreve wrote to his friend Keally that on the occasion when Eccles' music was played, "the whole thing was better worth coming to see than the jubilee."[22] *A Hymn to Harmony* was probably solicited for the celebration of St. Cecilia's Day in 1703.

His active career as a dramatist had ended when in August, 1700, Congreve made a journey to Holland and Belgium with Jacob Tonson and Charles Mein. Mein was the first to return home, Congreve followed, probably in October, and Jacob was back in London a few months later.[23]

Five brief letters from Congreve to Tonson throw some further light on Congreve's personal relations with his publisher. In these slight epistles Congreve thanks Tonson for favors, expresses a desire to meet him, and concludes with most affectionate greetings. It was "agreeable news" when *Love for Love* was reprinted, and Congreve hoped "to hear more of the same kind every post."[24] When Tonson was again in Holland in 1703, Congreve reported that he and Jacob junior were printing "the Pastoral" (*The Tears of Amaryllis*) themselves to forestall a pirated edition. Congreve had a longing to see Barn Elms, but not until Jacob's return.[25] Because of ill health and his preoccupation, so greatly resented by Pope,[26] with Henrietta, Duchess of Marlborough, Congreve became less accessible. Nevertheless, the dramatist and his publisher remained on the most cordial terms. In his last surviving letter to Jacob (August 8, 1723), Congreve declared himself "with unalterable esteem and friendship Dear Jacob / *Ever Yours*."[27]

Although Congreve wrote no more plays after *The Way of the World*, he contributed Book III, a witty paraphrase in heroic couplets of advice to ladies, to Tonson's publication of *Ovid's Art of Love* and translated episodes in Book X of Garth's edition of *Ovid's Metamorphoses*. As a labor of love, he supervised for Tonson the first collected edition of *The Dramatick Works of John Dryden* in six volumes. In his Dedication of this work to the Duke of Newcastle, Congreve paid Dryden a tribute which was both judicious and affectionate. "I had the happiness," he recalled, "to be very Conversant, and as intimately acquainted, with Mr. *Dryden*, as the great Disproportion in our Years could allow me to be." He had been "most sensibly touched" by Dryden's request that he should be "*kind to his Remains.*" Of Dryden's writings it could be said, "No man hath written in our Language so much, and so various Matter, and in so various Manners, so well." Himself a master of exquisite prose, Congreve rightly claimed for Dryden: "His Prose has all the Clearness imaginable, together with all the Nobleness of Expression; all the Graces and Ornaments proper and peculiar to it, without deviating into the Language or Diction of Poetry."[28]

Tonson published in three volumes in 1710 a collected edition of Congreve's *Works*, which Congreve described in his Preface as "the least faulty Impression which has been printed." The three volumes were distinguished by an excellent format, with good paper and large print. The plays had decorative headpieces and tailpieces, ornamented first initial letters for each act, and ornamental lines separating the scenes. In the second volume the opera of "Semele" appeared for the first time. The third volume consisted of poems "written occasionally at distant times," with some pieces, chiefly prologues and epilogues, not previously printed. Tonson subsequently published a reissue of Congreve's *Works* in three volumes, followed by an edition in two volumes, "Revis'd by the Author." A collected edition in three volumes was published by Tonson's nephew, Jacob junior, in 1730, after Congreve's death.

It is a safe guess that Congreve, "unreproachful man,"[29] was the most considerate among the writers who employed Tonson as publisher. By recognizing that publishers, as well as authors, have problems for which allowances must be made, Congreve must have earned Tonson's unceasing gratitude. In a note "To the Reader" in *The Tears of Amaryllis for Amyntas*, Congreve stated that he had intended these verses "rather privately to Condole, than publickly to Lament." But since one copy of them had by accident been shown to a bookseller, "it was high time for me to prevent their appearing with more Faults than their own, which might probably have met with Encrease, if not from the Malice, or Ignorance, at least from the Carelessness of an under-hand Publisher."[30] While conceding in his Preface to the 1710 edition of his *Works* that there were still "too many Errata" in those volumes, Congreve remarked with good-humored composure that "those of the Press, are to be reckoned amongst things which no Diligence can prevent." And he quoted with approval Bayle's comment in the preface to the first edition of his Dictionary on the vexation of ineffectual supervision of the press: "*Je l'oublie autant que je puis, animus meminisse horret.*" One reason for publishing the collected *Works* was that in a recent spurious edition[31] the five plays had been "very faultily, as well as indirectly Published: in Prejudice both to the Author, and the Bookseller [Tonson] who has the Property of the Copy."[32]

Many of Tonson's "eminent hands" had varying degrees of success yet failed to reach the top of Jacob's ladder. Three others who did achieve enduring fame were Prior, Addison, and Steele.

Matthew Prior was discovered at an early age by the Earl of Dorset. The Earl found the boy, in the tavern where he assisted his uncle, poring over a copy of Horace, and saw that the lad was capable of making graceful translations of what he was reading for the diversion of gentlemen of literary taste who frequented the tavern. Dorset paid for the continued education of "Matt" at Westminster School, and it was probably Dorset who introduced Prior to Tonson and recommended him for membership in the Kit-Cat Club.

Not long after Matt received his B.A. degree at St. John's College, Cambridge, he joined his friend and fellow alumnus, Charles Montague, in the composition of *The Hind and the Panther Transvers'd To the Story of The Country-Mouse and the City-Mouse*, published anonymously by W. Davis in 1687. At a time when Dryden's *The Hind and the Panther* was "in everybody's hands" and "very much cried up for a masterpiece," Prior and Montague, and no doubt many other readers, were struck by the absurdity of four-footed beasts' engaging in religious controversy. According to James Montague, Charles's brother, when Matt and Charles met one day at James's chambers in the Middle Temple, Charles picked up a copy of *The Hind and the Panther* which lay open on a table and read aloud the first four lines, then proposed writing a parody of the poem in the manner of Horace's fable of the city mouse and the country mouse. Matt took the book from Charles's hands and quickly composed the first four lines of the parody, the reading of which "set the Company in Laughter." On a loose sheet of paper Charles wrote four more lines, and between them the two produced in due course a merry satire which, when published, became immediately popular.[33] It was soon known who were the authors, and, as has been noted, the reputation "Mouse Montague" acquired for the poem was the foundation of his diplomatic career.

Although Prior's political advancement came slowly and brought him more hard work and vexation than honor, he attracted early and favorable notice by poetical contributions to contemporary periodicals. His verses "To the Honourable Charles Montague" were published in *The Gentleman's Journal* in 1692, introduced by a puff from Motteux, the editor: "Whilst things like the following Stanza's made by Mr. Prior, shall be given or sent me, you may believe I shall be prouder of making them publick than my own."[34] In the same journal in the same year appeared two of Prior's lyrics, "Whilst I am scorch'd with hot desire" and "An Ode—While blooming youth and gay delight." Also in 1692 Prior contributed to Gildon's edition of *Miscellany Poems Upon Several Occasions* "A Letter from Mr. Prior to Mr. Fleetwood Sheppard," in which Prior offered Dorset's steward at Copt Hall a pleasant, jesting account of a day in the country. Tonson would have noted with amusement the reference to himself:

> T——n, who is himself a Wit,
> Counts Authors Merits by the Sheet;
> Thus each should down with all he thinks,
> As Boys eat Bread to fill up Chinks.[35]

Prior published anonymously before 1700 three poems which he persistently refused to acknowledge as his. Written c. 1687, "Satyr on the Poets, in imitation of the Seventh Satyr of Juvenal," was first published in *Chorus Poetarum* in 1694, again in *Poems on Affairs of State* in 1698. The poem is so severe a satire on contemporary poets, including "Drudge Dryden," that Prior admitted:

> More I cou'd say; but care not much to meet
> A Crab-Tree Cudgel, in a narrow Street.

He attacked Mulgrave, the Lord Chamberlain, who had satirized Dorset, in the biting couplet:

> Dance then Attendance in slow Mulgrave's Hall,
> Read Mapps, or count the sconces till he call.[36]

Later on, when Mulgrave had become his patron, Prior had no desire to claim the authorship of this poem. "A Satire on the Modern Translators," published in 1697 in *Poems on Affairs of State*, may later have struck Prior as too harsh an indictment of contemporary writers. A second letter "To Mr. Fleetwood Shepherd" was also printed in 1697 in *Poems on Affairs of State*. With unbecoming levity in this poem, as he ultimately concluded, Prior complained to Dorset, by way of the Earl's steward, that he had been neglected while his fellow "mouse" had received advancement:

> My Friend C———s M———ue's Preferr'd;
> Nor would I have it long observ'd,
> That one Mouse eats, while t'other's starv'd.[37]

As his recent editors have remarked, Prior's subsequent relations with Montague "were not such as to permit much joking."[38] When Prior became a convert to Toryism, Halifax remained his best friend among the Kit-Cats.

Although his Tory alliances cost Prior his much-prized membership in the Kit-Cat Club, he enjoyed for a quarter of a century the unbroken author-publisher relationship that early in his career he established with Jacob Tonson. Tonson was Prior's publisher for the first time in 1692, when he printed Prior's "political panegyric," *An Ode in Imitation of the Second Ode of the Third Book of Horace*, Prior's fulsome tribute to King William in celebration of the naval victory of La Hogue in May of that year. In 1693 Prior had the pleasure of filling up half a dozen "chinks" in Tonson's Third Miscellany. Tonson reprinted in this volume Prior's "Letter to the Honourable Mr. Charles Montague" and "An Ode—While blooming youth and gay delight," as well as several new pieces. In 1694 two more poems by Prior were included in Tonson's Fourth Miscellany: "To Lady Dursley" and "For the New Year: To the Sun," a New Year's greeting to King William from The Hague, where Prior was then acting as secretary to the English Ambassador.

Tonson sent two urgent requests to Prior in Holland, relayed by Sir William Trumbull, Secretary of State, to compose a poem on the death of Queen Mary. Begging pardon for his "sin of omission," Prior wrote to Trumbull in April, 1695, that he now had "a poem on the stocks to be given to his Majesty at his arrival here, which I will send to Mr. Tonson to be reprinted in England, and since that cur instigated the writing of it, I hope it may lie unsold and contribute to the breaking of him."[39] It may be assumed that Trumbull knew better than to take this remark at its face value, for Prior was sensitive to criticism and set a high value on his poetical talents. The poem, published by Tonson in May, 1695, was entitled *To the King, An Ode on His Majesty's Arrival in Holland.* In the same extravagant vein which mars all of Prior's political panegyrics, as well as those of his contemporaries, King William is assured that

> Mary reigns a Saint in Heaven,
> And Thou a Demi-God below.[40]

Prior continued, for over a decade, to produce at intervals other topical pieces, first in honor of William and his victories and then, with more genuine conviction, in honor of Anne.

At the expense of Boileau, Prior indulged his wit anonymously in *An English Ballad: In Answer to Mr. Despreaux's Pindarique Ode on the Taking of Namure,* published by Tonson in September, 1695. Enclosing the poem in a letter to Tonson, Prior commented: "If you think this trifle worth yor printing, 'tis at yor service," though it "probably may lye the lumber of yor shop with some of my former works." He instructed his publisher to show the piece "immediately" to Mr. Montague, who possibly might "alter a line or two in it" and to print the French text on one side of the page and his own English text on the other. He cautioned: "I will positively have no name sett to it, for a secretary at thirty is hardly allowed the privilege of burlesque." Perhaps Sir Fleetwood Shepherd could suggest a better title.[41] Trumbull supervised the publication of the poem and again enjoined Tonson's silence as to the authorship.[42] The poem appeared with the text of Boileau's dull ode in neat small print opposite Prior's poem in very large print.

Prior returned to formal eulogy in *Verses Humbly Presented to the King. At His Arrival in Holland After the late horrid Conspiracy against His most Sacred Person* (1696) and *Carmen Saeculare for the Year 1700* (1700). He honored Anne's birthday with his *Prologue Spoken at Court Before the Queen* (1704) and offered her a New Year's greeting in *An Ode to the Sun for the New Year* (1707). He celebrated the battle of Blenheim in *A Letter to Monsieur Boileau Depreaux Occasion'd by the Victory at Blenheim* (1704), and the battle of Ramillies in *An Ode, Humbly*

Inscrib'd to the Queen (1706) and *An Epistle from the Elector of Bavaria to the French King* (1706).

Always dubious about the merits of the heroic couplet, Prior experimented in *An Ode, Humbly Inscrib'd to the Queen*, with the Spenserian stanza, thereby initiating the vogue of imitating Spenser. Less than a month after Tonson had published the *Ode*, Prior wrote to Lord Cholmondeley, "As to Spenser, my Lord, I think we have gained our point, every body acknowledges him to have been a fine Poet, tho three Months since not one in 50 had read him: Upon my Soul, 'tis true, the Wits have sent for the Book, the Fairy Queen is on their Toilette table, and some of our Ducal acquaintance will be deep in that Mythologico-Poetical way of thinking."[43]

In 1702 Tonson printed in a single folio sheet one of Prior's half-cynical, half-wistful amorous tales, *To a Young Gentleman in Love*. Tonson's Fifth Miscellany included several of Prior's most charming lyrics, notably "To a Child of Quality," "The Lady's Looking Glass," and "The Despairing Shepherd," as well as the lubricious, witty, and well-told tales, "Hans Carvel" and "The Ladle." An unreliable judge of his own poetry, Prior never chose to reprint "To a Child of Quality," which he had addressed to Lady Mary Villiers, the engaging little daughter of Edward Villiers, first Earl of Jersey. It is possible that Prior's original admiration for Lady Mary cooled because his friendship with her Jacobite family was a contributing factor to his political disgrace. This brightest jewel of the Fifth Miscellany, which Swinburne was to praise as "the most adorable of nursery idyls that ever was or will be in our language,"[44] did not appear in a collected edition of Prior's poems until 1740, nearly twenty years after his death.

As the most popular poet of his time, Prior could not escape the doubtful compliment of pirated editions. One of his prettiest amorous tales, "The English Padlock," written for the diversion of the Kit-Cats,[45] appeared in a spurious version in *The Diverting Post* in January, 1705. A second spurious version appeared soon afterward, published by "Jocab Tompson [*sic*]." Then Tonson himself published in the same year an authentic text. Unfortunately, more serious piracies of Prior's verses were to follow, the chief culprit being "the unspeakable Curll."

Edmund Curll was the most unscrupulous publisher of the eighteenth century, a thorn in the flesh of despairing authors and of all reputable publishers.[46] If a writer complained that one of his books had been published by Curll without his consent, Curll might retaliate by advertising a second volume as "corrected by the author." When Curll stole works for which Tonson held the copyright, Tonson could and did protest, but in vain. By devious means Curll managed to acquire good works which he published repeatedly among many worthless ones. His editions of Prior's poems are examples of his flagrant methods.

On January 24, 1707, Tonson advertised in *The Daily Courant* that all "Genuine Copys" of Prior were in his hands and he intended speedily to publish "a correct Edition."[47] A week later, on January 31, Curll advertised in the same newspaper: "This day is publish'd *Poems on Several Occasions*; consisting of Ode's, Satyrs, and Epistles: With some Select Translations and Imitations. By Mr. Prior, Gent. (now first Correctly Printed.)"[48] Curll listed the publishers as R. Burrough, J. Baker, E. Curll, E. Place, and E. Sanger. On February 6 Prior published in *The Daily Courant* an indignant denunciation of Curll's volume. "Whereas there is lately Printed and Publish'd Poems on several Occasions by Mr. *Prior*, Mr. Prior thinks himself obliged to certify that the said Poems were Printed and Publish'd without his knowledge and consent, that some Pieces in the said Collection are not Genuine, the Copies of the rest Spurious and Defective, particularly as to the Names of Persons, and the Errata innumerable."[49] Undeterred by Prior's intervention, Curll again advertised his edition on March 27 as "now publish'd and correctly Printed."[50] This time the publishers were listed as Edmund Curll, Charles Smith, and J. Baker.

Curll found it expedient to preface his 1707 edition with the following publisher's note:

> The name of Mr. Prior is a more Satisfactory Recommendation of the following Sheets to those Gentlemen who are Judges of Poetry, than whatever can be offer'd in their Behalf.
>
> All that I have endeavour'd, (and which by the Assistance of some Friends, I have accomplish'd) is, that the several Pieces herein contain'd, should appear more Perfect and Correct by their Publication, than they have hitherto done elsewhere; and that no Copy should be inserted, 'till I was assur'd of its being Genuine.[51]

Curll reprinted seventeen poems by Prior, several from the miscellanies and a number of others. He published the first of Prior's epistles to Fleetwood Shepherd with the title, "A Second Epistle to Sir Fleetwood Sheppard."

Included in the collection were four poems which Prior particularly objected to having associated with his name: "A Satyr on the Modern Translators of Ovid's Epistles"; "The Seventh Satyr of Juvenal, imitated" ("Satyr on the Poets"); "An Epistle to Sir Fleetwood Sheppard" (the letter "To Mr. Fleetwood Shepherd" printed in 1697); and "Some Passages of Mr. Dryden's Hind and Panther; Burlesqu'd or Varied," with parallels from Dryden's poem printed on opposite pages. Apropos of the parody of Dryden, Prior lost no time in writing to Halifax:

> Some rogue of a bookseller has made a very improper Collection of what He calls my writings, the Whole is mutilated, Names printed at length and things written near Twenty years since, mingled with some written the other Day; in such a Manner as may do Me harm, part of the Mouse is likewise inserted, which I had little to say to otherwise than as I held the pen to what Mr. Montague dictated; I mention this, my Lord, desiring your Lordship to believe this book was printed without my knowledge or consent.[52]

Prior's disclaiming his share of the parody has been commonly regarded as merely an extravagant gesture of compliment to an influential friend whom he could not afford to offend.

When Tonson published his collected edition of Prior's *Poems on Several Occasions* in 1709, Prior repeated in the Preface his grievance against Curll:

> The greatest Part of what I have Writ having already been Publish'd, either singly or else in some of the Miscellanies, it would be too late for me to make any excuse for appearing in Print. But a Collection of Poems has lately appeared under my Name, tho' without my Knowledge, in which the Publisher has given me the Honour of some things that did not belong to me, and has Transcribed others so imperfectly, that I hardly knew them to be mine. This has obliged me in my own Defence, to look back upon some of those lighter Studies, which I ought long since to have quitted, and to Publish an indifferent Collection of Poems, for fear of being thought the Author of a worse.
>
> Thus I beg Pardon of the Publick for Reprinting some Pieces, which as they came singly from their first Impression, have, I fancy, lain long and quietly in Mr. Tonson's Shop; and with others which

were never before Printed, and might have lain as quietly, and perhaps more safely, in a Corner of my own Study.[53]

As often happened in that age, when author and publisher needed to defend the superior merits of a new edition, in this instance a genuine one, Prior overstated his case. All of the poems printed by Curll were by Prior, and none was mutilated beyond recognition. To be sure, the earlier edition was incomplete, and there were many errata, some of them quite ridiculous.[54]

It may be wondered why Tonson chose to publish the 1709 edition of Prior's poems after Prior had already defected to the Tories. Tonson's honor as a publisher had, of course, been involved in the dispute with Curll. Moreover, Tonson never allowed political differences to divorce him from a writer whose works he found it lucrative to publish. As the "Augustan Horace," Prior was much in vogue. His lyrics were frequently set to music, and one of them, "The Despairing Shepherd," appeared in as many as fourteen song books.[55] Prior continued to be pirated, and Tonson continued to be his legitimate publisher.

Tonson published fifty-seven of Prior's poems in the 1709 edition, presumably omitting only those poems Prior did not wish to claim. Among the hitherto unpublished poems were such memorable pieces as "An Ode: The Merchant to secure his Treasure," "To Cloe Weeping," "Cupid Mistaken," "Venus Mistaken," and "Reading Mézeray's History of France," with that haunting last line which Scott was to consider one of the finest cadences in English verse.

In 1716 Curll brought out a *Second Collection of Poems on Several Occasions*, a still slenderer edition of Prior than he had published in 1707. Prior at once disowned the book in *The London Gazette.*[56] Among the thirteen poems in Curll's collection, only four had been printed since Tonson's 1709 edition, two of which Curll had already pirated.[57] One of these, "Erle Robert's Mice," a humorous plea to the Earl of Oxford for advancement, written in imitation of Chaucer, was the only one of his "mouse" poems which Prior later collected.

Prior's difficult and worrisome activities in France during the last years of Anne's reign gave him almost no time and perhaps little inclination for writing poetry. The fall of the diplomats whom he had loyally but somewhat uncomfortably served involved his own.

Although the Secret Committee appointed to investigate the conduct of the discredited Tory ministry was unable to bring specific charges against Prior, he was kept in custody from June 9, 1715, to June 26, 1716, and was never granted a pardon. Friends did rally around him; Edward Harley, second Earl of Oxford, gave him a country retreat; and an expensive edition of his poems was undertaken in his behalf.

The 1718 edition of Prior's verse, published by Tonson and Barber, launched the long poems, "Alma" and "Solomon," which have not enhanced Prior's posthumous reputation, and a new little sheaf of delicious Cloe poems, including "A Better Answer to Cloe Jealous," which have. Prior had ambitious plans for this collection and devoted much time and thought to work on it. Tonson was cooperative, and the result was one of the handsomest and literally the weightiest volume that Tonson's press produced. The list of subscribers filled thirty-nine columns, and Prior made a needed profit of four thousand guineas.

Prior had been dogged by misfortune. Addison, on the contrary, as his contemporaries would have agreed, was an eminently successful man. His rise to fame was swift, calm, and orderly, each step being carefully calculated. Besides possessing great literary gifts, Addison had an unsurpassed skill in calling public attention to them in the right quarters. As soon as he had set foot on Jacob Tonson's ladder, Addison knew very well how to help himself.

Addison's ten years of scholarly life in Oxford were profitably spent. His Latin poems attracted very favorable notice in Oxford and Cambridge "before he was talked of as a Poet in Town."[58] Dryden, who is said to have introduced him to Congreve and who probably introduced him to Tonson, could not have been otherwise than pleased by Addison's first English poem, "To Mr. Dryden," which Tonson published in his Third Miscellany. His own age would not have considered excessive Addison's claim for Dryden:

> Thy Lines have heighten'd Virgil's Majesty,
> And Horace wonders at himself in Thee.[59]

In the Fourth Miscellany, Addison is represented by four contributions: most of Virgil's "Fourth Georgic"; "A Song for St. Cecilia's Day"; "The Story of Salmacis," from the fourth book of Ovid's *Metamorphoses*; and "An Account of the Greatest English Poets,"

PLATE I. John Dryden

PLATE II. Charles Seymour, sixth Duke of Somerset (*left*)
PLATE III. Sir John Vanbrugh

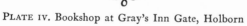

PLATE IV. Bookshop at Gray's Inn Gate, Holborn

M. Vander Gucht Sculp.

PLATE V. Frontispiece to Dryden's *The Works of Virgil* (1697)

PLATE VI. Scene in *As You Like It*

Thus Great, thus Gracious look'd BRITANNIA's Queen;
Her Brow thus smooth, Her Look was thus serene;
When to a Low, but to a Loyal Hand
The mighty Empress gave Her high Command,
That He to Hostile Camps, and Kings shou'd haste,
To speak Her Vengeance as Their Danger past;
To say, She Wills detested Wars to cease;
She checks Her Conquest, for Her Subjects Ease;
And bids the World attend Her Terms of Peace.

Thee, Gracious ANNE, Thee present I adore,
Thee, QUEEN of PEACE——If Time and Fate have Pow'r
Higher to raise the Glories of thy Reign;
In Words sublimer, and a nobler Strain,
May future Bards the mighty Theme rehearse.
Here, STATOR JOVE, and PHOEBUS King of Verse,
The Votive Tablet I suspend * * * *

PLATE VII. A Page from Matthew Prior's *Poems on Several Occasions* (1718)

PLATE VIII. Jacob Tonson Junior (about 1720)

PLATE IX. Anne and Mary Tonson (1734)

which ends the volume. Addison never chose to collect the "Account"; and indeed the pretentious poem betrays all too clearly the fact that the youthful poet, so well acquainted with classical authors, had a limited knowledge of the history of English poetry. Shakespeare is not mentioned; Chaucer is criticized for his "unpolish'd strain"; Spenser for his "fulsom" and "long-spun Allegories"; Milton because he varnished over "the Guilt of Faithless Men."[60]

In 1695 Addison acted as a sort of literary agent for Tonson in Oxford. Although a proposed translation of Herodotus, in which several Oxford scholars were involved, failed to materialize, Addison was encouraged by Tonson to continue work as a translator. On May 28, 1695, Addison wrote to Tonson that the latter's remarks on translating Ovid "made such an impression on me" that in his leisure hours he had "ventured" on the second book of Ovid's *Metamorphoses* and had it ready for Tonson to read.[61] The victory of Namur gave Addison an opportunity to show his loyalty to William and to the Whig ministry in *A Poem to His Majesty*, which Tonson published in an excellent folio edition. Addison dedicated the poem to Somers, whom he respectfully invited to receive the tribute of "a Muse unknown." Addison noted that the King confided to Somers

> His Inmost Thoughts, determining the Doom
> Of Towns unstorm'd and Battels yet to come.

If the Lord Keeper would but "Smile upon my Lays," the poet would be "Secure of Fame."[62] Somers was suitably impressed, and his patronage secured for Addison a fellowship for three years of travel on the Continent. Before leaving England, Addison was serviceable to Dryden by writing an essay on the "Georgics," as well as all of the prose arguments for the "Aeneis" for Dryden's *Virgil*, although preferring to have his name "concealed"; and Dryden expressed his gratitude in generous praise of the "most Ingenious Mr. Addison of Oxford" for his "Fourth Georgic." "After his Bees," wrote Dryden, "my latter Swarm is scarcely worth the hiving."[63]

At the conclusion of his European tour, Addison met Tonson in Amsterdam in 1703. Somerset had commissioned Tonson to offer Addison the post of traveling tutor to his son Algernon, Earl of Hertford. One of the very few lapses in tact of which Addison was ever guilty was so chilly a reaction to the financial arrangements proposed for him by Somerset that Somerset considered himself rudely rebuffed and abruptly broke off the negotiation. To Tonson as intermediary this awkward affair must have been embarrassing, although Somerset confined his resentment to Addison. The "Proud Duke" wrote "finis" to the episode with a gracious apology to Tonson: "I am very sorry that I have given you soe much trouble in it but I know you are good & will forgive it, in one that is soe much your friend & humble servant / Somerset."[64]

Addison chose to address to Halifax his "Letter from Italy" written in 1701, which Tonson published as the opening poem in his Fifth Miscellany, where he also published substantial portions of Addison's translations from Books II and III of Ovid's *Metamorphoses* and an episode from the third book of Virgil's *Aeneid*. According to Tickell, the "Letter" was admired as "the most exquisite" of Addison's "poetical performances."[65] Halifax, who, like Somers, could lend an attentive ear to suave flattery, soon found an opportunity to befriend the promising young emulator of his own superior "Muse." When the services of a Whig poet were required to celebrate the victory of Blenheim, Halifax advised Godolphin to summon Addison, who was then living in very humble London lodgings, to undertake that task.

The result was *The Campaign*, which Tonson published on December 14, 1704, on the very day of Marlborough's return to London in triumph. *The Campaign* was an immediate success and brought Addison an appointment as Commissioner of Appeals in the Excise. The imagination of Addison's contemporaries was charmed by the comparison of Marlborough to an angel who

> pleas'd th' Almighty's orders to perform
> Rides in the whirl-wind and directs the storm.[66]

The poem was quickly reprinted and acquired a fifth edition by 1713.

Addison once more commended himself to Somers in dedicating to him *Remarks on Several Parts of Italy*, printed by Tonson in 1705. In his Dedication, Addison observed: "should I publish any Favours done me by your Lordship, I am afraid it would look more like Vanity than Gratitude." The journey and the book had been carefully planned in advance, and Addison had brought with him from England passages from classical authors for use as illustrations.[67] Addison's preoccupation with ancient, rather than modern,

Italy did not strike his contemporaries as pedantic. The sale of the book "increased from year to year, and the demand for copies was so urgent, that the price rose to four or five times the original value, before it came out in a second edition."[68] The *Remarks* had many editions. The book was translated into French, and it became "the indispensable companion of every young man upon the grand tour."[69]

Addison's opera *Rosamond*, published by Tonson in 1707, failed on the stage, although it had a second edition that same year and a third in 1713. Meanwhile, Addison was succeeding politically. He had become an under-secretary of state and in 1709 received the post of chief secretary to Wharton, who had been appointed Lord Lieutenant of Ireland. He contributed to Tonson's Sixth Miscellany a graceful paraphrase of the third ode of Book III of the *Odes* of Horace.

Addison was in Ireland when Steele, under the pseudonym of Isaac Bickerstaff, began publishing *The Tatler*, which appeared three times a week from April, 1709, to January, 1711. The journal was not printed by Tonson but by Lillie and Morphew, who also brought out a collected edition in four volumes in 1710–1711. By the middle of 1711, however, the Tonsons took over the edition.[70] *The Tatler* proved to be the most successful periodical the English press had thus far achieved. Although the paper was essentially Steele's, Addison contributed anonymously 42 of the 271 numbers. In his preface to the fourth volume Steele handsomely acknowledged the help of "one gentleman [Addison] who will be nameless" and confessed that he was "undone by my Auxiliary; when I had once called him in, I could not subsist without him."[71]

The Spectator, to which Addison contributed nearly half of the numbers, appeared six times a week, from March, 1711, to December, 1712, and was revived by Addison alone from June to December, 1714. The early issues were printed by Samuel Buckley. Charles Lillie's name was soon added to Buckley's but dropped in October, 1712, when Tonson replaced Lillie.[72] The collected papers were published in eight volumes: I–IV in 1712, and V–VII in 1713 by Buckley and Tonson; VIII in 1715 by Tonson. On November 10, 1712, Addison and Steele sold their title to the first seven volumes, a half share to Buckley and a half to Tonson's nephew, Jacob junior, each paying £575. On October 13, 1714, Buckley reassigned his half share to Tonson for £500; and on

August 27 the following year, the title to Volume VIII was sold by Addison to Tonson for £53 15s.[73] It is usually impossible to determine what portions of the Tonson publishing business became the immediate responsibility of Tonson's nephew, but the Buckley-Tonson agreement which Jacob junior signed has been preserved.[74] It is not unlikely that Jacob junior handled directly the negotiations for all of the journals which the two Jacobs, uncle and nephew, published for Addison and Steele.

A Whig, but a cautious Whig, Addison determined the non-party tone of *The Spectator*, being "resolved to observe an exact Neutrality between the Whigs and Tories."[75] The two essayists likewise effected Addison's objective of bringing "Philosophy out of Closets and Libraries, Schools and Colleges, to dwell in Clubs and Assemblies, at Tea-Tables, and in Coffee-Houses."[76] The paper was taken in to Queen Anne every morning with her breakfast. It became a part of a polite lady's tea equipage, and its circulation spread to the provinces, where it was sometimes read aloud to village groups. In the second year of publication *The Spectator* had a daily circulation of between three and four thousand copies.[77] Each published volume sold about nine thousand copies.[78]

The Guardian, a daily paper by "Nestor Ironside," printed by Tonson, ran from March to October, 1713. Addison joined Steele in the journal with No. 67 and contributed fifty papers. A collected edition was published by Tonson in 1714. As in *The Tatler* and *The Spectator*, Addison did not publicly acknowledge his participation, but the tribute Steele paid to his unnamed collaborator could have left no doubt as to his identity. In a note to the reader in the collected edition, Steele explained that a hand at the end of certain papers indicated contributions "by a Gentleman [Addison] who has obliged the World with Productions too sublime to admit that the Author of them should receive any Addition to his Reputation from such loose occasional Thoughts as make up these little Treatises. For which reason his name shall be concealed."[79] Steele took advantage of the excellent facilities offered in *The Guardian* for advertising Addison's classical tragedy, *Cato*, the phenomenal vogue of which conveniently coincided with the period when the journal was appearing daily.

On April 14, 1713, Steele announced in *The Guardian* that *Cato* would be acted "this day" at Drury Lane, with Prologue and Epilogue by Pope and Garth, respectively. On April 27 Tonson published the first edition, on May 7 the third, and on May 9 the fourth. *The Guardian* announced on May 19: "There is sold a Pyrated Edition of this Play, wherein are numberless gross Faults and several Scenes left out. The Edition Published and Corrected by the Author, and printed for J. Tonson, has a head of Cato taken from an old Medal, Printed in the Title Page to distinguish it from that which is Spurious and Imperfect."[80] On May 22 the fifth edition of the play was published, on June 5 the sixth, on June 26 the seventh, a small number being printed on very fine paper and "curiously bound"; and on August 31 the eighth edition appeared in a neat pocket volume. In July, Tonson published a French translation of the play.

Addison had written part of this tragedy during his travels. He was encouraged to complete it because the Whigs were in need of political ammunition. Characteristically, however, Addison took pains to make *Cato* seem a non-partisan plea for liberty, and both parties gave it their seal of approval. The stage production had an unprecedented run of thirty-five nights and ended in May only because Mrs. Oldfield, who played Cato's daughter Marcia, was expecting a child and had been keeping a midwife behind the scenes for several nights.[81] The play attracted such crowds of spectators that "every Night seem'd to be the first."[82] On April 30 Pope wrote to Caryll: "The town is so fond of it, that the orange wenches and fruit women in the Park offer the books at the side of the coaches, and the Prologue and Epilogue are cried about the streets by the common hawkers."[83] By the end of the year *Cato* had cleared £1,350 to each of the managers of Drury Lane.[84] The play was translated into various European languages, the Italian translation by Antonio Mario Salvini being particularly admired. Well might Tonson consider that the large sum of £107 10s. which he paid Addison for the copyright of *Cato*[85] was one of the best investments of his publishing career.

During the last years of his life, Addison's official duties and ill health reduced his literary activities. His social position, but apparently not his happiness, was enhanced by his marriage in 1716 to the Countess of Warwick, a coolly calculated maneuver in the opinion

of Jacob Tonson, who seems never to have liked Addison personally.[86] In 1717 Addison's ambition was further gratified by his
appointment as Secretary of State for the Southern Department.

In comparison with Steele's, Addison's efforts in political journalism were limited and discreet. *The Whig Examiner* (1710) had
only five numbers. *The Freeholder* (1715–1716), published twice
a week for fifty-five numbers, was regarded by Steele as far too
mild in tone, although Addison defended Whig principles in that
paper with more vigor than he would have considered advisable in
the last years of the reign of Queen Anne. Midwinter and Tonson
printed *The Freeholder* in a collected edition in 1716; the volume
had many editions and was translated into French. In December,
1715, Tonson published Addison's *To Her Royal Highness the
Princess of Wales, with the Tragedy of Cato*, and *To Godfrey
Kneller on His Picture of the King*. There were three editions of
these two poems the following year. A comedy, *The Drummer*,
which he had written many years before, was handed over by Addison to Steele and published anonymously by Tonson in 1716. *The
Drummer* did not attract attention until the play was published
posthumously under Addison's name; by the end of the century it
had had nine English editions, and it was translated into French,
German, and Italian. *The Campaign* was reprinted in the 1716
edition of Tonson's Sixth Miscellany.

In the midst of a needless and unresolved quarrel with Steele,
Addison died in 1719. The two friends had taken opposite sides in
The Old Whig and *The Plebeian* concerning a bill, ultimately
abandoned, to limit the creation of peers by the king. Sadly and
abruptly, an intimate friendship of many years was thus destroyed.

Richard Steele did not, like Addison, have a long and peaceful
literary apprenticeship as a university student. He left Merton College, Oxford, without a degree in 1692, enlisted as a soldier, and
joined the Royal Horse Guards. Steele's military life did not preclude, however, a strong bias toward literature; and like Congreve,
Addison, and so many other young writers, he paid tribute to the deceased Queen Mary in a funeral poem in her memory, *The Procession*, published by Tonson in 1695 as "By a Gentleman of the
Army." Steele dedicated this undistinguished poem to Lord Cutts,
colonel of the Coldstream Guards, who transferred Steele to his

own company and made him his secretary. Steele became an ensign in Cutts's company, later a captain.

Too easily tempted to lead the life of a careless but by no means heartless young rake, Steele undoubtedly counted among his sins the seduction of Elizabeth Tonson, the sister of Jacob junior, who bore him a daughter, Elizabeth "Ousley," in 1699 or 1700.[87] The life of the child's mother remains almost a blank. Elizabeth Tonson lived with her mother in her brother's family, perhaps assisting in the bookshop and, like her mother, receiving a quarterly annuity from her brother.[88] She died in 1726 at the age of forty-six.[89] Steele had a warm affection for his illegitimate daughter. He sent her to boarding school, eventually transferred her to his own household, and arranged, probably with the Tonsons, her marriage to William Aynston,[90] a glove manufacturer of Almeley, Herefordshire. Steele left her £100 in his will. "The witty Mrs. Aynston" addressed verses to her cousin, Mary Tonson, Jacob junior's eldest daughter, as "dear nymph," and was evidently a welcome guest at Barn Elms.[91]

In the mood of one who has erred and repents, Steele produced his first prose work, a sober moral treatise, *The Christian Hero*, published by Tonson in 1701. He dedicated this volume to Lord Cutts and hoped that it would be read by "Men of Wit and Gallantry," especially by his fellow soldiers. Some years afterward, Steele disclosed that he had written the tract for his private use, to fix on his mind a strong impression of virtue and religion; but since this "secret Admonition was too weak," he had printed the book with his name "as a standing Testimony against himself," that he might be "ashamed of understanding and seeming to feel what was Virtuous, and living so quite contrary a Life."[92] In a review and comparison of pagan and Christian ethics, unfavorable to the former, Steele affirmed his conviction that we are "framed" for mutual kindness, good will, and service. Popular at a time when "morality" was becoming fashionable in literature, the book reached a sixth edition in 1712 and had twenty editions in the course of the century.

Steele soon discovered that the yardstick of his ideal hero was being too scrupulously applied to his own conduct, and "to enliven his Character"[93] he wrote his first comedy, *The Funeral*, which Tonson published in 1702. Lintot printed Steele's second comedy,

The Lying Lover (1704), perhaps offering Steele a better price for it (£21 10s.) than Tonson. Finding that the play was "damn'd for its piety,"[94] Steele combined mirth and morality more successfully in his next comedy, *The Tender Husband*, which Tonson published in 1705 and which Steele dedicated to Addison as a "Memorial of an Inviolable Friendship."[95] *The Funeral* and *The Tender Husband* were printed together by Tonson in an attractive edition in 1712 and reprinted in 1717.

Steele began editing *The London Gazette* in late April or early May, 1707, and Jacob junior took over the printing of the paper the following year. With the change in ministry, Steele was removed as editor in October, 1710. Irked by the lack of freedom which this conservative newspaper offered him, he had already embarked on *The Tatler* as a more suitable vehicle for independent journalism. Here his taste for political controversy was held in check by Addison, but not sufficiently to prevent the sudden demise of this popular paper, in which Steele had risked attacking leading Tories after the fall of the Whig ministry. It was Addison who determined that *The Spectator* should be a purely literary journal with nothing partisan about it. Gay, who had the highest praise for both *The Tatler* and *The Spectator*, regretted Steele's "unaccountable Imprudence" in attacking the Tories when his reputation was at its height and noted that the disappearance of *The Tatler* "seem'd to be bewailed as some general Calamity."[96] The ensuing "Blaze" of *The Spectator* had delighted all "unbyassed well-wishers to Learning"; and it must be hoped, cautioned Gay, that "the known Temper and Prudence" of one of the two editors (Addison) would hinder the other (Steele) from again "lashing out into Party."[97]

But Steele's ardent political convictions as "a lover of his country" could not be suppressed, and he elected to follow a bold course as a political journalist. On August 7, 1713, in No. 128 of *The Guardian*, Steele protested the failure of the French to demolish the fort and harbor of Dunkirk, as agreed in the Treaty of Utrecht. At Addison's request, he continued his strictures on this subject outside of *The Guardian*. He published on September 22 *The Importance of Dunkirk considered*, which did lead at once to some steps in the direction he advocated. Addison withdrew from *The Guardian*, Steele ended the paper on October 1, and the two essayists went their separate ways. On October 12, Addison wrote to John Hughes:

"I am in a thousand troubles for poor Dick, and wish that his zeal for the public may not be ruinous to himself: but he has sent me word that he is determined to go on, and that any advice I may give him in this particular, will have no weight with him."[98]

Two days after the last *Guardian*, Steele started *The Englishman*, published by Samuel Buckley. The paper appeared three times a week for fifty-seven numbers. In this new journal, devoted exclusively to politics, Steele kept advertising *The Crisis*, published by Ferdinand Burleigh, the most important of his political tracts, in which he rashly stressed the threat of the Queen's government to the Hanoverian succession. *The Crisis* and two papers in *The Englishman* cost Steele his recently acquired seat in the House of Commons. Invectives against him, Steele observed, "came out stitch'd, bound, and in loose Papers for some Months every Week."[99] When Steele wrote *The Tatler*, persons of all classes, said Colley Cibber, were Steele's friends, "and thought their Tea in a Morning had not its Taste without him"; but when he wrote as a patriot, half of the nation denied he had wit, sense, or genius.[100] At any rate, Steele had an impressively large reading public. An eighteenth-century historian alleged that "perhaps there never was in the annals of political literature a book more universally read, or so much the subject of conversation as *The Crisis*."[101]

Preoccupied with politics, Steele had little time for non-political writing. He was at work as one of the editors of Tonson's Sixth Miscellany in the winter of 1709. In one of his numerous brief notes to his wife, he referred to this enterprise, informing her that he was "indispensably obliged" to dine at Tonson's, where, after dinner, some papers were to be read, "whereof, among others, I am to be a Judge."[102] In 1714 Tonson published Steele's *Poetical Miscellanies*. The small volume included poems by Pope and Gay and such examples of a new romantic lyricism as Parnell's "Hymn on Contentment" and Lady Winchilsea's "A Sigh." Besides reprinting here his own complimentary verses on *The Way of the World*, Steele ended the volume with "The Procession," the poem in which he had first proclaimed his Whig sympathies. For a few months in 1714 Steele edited and Tonson published two literary journals, *The Lover* and *The Reader*, which Tonson, J. Brown, and O. Lloyd printed in a collected edition at the end of the year. *The Ladies Library* (1714), published by Tonson, is only a compilation of

Steele's borrowings from edifying moral essays. Advertised, like similar works, as "very proper for a New Year's Gift for the Ladies," the book had a large sale.

Mr. Steele's Apology for Himself and His Writings, Occasioned by his Expulsion from the House of Commons, was published by Burleigh in October, 1714. The essay had been printed shortly before the death of Queen Anne, "but upon that Accident," said Steele, "the Publication was deferred."[103] With warmth and eloquence Steele defended his political activities, being much less concerned for his fame as a writer than as "an honest Man." By every means that his pen afforded, he had sought to rouse his country "from a Lethargy from which she has awaked only to behold her Danger, and upon seeing it too great has only sighed, folded her Arms, and returned to her Trance."[104]

The joint labors of Steele and Jacob junior as editor and printer involved late hours for Steele at the printing house of the Tonsons in Earl's Court, Bow Street, near Covent Garden,[105] as Steele's hurried notes to his wife testify. Proof must be corrected, late news waited for, accounts made up. Steele's business affairs required him to spend more time with Jacob junior than with the elder Tonson; and Steele may have preferred the company of the younger man, his contemporary.

Pope's claim[106] that Steele ended *The Guardian* because of a quarrel with Tonson and therefore turned to another publisher for *The Englishman* has been viewed with scepticism. It is more in accordance with Steele's well-known humanity to assume that he felt personally responsible when the printing of the *Gazette* was transferred from Jacob junior to Benjamin Tooke and John Barber in August, 1711, and preferred to spare Jacob junior further involvement in his own serious feud with the Tory ministry. The Tonsons had vainly sought Swift's intervention in their behalf. When this was not forthcoming, Steele wrote, likewise in vain, to James Brydges:

> What I presume to trouble you now upon is in behalf of my friend Jacob Tonson Junr Printer of ye Gazette. There may be very good reason to remove a writer of that paper [Steele], that should not be altogether agreeable to ye Ministry, but that reason, methinks, cannot bear against ye Printer of it, who is mechanically to do what he is ordered. Mr Moore is ye person, who now presses hard in behalf of

one Barber against Tonson. I believe you can persuade him to lay
aside that application. If you please to speak to Mr Moore, or use any
other method by speaking to Mr St John your self, you would oblige
a very honest young man & do an act worthy yr own noble nature.[107]

Not only for *The Englishman*, but also for the political tracts which
followed it, with such serious reverses for himself, Steele employed
other publishers until he could return to the Tonsons with a clear
conscience after the accession of George I.

Steele's honors in the new reign were less substantial than he had
hoped for, but they included a knighthood and a share in Drury
Lane Theatre. In 1715 Tonson published a collected edition of
The Political Writings of Sir Richard Steele, which Steele dedicated
to the young Earl of Clare, soon to become Duke of Newcastle.
That same year Tonson also published *A Letter from the Earl of
Mar to the King*, Steele's attack on one of the leaders of the Jacobite
rebellion in that year.

Steele dissipated his energies in the final, harassed years of his life.
He edited briefly a number of journals of minor importance. He
was plagued by debts, saddened by domestic griefs, deprived for a
time of his post as comptroller of Drury Lane Theatre, and embit-
tered by his quarrel with Addison. In 1719 he wrote angrily to
Jacob junior, protesting against the separation of Addison's essays
from his in Tickell's forthcoming edition of Addison's writings.[108]
Steele had a further grievance against Tickell for excluding from
Addison's collected *Works* (1721) *The Drummer*, which Steele
had had Tonson publish for his friend, as Addison had requested.
Jacob junior, who had given Steele fifty guineas for the anonymous
play, believing it Addison's, now hastened to sell the copyright to
another publisher, J. Darby, considering that Steele had misled him.
In self-defense Steele sponsored a new edition of *The Drummer*,
with a preface to Congreve, in which he reaffirmed Addison's authorship of the play and his own devotion to one who had exercised
"such natural Power over me."[109]

Steele's last play, *The Conscious Lovers* (1723), was published
by Jacob junior after his uncle's retirement. Steele dedicated the
comedy to George I, from whom he received a gift of five hundred
guineas. The play had an initial run of eighteen nights and two
editions within a month of its first performance. Despite some comic
episodes, *The Conscious Lovers* was a farewell to laughing comedy

and was thus welcomed by Steele's contemporaries, who had rejected the values of the Restoration comic tradition. A long twilight in English comedy had begun.

Steele was the last survivor of the distinguished writers for whom Tonson became the regular publisher. Congreve, Addison, and Steele were all in their early twenties when Tonson's keen detective eye recognized their literary potentialities. It was Tonson who gave them their expanding reading public. In his late twenties Prior was the author of a few popular poems. Tonson made him more popular and published the authorized collected editions of Prior's verse. Where prodding was necessary, Tonson supplied it; his persuasive advertising was unfailing; and the respective interests of these gifted men, their publisher, and their readers were well served.

v.

The Routine
of Publishing

owever much in-
volved Tonson was
with authors for whom
he published regularly, he
also found time to print each year an astonishingly large number
of books, old and new, in a wide variety of fields. It has been
estimated that in forty years of publishing Tonson published between seven hundred and fifty and eight hundred and fifty books.[1]
A descriptive account of all of them is the task of a bibliographer,
rather than a biographer, and would require a separate volume.
Useful lists of Tonson's publications already exist[2] to provide the
groundwork for a critical bibliography of the type available to
students of Dryden and Prior.[3] Even a selective review of the out-
put of forty years throws helpful light on the career of a man who
subordinated all other interests to the advancement of his profession.

Aside from a certain amount of restrictive legislation and inevitable evasions of it, the times were auspicious for enterprising
publishers, although less so for authors. Although the Licensing Act
of 1662[4] expired in 1679, it was revived in 1685 and imposed a
government censorship of the press which no doubt was irksome to
Tonson, as well as to other publishers. With the final lapse of this
act in 1695, the press became free of censorship, except in cases
where the law of libel was invoked.[5] The new freedom tended to
endanger copyrights, and the publishers themselves were responsible
for the Copyright Act of 1709,[6] which gave authors the first protection of their rights. The full implications of this act were not
felt until after Tonson's retirement, and throughout his career he
enjoyed the benefits of perpetual copyright. In most cases he purchased their copies from the authors, who sold them outright as
they might have sold any other piece of property. He could thus
reap the entire profits of all editions, unless by agreement the authors were to have some share in them. Rights to the works of de-

ceased writers could be obtained, as the opportunity arose, from publishers who controlled them. A publisher with his wits about him could gradually build up a very lucrative business.

Early in his career Tonson became aware that customers and prospective writers might be drawn to his bookshop in a variety of ways. Jacob Tonson tried all of those ways. Advertising was one fruitful expedient. In his first newspaper advertisement, in *The London Gazette* of February 6, 1679, Tonson announced that persons who would bring to his bookshop any of the books dispersed in the late fire in the Temple would receive "reasonable satisfaction" from the owners. As time went on, he frequently advertised his new publications in the London newspapers and on the final page of the books themselves. Busy though he was in his shop, he realized the importance of leaving it to "feel the pulse of the City." He visited taverns and coffee houses, read newsletters and newspapers, discussed public affairs with politicians, and became one of the best informed men of his time. His master stroke, of course, was the founding of the Kit-Cat Club.

In the era of the "unspeakable" Edmund Curll and some other less unscrupulous publishers, Tonson refused to print obscene, sensational, or libelous works. His press was genteel. He took legal action against Henry Dickinson, who failed to sign a statement that a work which Tonson had intended to publish for him contained nothing "but wt was agreeable to sound doctrine & good Manners."[7] Some of Tonson's fellow publishers stood in the pillory and paid fines for seditious publications, but his own record remained clear. It is unlikely that he ever published pirated works.

Tonson was a shrewd but honest bargainer, who kept his word and expected others to do likewise. According to the standards of his time, he paid his writers fair, never too high, prices, and few of them left him for other publishers. At a time when brown paper and poor print reduced the cost of books, Tonson paid well for imported Dutch type and paper. As agreeable fringe benefits to his "hands," he circulated manuscripts, wrote complimentary verses, waited upon writers when summoned, gave them gifts of food and wine, loaned them money, collected rents (for Dryden), and forwarded mail.

Tonson was respected by other publishers, and his relations with them seem to have been cordial. Henry Prideaux begged Tonson to deliver him from Curll, on whom Prideaux showered the epithets of "this wretch," "this villian," "this vile knave."[8] But although he called Curll firmly to account more than once, as he had every reason to do, Tonson tolerated the rascal and shared an occasional copyright with him.

Tonson's early interest in politics appears in two newsletters (he may have written more) which, as requested, he sent from London to Narcissus Luttrell in Staffordshire, who was collecting news for his manuscript "Diary." The two letters, dated August 31 and September 11, 1680,[9] have been preserved in the Library of All Souls College in Oxford in a manuscript volume once belonging to Luttrell, which contains other newsletters of about the same dates. Tonson complained that the news was "exceeding barren." What he could supply was mainly hearsay. The proceedings of the Privy Council regarding the Popish Plot[10] had been "kept very secret." Fitzpatrick's report concerning the conduct of the plot in Ireland had not been confirmed. Further news from Tangier was being awaited. Colonel Blood,[11] reported dead and buried, had been seen in Calais. John Giles had stood in the pillory for the third and last time, protected by the constables and watchmen. The papers of Mrs. Cellier, the Popish midwife,[12] had been seized at her home, and she had been tried at the Old Bailey for publishing her narrative, "wch is a Libell upon the whole Government." Several of these items were included by Luttrell in his faithfully kept "Diary,"[13] which was published many years later.

Tonson's second newsletter has a rather cryptic personal postscript. "I would write larglyer to you had I time," explained Tonson, "but it is now past 11. Ye books are sent home, & ye woemen are very earnest for bawdrys & teas'd me perpetually. I long earnestly to see you & pray oblieedge me wth one line from you when you possibly can."[14] Was Tonson, who never married, amorous as a young man? The evidence of this postscript, if evidence it can be called, is too vague to invite conjecture. Whatever further services to Luttrell in the way of newsletters Tonson may have undertaken, he was soon fully occupied in publishing activities.

Tonson was a very methodical man. He developed a pattern in publishing which he found satisfactory and to which he consistently adhered. He preferred to print quarto texts of plays, which sold for a shilling and which might or might not have a second edition, as well as other short pieces, between editions of larger scope, which would have a larger sale: translations, miscellanies, histories, reprinted English masterpieces. The more extensive works appeared at fairly regular intervals, often after several years in the making, and sometimes in installments. Tonson perceived that Dryden's name attached to a volume to which a fair number of youthful collaborators had contributed was a sufficient guarantee of its financial success. The collaborators received modest remuneration, and some of them proved worthy of more important assignments. The search for talent was congenial to the aging poet, who required competent assistance in his burdensome labors; and under such distinguished auspices Tonson achieved a head start over other contemporary publishers.

In the first five years of his publishing, Tonson published with his brother, with Richard Bentley, or alone plays by Nahum Tate, Nathaniel Lee, Thomas Otway, and Aphra Behn, in addition to plays by Dryden. Tate's *The History of Richard the Second*, published by Jacob with his brother in 1681, is the least interesting of these plays. This tragedy, which had been banned on the stage for political reasons, is an unfortunate new modeling of Shakespeare's *Richard II*. It may be considered a cause for rejoicing that Tonson's reputation was not sullied by the publication in the same year by another publisher of Tate's debased version of *King Lear*, which was to hold the stage for a century and a half.

Tonson had occasion to witness the plight of erratic genius in the tragic lives of Otway and Lee, both of whom had run their brief literary course by 1684. In 1681 Jacob with his brother published Lee's *Lucius Junius Brutus*, banned on the stage for expressions suggesting a Whiggish slant but often praised as Lee's finest tragedy. The next year Bentley and Tonson published *The Duke of Guise*, a Tory play in which Lee collaborated with Dryden. Not long before Lee became insane, Bentley and Tonson published without prologue or epilogue Lee's last play, *Constantine the Great*, which reflects, like *The Duke of Guise*, Tory sentiments. In a pathetic prologue for this tragedy, which Tonson claimed for Otway and later published in his collected edition of Otway's *Works*, starving poets are compared to

Rats in Ships . . .
All hated too as they are, and unfed.[15]

Otway's fate was no less melancholy than Lee's. Not long before Otway died obscurely in desperate poverty, Tonson and Bentley published Otway's last play, *The Atheist; or, The Second Part of the Souldier's Fortune* (1684). Otway's only surviving "letter" is the following revealing note to Jacob Tonson, dated June 30, 1683: "All accounts evend between Mr Thomas Ottway Jacob Tonson. The said Mr Otway does hereby acknowledge himself indebted to Jacob Tonson in the Sum of eleven pounds wch hee hereby engages to pay upon demand witness his hand—Tho: Otway."[16] It is obvious that *The Atheist,* an inferior comedy, was hastily written to clear off this nagging debt of eleven pounds.

Tonson's connections with Aphra Behn were more exhilarating. She was another impoverished writer, but her gaiety, courage, and resilience contributed to a very pleasing personality. All clouds of dullness were dissipated by her engaging presence and her lively writings. "For years," it has been claimed, "her name to a new book, a comedy, a poem, an essay from the French, was a word to conjure with for the booksellers."[17] The great vogue of *The Rover, or, The Banish't Cavaliers,* Mrs. Behn's most famous and most frequently acted play, probably induced Tonson to publish alone in 1681 the sequel to that play, *The Second Part of The Rover,* a poorer and less popular play than its predecessor. Mrs. Behn's effusive Dedication to the Duke of York included an avowal of those emphatic Tory sentiments which led to her neglect after the Revolution. In 1682 Tonson published alone Mrs. Behn's successful farce, *The False Count, or, A New Way to Play an Old Game.* Having received a reprimand from the Lord Chamberlain for a bold attack on Monmouth in a recently written epilogue,[18] Mrs. Behn withdrew from politics in this non-political play.

In 1684 the Tonson brothers brought out Mrs. Behn's *Poems Upon Several Occasions: With a Voyage to the Island of Love.* In a very beguiling letter to Jacob, probably written late in 1683, Mrs. Behn set forth the merits of her forthcoming work and pled for a much-needed five pounds more than had been offered her for the copyright. She wrote:

> As for ye verses of mine, I shou'd really have thought 'em worth thirty pound; and I hope you will find it worth 25 l.; not that I shou'd dispute at any other time for 5 pound wher I am so obleg'd; but you can not think wt a preety thing ye Island[19] will be, and wt

a deale of labor I shall have yet with it: and if that pleases, I will do the 2d voyage, wch will compose a little book as big as a novel by it self. But pray speake to yor brothr to advance the price to one 5 *lb* more, 'twill at this time be more than given me, and I vow I wou'd not aske it if I did not really believe it worth more. Alas I wou'd not loose my time in such low gettings, but only since I am about it I am resolv'd to go throw wth it tho I shou'd give it. I pray go about it as soone as you please, for I shall finish as fast as you can go on. Methinks ye Voyage shou'd come last, as being ye largest volume. You know Mr Cowley's David is last, because a large poem, and Mrs. Philips her plays for ye same reason. I wish I had more time, I wou'd ad something to ye verses yt I have a mind too, but good deare Mr. Tonson, let it be 5 lb more, for I may safly swere I have lost ye getting of 50lb by it, tho that's nothing to you, or my satisfaction and humour: but I have been wthout getting so long yt I am just on ye poynt of breaking, espesiall since a body has no creditt at ye playhouse for money as we usd to have, fifty or 60 deepe, or more; I want extreamly or I wou'd not urge this. / Yors / A. B.[20]

We do not know whether Jacob Tonson yielded to Mrs. Behn's urgent request for five pounds more. We do have her note for a loan of six pounds which Tonson provided the following year:

Where as I am indebted to Mr. Bags the sum of six pound for the payment of which Mr. Tonson has oblegd him self. Now I do here impowre Mr. Zachary Baggs, in case the said debt is not fully discharg'd before Michaelmas next, to stop what money he shall hereafter have in his hands of mine, upon the playing my first play till this aforesaid debt of six pound be dischargd. Witness my hand, this 1st August, — 85. A / Behn[21]

Tonson's admiration of Mrs. Behn's talents found a less tangible expression in anonymously published verses which he wrote in her praise, as he confided years afterward to his nephew.[22] These verses he published, among other commendatory poems prefixed to her *Poems Upon Several Occasions*, under the title, "*To the Lovely Witty* Astraea, *on her Excellent Poems.*" Not unmindful of his timely opportunity to encourage the sale of the volume, Tonson wrote:

Your Wit wou'd recommend the homeliest Face,
Your Beauty make the dullest Humour please;
But where they both thus gloriously are join'd,

All Men submit, you reign in every Mind.
What Passions does your Poetry impart?
It shews th' unfathom'd thing a Woman's Heart,
Tells what Love is, his Nature and his Art.
Displays the several Scenes of Hopes and Fears,
Love's Smiles, his Sighs, his Laughings and his Tears.
Each Lover here may reade his different Fate,
His Mistress kindness or her scornfull hate.
Come all whom the blind God has led astray,
Here the bewildred Youth is shew'd his way:
Guided by this he may yet love and find
Ease in his Heart, and reason in his Mind.[23]

In 1681 Tonson published with Charles Harper the fourth edition of *The Second Part of The Works of Mr. Abraham Cowley*. Eventually, after acquiring the entire valuable copyright, Tonson was able to publish alone the eleventh edition of Cowley's *Works* in 1710. In 1683 Tonson was flattered, no doubt, to be one of the publishers of the sumptuous folio edition of François Eudes de Mézeray's *A General Chronological History of France*, translated by John Bulteel. The name of Thomas Basset, Jacob's former master, headed the list of publishers on the title page, followed by Samuel Lowndes, Christopher Wilkinson, William Cademan, and, albeit the last, Jacob Tonson.

In the midst of his publishing activities, Tonson found time for a curious service to Thomas Creech, the gifted Oxford scholar whose translation of Lucretius was one of the most acclaimed translations of the age. As Tonson later reported to his nephew,[24] Creech had begged Tonson to try to obtain commendatory verses by Dryden and Waller to be prefixed to his second edition of *T. Lucretius Carus* (1683). Since he felt obliged to Creech for his contribution to *Plutarchs Lives* and for promising him the printing of *Horace*, Tonson wished to help the young poet. Unable to obtain the desired poem from Dryden, Tonson wrote himself, in imitation of Dryden's style, verses beginning, "How happy had our English tongue been made." The verses, unsigned, were among those prefixed to Creech's *Lucretius* and were taken by Creech and everyone else for Dryden's. Knowing that it was also "to no purpose" to hope for a poem from Waller, Tonson tried his hand again with another set of verses, in Waller's style, beginning, "What all men wisht, tho few cou'd hope to see." These verses he signed with the initials "E. W.," and they were printed among the other commendatory poems. Masquerading thus pleasantly as Dryden and Waller, Tonson appeared in print in the company of John Evelyn, Nahum Tate, Thomas Otway, and Richard Duke.

The very popular translation, *Ovid's Epistles*, convinced Tonson that translations would be a thoroughly dependable source of income. Early in his publishing career, he issued also the first three volumes of *Plutarchs Lives*, Creech's *Horace* (1684), and various translations of Latin authors in his First Miscellany. Virgil's "Eclogues" occupied nearly one hundred pages in the Miscellany and were the work of Dryden (two eclogues), the Earl of Roscommon (one eclogue), Creech (two eclogues), and a few lesser "hands." Dryden made one contribution to Ovid's "Elegies," and Creech made several. George Stepney contributed to both Ovid's "Elegies" and Horace's "Odes," as did the lesser hands. There were brief translations from Theocritus and a part of Virgil's "Fourth Georgic." Considerably more space in this volume was given to translations than to original poems (mainly Dryden's).

His successive Miscellanies brought Tonson new contributors, among them Congreve, Addison, and Prior. The Second Miscellany was almost wholly given over to translations, chiefly by Dryden, with many unsigned shorter pieces. Among the unsigned poems appeared Tonson's own modest blank verse elegy, "On the Death of Mr. Oldham,"[25] which no one suspected as Tonson's.[26]

Tonson prefaced his Third Miscellany with a note, "The Bookseller to the Reader," in which he explained that this volume had been delayed by work in connection with the publication of *Juvenal*. Tonson had received so many "Ingenious Copies" for this Miscellany that some of them, to be augmented by copies from persons now out of England, must be reserved for another volume. He would "likewise willingly try if there could be an Annual Miscellany, which I believe might be an useful diversion to the Ingenious," as well as a means of preserving choice copies that might otherwise be lost.[27] He concluded: "If I should go on with the Design of an Annual Miscellany, after I have procur'd some Stock to proceed upon, I will give Public Notice of it. And I hope the Gentlemen who approve of this Design, will promote it, by sending such Copies as they judge will be acceptable. / Your very humble Servant / Jacob Tonson."[28]

The Third Miscellany offered extensive translations, especially Dryden's from Ovid, and many unsigned original poems. The Fourth Miscellany, hopefully entitled *The Annual Miscellany*, proved to be a rather slender volume. Dryden's now limited contributions were supplemented by a fair number of original poems. According to their title pages, both the Third and the Fourth Miscellanies were printed for Tonson by Robert Everingham, who was probably the printer of Dryden's works and most of Tonson's other publications throughout the last decade of the century.

His involvement in literary projects did not preclude Tonson's increasing interest in politics. He would have shared with his Whig friends, notably Somers and Dorset, the growing resentment against the despotism of James II during his brief and unpopular reign. In 1681 Somers had published *A Brief History of the Succession*, in defense of the legality of excluding the Duke of York from the throne. This tract was reprinted by Awnsham Churchill and Jacob Tonson in 1687. James had already entrenched his position by the execution of Monmouth, "the Protestant Duke," beloved in the City and befriended by William of Orange. The King's dangerous policies accelerated, and the need to check them became more urgent. In May, 1688, Somers acted as their junior counsel in the trial of the Seven Bishops, who had opposed the reading in the churches of James's second Act of Indulgence, designed to favor Roman Catholics and issued without the assent of Parliament. Somers's appeal to the jury, in defense of the bishops, backed by his thorough knowledge of the Constitution, was instrumental in bringing a verdict of "not guilty," much to the satisfaction of the majority of Londoners. Tonson would have followed with interest the progress of so important a trial, in which Somers played so decisive a role. The Kit-Cat Club, evolving about this time, provided a serviceable forum for Whig agitation against the King.

Political tensions may have fired Tonson's enthusiasm for Milton, whose eloquent defense of politcal freedom was peculiarly gratifying to the Whigs. In 1683 Tonson purchased from Brabazon Aylmer half of the copyright of *Paradise Lost*, and seven years later, the remaining half of it, "with a considerable advance in price" over the amount which Aylmer had paid.[29] Tonson was not deterred in this enterprise by his very limited capital, nor by the fact that Milton's well-remembered Commonwealth activities were not likely to recommend him to the reading public. In his venturesome undertaking the young publisher received welcome encouragement from John Somers.

As was his custom in the case of expensive editions, Tonson devoted some years to the careful preparation of Milton's text. *Paradise Lost, A Poem in Twelve Books, The Author John Milton, The Fourth Edition, Adorned with Sculptures,* was not published until 1688. Tonson still owned only half of the copyright, and Richard Bentley was joint publisher with him; but Tonson had a separate title page made for his own copies. The poem was printed by M[iles] Flesher, son of James and Elizabeth Flesher, and grandson of Miles Flesher, a well-known printer and master of the Stationers' Company. The young printer and Jacob Tonson had been admitted freemen of the Stationers' Company on the same day, January 7, 1678. Miles Flesher also printed for Tonson Dryden's translation of Maimbourg's *The History of the League* and probably other works. Flesher's widowed mother, Elizabeth Flesher, had printed Mrs. Behn's *Sir Patient Fancy* for Richard and Jacob Tonson.

To avoid the risk of financial loss, Tonson and Bentley published *Paradise Lost* as a subscription edition. It was the first of fifteen important subscription editions undertaken by Jacob Tonson.[30] As with the Miscellanies, Tonson popularized a method of publication which he did not initiate. Among the 538 subscribers to *Paradise Lost* were many distinguished persons.

In securing subscriptions in Oxford for this new edition Tonson had the services of Francis Atterbury, then a young Oxford tutor. In a letter dated November 15, 1687, Atterbury assured Tonson that he had bestirred himself in Tonson's behalf, and he appended a list of thirty-one Oxford subscribers. He complained, however: "The thinness of ye University, particularly our house [Christ Church], and ye expectations people are in of greater affairs have been ye cause that this Thing has not gone forward so well as it would have done at another time; especially if you had gone on immediately with it. upon ye first proposal all people were strangely fond of it." Oxford was seething over King James's highhanded acts, including the transformation of Magdalen College into a Roman Catholic seminary. News from London was perhaps little more encouraging. Atterbury wrote cautiously: "If you have any thing that's told on your side of ye world, ye Coach is a safe way of conveyance." He added the postscript: "Creech preach'd a bold sermon on Gunpowder Treason day."[31] We may infer that Atterbury could rely on Tonson to share his political views.

Tonson was never more active than in the last decade of the century, nor was his interest in translations ever more pronounced. Dryden's three major translations, *Juvenal and Persius*, *Virgil*, and the *Fables*, were spaced a few years apart, giving the elderly poet no respite from the overwork which was wearing him out. Another translator who was extensively read was Sir Roger L'Estrange, who, in his heyday, as Licenser of the Press, had wielded immense authority. The Revolution had ruined L'Estrange's private fortunes, but the fame of his vigorous translations continued unabated. Tonson was pleased to have a share in reprinting L'Estrange's popular works. In 1688 Tonson joined Richard Bentley and Joseph Hindmarsh in publishing the fourth edition of *Tully's Offices*, and in 1699 he published alone the seventh edition of *Seneca's Morals by Way of Abstract*. In 1697 Tonson published Creech's last translation, *The Five Books of M. Manilius*.

Tonson's interest in massive historical works is reflected in the fourth edition, which he printed with Richard Bentley, of William Camden's *The History of the Most Renowned and Religious Princess, Elizabeth* (1689), and the first installment of Laurence Echard's *The Roman History* (1695), a publication which he shared with M. Gilliflower, H. Bonwicke, and R. Parker. He had sound judgment as to works that were likely to have a continuing sale. He printed with Awnsham Churchill the fifth edition of Sir William Temple's *Observations upon the United Provinces of the Netherlands* (1690) and with Awnsham and John Churchill the third edition of Temple's *Miscellanea* (1693).

In the busy decade of the 1690's Tonson published many shorter works. He reprinted with Hindmarsh a pocket edition of Mrs. Behn's first and popular romance, *Love-Letters Between a Noble-Man and his Sister* (1693). He published poems by Walsh, Hopkins, and Blackmore; a travel diary by Lister;[32] and plays of varying merit by Betterton, Settle, Bancroft, Southerne, Hopkins, and

Dennis. It was in this decade that Tonson had the privilege of publishing all but the first of Congreve's plays.

The Collier controversy near the end of the century did not leave Tonson unscathed. Shortly after the appearance of Collier's *A Short View of the Immorality and Profaneness of the English Stage*, the justices of Middlesex prosecuted Congreve for writing *The Double-Dealer* and Tonson for printing it.[33] In his verse-allegory, *The Pacificator* (1700), Defoe defended Blackmore and Collier against the Troops of Wit, who are overthrown by the Men of Sense, yet may revive. For the marshaling of the Wits, Tonson is held responsible:

> T——n, even Hackney T——n, would not Print,
> A Book without Wits Imprimatur in't.[34]

Whatever he may have thought of Defoe, for whom he never published, Tonson seems good-humoredly enough to have borne no malice toward either Blackmore or Collier.[35]

It became Tonson's practice to publish occasional poems in honor of England's monarchs or in praise of her military victories. These poems he printed in folio editions, with large type on paper of the best quality. In 1695 Congreve, Prior, and others provided him with poems on the battle of Namur; and numerous poets produced elegies written in rather similar vein on the death of Queen Mary. If not the best of the elegies, George Stepney's[36] was perhaps the most painstakingly composed. Stepney was abroad on diplomatic service and sent Tonson his verses, accompanied by the most precise queries concerning their possible revision.

In the letter enclosing his elegy, Stepney disparaged it as "ye product of Westphalia dyet and no sleep." Nevertheless, he is sending it, because "they that will have a poem, must have a poem." He would have liked to have his friends about him to "judge and correct" his verses. Since that is not possible, he depends on Tonson to show them to Dryden, to Montague, if Tonson "goes early in a morning" to him, and to Congreve. He is sending a copy to Prior for further suggestions. He is "sure Mr Dryden at one minute" can set certain lines right, and Mr. Montague "with a cast of his eye" will recognize where the poem fails. But he frankly depends also on Tonson for editorial improvements. Some lines are too stiff, others too flat. He confides, "I may confess to you (for you cannot but observe it) that all beginnings come hard to me; but when I am once gott into ye right road, I can make shift to Canterbury it on, as Sir Godfrey calls it." Stepney is displeased with his reference to William and Mary as "this couple," for "couple is a mean word." (Tonson, or someone else, substituted "happy Nuptials.") Tonson has "read the Bible later than I" and will know whether it was Elijah or Elisha who fled "in the fiery Car." Tonson must strike out lines ninety-two and ninety-three if he notes that Stepney stole them, for "You have a better memory." At the publisher's discretion certain other lines may be omitted. It is Stepney's hope that the poem may come out before the Queen's funeral, "else ye market may be spoiled."[37]

Little is known of Tonson's private life during these years. On August 20, 1688, his mother assigned to her elder son Richard the shops under the two gatehouses of Gray's Inn which had been her property.[38] She was evidently still alive in 1690, because in January of that year a young Irish cousin, Jacob Tonson (a younger son of Jacob's uncle Richard?), wrote from Bristol to the publisher regarding a project to "turn volunteer," thanked his cousin for some assistance in this matter, and sent his regards to "my Aunt, Cos. Tonson, & all the rest of my relations."[39] The death of Jacob's brother Richard that same year brought to an end the occasional sharing of copyrights by the two brothers. By the summer of 1694 Tonson had moved his bookshop, still retaining the sign of the Judge's Head, to a site near the Inner Temple Gate in Fleet Street.[40] About October, 1698, he moved again to his brother's old shop at Gray's Inn Gate next to Gray's Inn Lane.[41] By this date Mary Tonson may have wholly given up her husband's business.

In the summer following Dryden's death, Tonson, Congreve, and Congreve's jovial friend, Charles Mein, made a trip to Holland. A disconcerting example of the survival of the irrelevant is Congreve's detailed description of the crossing to Calais and his almost total silence concerning the rest of the expedition. On August 11, 1700, Congreve wrote to Edward Porter from Calais:

> Charles and Jacob and I have never failed drinking your healths since we saw you, nor ever will till we see you again. We had a long passage but delicate weather. We set sail from Dover on Saturday morning 4 aclock and did not land till 6 the same evening; nor had we arrived even in that time, if a french open boat with Oars had not

been stragling towards us when we were not quite half-seas over, and rowed us hither from thence in 5 hours; for the packet boat came not till this morning.[42]

For Congreve and Mein the journey was a pleasure excursion, but for Tonson, like his other journeys, it was a business trip. Congreve, who knew Tonson well, once observed to his friend Keally that Tonson would never come to Ireland "for having said so, unlesse some considerable subscription may be set afoot to induce him."[43] Tonson's objective was to select Dutch paper and Dutch type, the finest which any English publisher could obtain anywhere, for his forthcoming publications. His headquarters were in Amsterdam, where he received many civilities from a Scottish merchant, John Drummond, whom he later supplied with books.[44] Tonson was still in Holland in October.

On April 23, 1703, Mary Tonson assigned to her son Jacob, who had reached the age of twenty-one, and to her daughter Elizabeth their half-shares in her late husband's property in Bell Court and "under Gray's Inn Gate, next Gray's Inn Lane," with all the books there, for £400 in "good English money." In a "Schedule of Exceptions," she reserved to herself: £40 of stock in Stationers' Hall; a feather bed with pillows, bed linen, and blankets; two sets of damask table linen; a silver tankard; four silver spoons; six "cain" chairs; a "standing looking glass"; a fire grate; a table; two small pictures; and four chests of drawers.[45] At about this time Tonson the Elder may have taken his young nephew, Jacob Tonson junior, into partnership with him. Possibly soon after uncle and nephew became partners, they set up their own printing house in Earl's Court, Bow Street.

Tonson was prospering. He could share his responsibilities with his nephew, and he could now afford the pleasure of a country residence. In 1703 he leased the attractive estate of Barn Elms in Surrey, six miles from London.[46] The property had a frontage on the Thames and "majestic elms." The Kit-Cats were to enjoy their secretary's hospitality at "Barnes" on many relaxing occasions, and their portraits were to adorn the walls of the bow-windowed room where the club members were to hold their meetings.

Tonson had no less than three long-term projects under way in the first decade of the eighteenth century: a translation of Bayle's Dictionary; an edition of Shakespeare; and a Latin text of Caesar's

Commentaries. On April 1, 1701, King William granted Tonson a royal license for the sole printing and publishing for fourteen years of an English translation in four volumes of Pierre Bayle's *Dictionnaire historique et critique*. Tonson proposed to supply "additional accounts of several English authors of note not mentioned by the said author, or at least not sufficiently enlarged upon."[47] The learned French philosopher, living in retirement in Rotterdam, brought out in 1702 an enlarged version of the imposing Dictionary. It was to confer with Bayle, as well as to secure type, paper, and illustrators for the edition of *Caesar*, that Tonson returned to Holland in the spring of 1703, leaving his nephew in charge of their business affairs.

Tonson arrived at The Hague with the Duke of Grafton in May, 1703,[48] and proceeded to Amsterdam, where he lodged "at Mr. Vatck's house near the Stadt House." Several letters from Vanbrugh in Vanbrugh's delightfully exuberant style kept Jacob posted as to events at home. Vanbrugh was supervising alterations in Tonson's new country residence at Barnes, where the work was progressing slowly, every room littered with "chips—up to your chin!" Soon, however, the house would be fit "for the reception of a King." "The compas window [bow window], below and above, is made, but the shashes [*sic*] not yet up; both the rooms are ten times the better for 't." Tonson's gardens abounded with vegetables and fruits. In a few days "a hundred thousand apricocks" would be ripe, and "such strawberrys as never were tasted," currants "red as blood," and other fruits "to gripe the gutts of a nation."[49] Vanbrugh regaled Jacob with his personal affairs and those of mutual friends, all of whom resolved "never to subscribe to another Book that must carry you beyond Sea."[50]

When Tonson met Addison in Amsterdam, the latter was evidently quite willing to make some amends for the failure of Tonson's mission from Somerset to secure Addison as traveling tutor for Lord Hertford.[51] At Tonson's request, Addison wrote from The Hague to Leibnitz, describing Tonson's project for a Latin text of Caesar's Commentaries and begging the assistance of the famous scholar in obtaining a drawing, to be engraved for this work, of a "urus" or wild ox owned by the King of Prussia. Addison explained that Tonson was prepared to spare no cost in the publication, "which will probably be the noblest Volume that ever came from the English press." Prince Louis of Baden and Prince Eugene already headed the list of subscribers.[52] Addison likewise commended the project to Lord Cutts, who offered his aid in securing subscribers.[53] A few months later, Lord Raby, envoy at the Court of the King of Prussia in Berlin, was able to assure Tonson that the painting of the urus was under way, a print would be ready in the near future, and the King of Prussia would subscribe for the volume.[54] Daniel Pulteney, a cousin of William Pulteney, and a visitor in Utrecht, helped Tonson to make contacts with designers and booksellers.[55]

Tonson's elaborate plans for publishing *Caesar* seem to have aroused the warmth of interest which had preceded the publication of *Virgil*. Henry D'Avenant, in diplomatic service in Frankfort, solicited subscriptions in 1704 from the Electoral Prince and Prince Louis.[56] Stepney obtained other royal subscribers and reported to Tonson that Prince Eugene was "very inquisitive" as to the date of publication of "your Caesar."[57] Tonson returned to Holland again in 1707[58] and 1710[59] for further business in connection with this work and other enterprises. In the latter year Johannes Rolij, a typefounder of Rotterdam, sold Tonson three hundred pounds' worth of Dutch type.

Tonson published *Poetical Miscellanies: The Fifth Part* with a footnote on the title page reminding purchasers that they might have at his bookshop "the four former Parts: Publish'd by Mr. Dryden." The Miscellany opened bravely with Addison's "A Letter from Italy" and continued with a few pieces by Dryden which had not been published previously. Other contributions by Addison and a number of the best lyrics of Prior and Congreve gave some distinction to a volume that proved to be mainly a rather heterogeneous collection of very minor poems.

Poetical Miscellanies: The Sixth Part begins with the "Pastorals" of Ambrose Philips and ends with Pope's "Pastorals." The Miscellany includes a large assortment of trivia, relieved by a few other pieces by Pope and a substantial translation from Lucan by Nicholas Rowe. Although in his prefatory note, "The Bookseller to the Reader," Tonson held out the hope of another Miscellany "at the beginning of the next Year," he did not go on with the series. He no longer had the services of anyone who, like Dryden, could command this type of access to the reading public.

Tonson did publish, however, a complete edition of the six Miscellanies in 1716, which he dedicated to the Duke of Newcastle. The poems are somewhat differently arranged than in the original editions, and poems by Milton, Donne, and other earlier poets were added. "Verses Written for the Toasting-Glasses of the Kit-Cat Club, in the Year 1703" first appeared in this edition, so shortly before the club expired.

In the main, Tonson's publications were popular and profitable. *Cato* repeated the spectacular sales of *Absalom and Achitophel.* The 1709 edition of Prior's poems must have sold well, for Prior was a favorite poet and the first eighteenth-century poet to be collected. Eighteenth-century plays and operas, of which Tonson published a fair number, were often ephemeral productions. But to his credit as a publisher, Tonson published the two best classical tragedies of the century, Ambrose Philips's *The Distrest Mother* (1712) and Addison's *Cato.* He published six of Rowe's plays,[60] including *The Fair Penitent* (1703) which influenced Samuel Richardson.

In only a few instances do we know which of the Tonson publications were undertaken by Tonson's nephew after 1703. We have Steele's testimony that it was Jacob junior who printed *The London Gazette* (1708–1711).[61] The printing of that government-controlled newspaper was one of the plums with which the Whig ministry, when in power, rewarded faithful Whig services. When the Whigs returned to power under George I, Tonson regained the printing of the *Gazette* (1714–1717).[62] Tonson was one of the official printers of the *Votes* of the House of Commons (1708–1710 and 1715 onward). In 1710 he received from the House of Lords the sole right to publish the official account of Sacheverell's trial. And on January 25, 1720, through the patronage of the Duke of Newcastle and Secretary Craggs, Tonson and his nephew by royal patent from George I were appointed official printers to many of the principal government offices for a term of forty years.[63] It seems probable that most, if not all, of these lucrative but heavy assignments of government publications to the Tonson press were delegated by Tonson the Elder to his junior partner.

It was also Jacob junior who took over the collected edition of *The Tatler* in 1711 and who negotiated the purchase from Buckley of seven volumes of *The Spectator* in 1712. Did Jacob Tonson the Elder assign to his nephew much, if not all, of the responsibility connected with the literary journals with which the Tonson press was associated and from which it derived so much prestige? Again, we do not know. Jacob junior, like his uncle, exerted himself in the purchase of copyrights. One important purchase, made by Jacob junior in 1707, was of over one hundred of Henry Herringman's copies and shares of works.[64] A purchase for the sum of £100, which the nephew made in 1709, was of over three hundred whole or part shares in works owned by George and Mary Wells, including a half copyright in twenty-five of Shakespeare's plays and a fourth part in thirty-four plays by Beaumont and Fletcher.[65]

Tonson published *The Works of William Shakespear* in 1709 in six volumes, edited by Nicholas Rowe. Tonson had published a number of Rowe's plays and may well have concluded that a successful dramatist was an appropriate choice among possible editors. The publication was delayed while Rowe made somewhat frustrated attempts to collect materials for the "Life." "Revis'd and Corrected," the work was reprinted in 1714. It may be inferred that it was the publication of Shakespeare which induced Tonson to give his bookshop the sign of "Shakespears Head" when he moved to new and final quarters "over against Catherine Street in the Strand" in October, 1710.[66]

Rowe's *Shakespear* holds first place among Tonson's eighteenth-century collected editions of English authors. But perhaps Tonson deserves almost as much recognition for his services to English literature in his eighteenth-century collected editions of other English writers. In 1709 he published the fifth edition of Sir John Denham's *Poems and Translations*, and *The Works of Sir John Suckling*; in 1710 the eleventh edition of *The Works of Mr. Abraham Cowley* in two volumes, and *The Works of Mr. William Congreve* in three volumes; in 1711 *The Works of Mr. Francis Beaumont and Mr. John Fletcher* in seven volumes, and the eighth edition of *Poems, &c Written by Edmund Waller*, with a "Life" of Waller which has been attributed to Atterbury; in 1712 *The Works of Mr. Thomas Otway* in two volumes; in 1715 *The Works of Mr. Edmund Spenser* in six volumes; and in 1717 *The Dramatick Works of John Dryden* in six volumes, edited by Congreve.

An Historical and Critical Dictionary, translated from Bayle's French text, appeared in 1710 in four volumes, "with many Additions and Corrections, made by the Author himself that are not in the French Editions." The work was too great a labor for a single publisher, and Tonson took on thirteen other publishers as his "assigns." He reprinted the license granted by King William, and it is probable that he wrote the unsigned Dedication to a loyal member of the Kit-Cat Club, the Earl of Essex, who had served "Our late Glorious King" in all of his campaigns in Flanders.[67]

For historical works Tonson relied heavily on that tireless historian, Laurence Echard. He published Echard's *A General Ecclesiastical History* (1702); his revisions of *The Roman History* (1703–1705), extending to five volumes; and *The History of England* (1707 and 1718),[68] extending to three volumes. With others Tonson published in 1717 *The Universal Bibliotheque of the Historians,* translated from the French text (1707) of Louis Ellies Dupin, which had aroused his interest when he was in Holland in 1707.[69] Other histories from the Tonson press were Temple Stanyan's *The Grecian History* (1707)[70] and Humphrey Prideaux' *The Old and New Testament Connected, in the History of the Jews and Neighboring Nations* (1716–1718) in two volumes.

The eighteenth century was an age when literary piracy was rampant,[71] especially in the form of cheap reprints of recently issued and popular works. Tonson's battles over unauthorized or pirated texts of his own editions, or alterations of them, added zest to the life of a man who relished a good fight but knew when to call it off. Edmund Curll was the most persistent invader of Tonson's prerogatives, and the most slippery, for more than half of the publications which were wholly or partly Curll's bore other names.[72] Tonson's publication of *The Tryal of Dr. Henry Sacheverell* in 1710, by order of the House of Lords, was immediately followed by *An Impartial Account* of the trial, "Done on such another Paper and Letter, and may therefore be bound up with the Tryal of the said Doctor. Printed for Jacob Tonson at Gray's-Inn-Gate in Gray's-Inn-Lane." Tonson protested in *The London Gazette* that the *Impartial Account* was spurious, and his name had been added to it without his knowledge.[73] Other spurious tracts on the proceedings promptly appeared; and as all of these were advertised as printed to be bound up with *The Tryal,* Tonson may have considered the free publicity more welcome than otherwise. In 1715, by order of the House of Commons, Jacob Tonson, Timothy Goodwin, Bernard Lintot, and William Taylor published a large folio edition of *A Report from the Committee of Secrecy*, dealing with the negotiations with France of the late Tory ministry. Curll, as "S. Popping," lost no time in bringing out at the price of one shilling *An Index to the Report of the Secret Committee*: "By which, in a Short View, the Reader is Presented with the Substance of it. In a Letter to a Friend." The publisher affirms that "no true Briton" should be without the *Report* itself, and the *Index* indicates where to turn to the more remarkable passages. Soon Curll was bolder. In 1716, by order of the House of Lords, Tonson published *The Tryal of George Earl of Wintoun*[74] in a pamphlet which sold for a shilling. Curll seized the opportunity to publish for twopence *An Account of the Tryall of the Earl of Winton*, as printed by "S. Popping." When it was discovered that Curll was S. Popping, Curll and his printer, Daniel Bridge, were taken into custody. They were summoned before the Lord Chancellor and obliged to express on their knees their "hearty sorrow" for their offense.[75]

Tonson's long-awaited Latin text of Caesar's Commentaries, *C. Julii Caesaris Quae Extant*, finally appeared in 1712. Shoals of less ambitious eighteenth-century classical texts and translations preceded and followed it. Cambridge editions (1699–1702) were printed for Tonson of Latin texts of Horace, Virgil, Terence, Catullus, Tibullus, and Propertius. A few years later, Maittaire's Classics (1713–1719)[76] provided another series of the same and other Latin authors. Maittaire's *Opera et Fragmenta Veterum Poetarum Latinorum Profanorum & Ecclesiasticorum* (1713) was published in two volumes by Tonson, J. Nicholson, and B. Tooke. A number of translators contributed to *Several Orations of Demosthenes* (1702), translated from the Greek; *Ovid's Art of Love*; and *The Odes and Satyrs of Horace* (1715). *Lucan's Pharsalia* (1718) was translated by Rowe. Tonson's most important French text was his *Oeuvres Meslees de Monsieur de Saint-Évremond* (1705), the first authentic collection of Saint-Évremond's works in England.

Jacob junior again assumed charge of the Tonson business during his uncle's absence from England in 1713–1714. It was Jacob junior who on May 4, 1714, negotiated a contract with Thomas Tickell,[77] still at Oxford, for a complete translation of Homer's *Iliad*. Tickell was to receive five hundred guineas for this work, which was a great deal less than the twelve hundred guineas for which Pope had agreed in March to translate the *Iliad* for Lintot. When Tickell learned of Pope's project, he cancelled all but the first book of his translation. The rival first books were published in June, 1715, within two days of each other, and became "the talk of the town."[78] The Tonsons may well have regretted the unfortunate bargain which thwarted their publication of Homer. Perhaps Tonson the Elder found compensation for this disappointment in the two luxuriously printed editions which ended his publishing career: *Ovid's Metamorphoses* and Prior's *Poems on Several Occasions*.

In the autumn of 1718, Tonson returned to Paris, where he was to remain until the spring of 1720. His life as a publisher was over. Before leaving England, he assigned his copyrights to his nephew for the sum of £ 2,597 16s 8d.[79] The chief events of his stay in Paris were a serious illness and his profitable speculations in French stocks. Rather unkindly, Robert Arbuthnot wrote from Rouen to Matthew Prior: "the Whigs are those who have run away with the 'rost.' Jacob Tonson has got 40,000 l. (sterling I mean) and I hear is to drop 'Thuanus'[80] that he was to reprint; riches will make people forget their trade as well as themselves."[81] Tonson was sufficiently a man of his century to wish for the life of a country gentleman at last. He would buy land and build, and own gardens and orchards like his noble friends. Unlike those noble friends he had not inherited such benefits; he had earned them.

Eminent
Publisher

onson profited from the labors of his "eminent hands"; they profited, less tangibly, from the services of an "eminent publisher." Tonson was discriminating. It was his ambition to follow in the footsteps of the best publishers who had preceded him, acquire, as opportunity afforded, the copyright of their best editions of ancient and modern authors, and surpass their achievement. Among his contemporaries, he published for gifted creative writers and reputable scholars. To be sure, for financial or political reasons he missed some of the prizes, notably masterpieces by Pope, Swift, and Defoe. But he frowned upon cheap editions of works devoid of any literary merit.

In a classically minded age, Tonson made a considerable contribution to classical translations and texts. There is every reason to suppose that he undertook a rigorous program of self-education. Tonson's chief rival in the publishing business, Bernard Lintot, cheerfully informed Pope that he had no knowledge of Greek, Latin, French, and Italian and had to employ correctors of unreliable translators and sometimes also call in "a civil customer" in his shop, "especially any *Scotchman*," to help him correct a corrector.[1] Tonson required no such elaborate precautions. His taste was cosmopolitan, his knowledge of foreign languages adequate. He had the valuable advice of Dryden and established fruitful contacts with young scholars.

Tonson took great pride in handsome folio editions of classical authors. First among these was the 1693 translation of *The Satires of Decimus Junius Juvenalis . . . Together with the Satires of Aulus Persius Flaccus*. As has been noted, Dryden edited this work. Also, he translated the first, third, sixth, tenth, and sixteenth satires of Juvenal and the six satires of Persius. Tonson had delayed publication so that Dryden could complete the translation of Persius himself, perhaps thereby increasing the prospect of a large sale.[2] The volume was printed on paper of the best quality, gilt-edged, with wide margins, and in large, clear type, and included Dryden's impressive introductory essay and notes for each satire.

Dryden supervised and corrected the translations of ten collaborators in *Juvenal*: his sons Charles ("Seventh Satire") and John Dryden, Jr. ("Fourteenth Satire"), Nahum Tate ("Second" and "Fifteenth Satires"), William Bowles ("Fifth Satire"), George Stepney ("Eighth Satire"), Stephen Hervey ("Ninth Satire"), William Congreve ("Eleventh Satire"), Thomas Power ("Twelfth Satire"), Thomas Creech ("Thirteenth Satire"), and one anonymous contributor (Richard Duke) ("Fourth Satire"). With disarming modesty, Dryden ascribed "the better though not the greater part" of the translation to the work of assistants whose "Excellencies" must "attone for my Imperfections and those of my Sons."[3] The assistants, some of whom were known to the public, shone, of course, in light reflected from their distinguished director. Tate was a dramatist and had recently been appointed Poet Laureate. Creech was admired as the translator of Lucretius. Stepney, whose contribution was his longest poem, was to prove a better diplomat than poet. Congreve, who translated the satire on "Gluttony," was to become the most famous of the collaborators.

Dryden's translations, occupying more than a third of the volume, overshadow the others and admirably achieved the purpose he intended. He remarked in his prefatory essay that he and his assistants had undertaken "not a literal Translation but a kind of Paraphrase; or somewhat which is yet more loose betwixt a Paraphrase and Imitation." He explained: "We write only for the Pleasure and Entertainment of those Gentlemen and Ladies, who tho they are not Scholars are not Ignorant: Persons of Understanding and good Sense; who not having made *Latine* Verse so much their business, as to be Critiques in it, wou'd be glad to find if the Wit of our Two great Authors, be answerable to their Fame and Reputation in the World."[4] Dryden conceded that the translators had made Juvenal "more Sounding, and more Elegant, than he was before in *English*," and had "endeavour'd to make him speak that kind of English, which he wou'd have spoken had he liv'd in England, and had Written to this Age." It must be admitted that "to speak sincerely, the Manners of Nations and Ages, are not to be confounded: We shou'd either make them *English*, or leave them *Roman*. If this can neither be defended, nor excus'd, let it be pardon'd, at least, because it is acknowledg'd; and so much the more easily, as being a fault which is never committed without some Pleasure to the Reader."[5]

Dryden's readers found his "more elegant" English very much to their taste. They could appreciate the vigorous antithesis and grace of such well-turned couplets as:

> Look round the Habitable World, how few
> Know their own Good, or knowing it, pursue.[6]

and

> What Musick, or Enchanting Voice can chear
> A Stupid, Old, Impenetrable Ear?[7]

or the description of a harlot:

> She knows her Man, and when you Rant and Swear
> Can draw you to her, *with a single Hair.*[8]

The greatest distinction of the *Juvenal* is Dryden's prefatory "Discourse concerning . . . Satire." For the benefit of those who were neither scholars nor ignorant, Dryden provided brief, trenchant, illuminating comparisons of Horace, Juvenal, and Persius. He found Persius "not sometimes, but generally obscure"[9] but excelling, in his spirit of sincerity, Horace, "who is commonly in jeast and laughs while he instructs," and equal to Juvenal, "who was as honest and serious as *Persius,* and more he cou'd not be."[10] Juvenal was wholly employed in lashing vices, whereas "'Folly was the proper Quarry of *Horace,* and not Vice: And as there are but few Notoriously Wicked Men, in comparison with a Shoal of Fools, and Fops; so 'tis a harder thing to make a Man Wise, than to make him Honest: For the Will is only to be reclaim'd in the one; but the Understanding is to be inform'd in the other."[11] The essay includes one of the finest passages of Dryden's incomparable prose:

> I must confess, that the delight which Horace gives me, is but languishing. Be pleas'd still to understand, that I speak of my own Taste only: He may Ravish other Men; but I am too stupid and insensible, to be tickl'd. When he barely grins himself and, as Scaliger says, only shows his white Teeth, he cannot provoke me to any Laughter. His Urbanity, that is, his Good Manners, are to be commended, but his Wit is faint; and his Salt, if I may dare to say so,

almost insipid. *Juvenal* is of a more vigorous and Masculine Wit, he gives as much Pleasure as I can bear: He fully satisfies my Expectation, he Treats his Subject home: His Spleen is rais'd, and he raises mine: I have the Pleasure of Concernment in all he says; He drives his Reader along with him: If he went another Stage, it wou'd be too far, it wou'd make a Journey of a Progress, and turn Delight into Fatigue. When he gives over, 'tis a sign the Subject is exhausted; and the Wit of Man can carry it no farther. If a fault can be justly found in him; 'tis that he is sometimes too luxuriant, too redundant; says more than he needs . . . but never more than pleases. Add to this, that his Thoughts are as just as those of *Horace* and much more Elevated.[12]

Dryden's *Juvenal* had been the first folio edition of the Latin poet to be published for twenty years. A second edition in 1697 was illustrated with engravings by the Dutch artist Michael Van der Gucht. The continuing popularity of the translation is attested by the fact that Tonson printed a fifth edition in 1713.

The Works of Virgil was a far more ambitious undertaking than *Juvenal* for both Dryden as translator and Tonson as publisher. As he proceeded with the translation, Dryden found it increasingly burdensome. He complained: "Virgil called upon me in every line for some new word; and I paid so long, that I was almost bankrupt . . . the twelfth *Aeneid* cost me double the time of the first and second."[13] Of the completed work, however, he could feel that in spite of declining years, poverty, illness, and judges prejudiced against him, he had "in some measure" acquitted himself of "the Debt which I ow'd the Publick, when I undertook this Work."[14] The publication was welcomed with enthusiasm. On September 30, 1696, Basil Kennett wrote to Tonson: "It's ye best News in ye world that your great Friend is so near the height of his glory: when 'twill be as impossible to think of Virgil without Mr Dryden as of either without Mr Tonson."[15]

The very great success of *Virgil*, Dryden remarked, was "beyond its desert or my Expectation."[16] The translation superseded Ogilby's *Virgil*, which for nearly half a century had been much admired by English readers. Dryden's version "still has more vitality,"[17] it has been justly observed, than any other translation of Virgil. "Whatever may be our opinion of Dryden's *Virgil* as a translation," comments one modern critic, "we must admit that it is a splendid example of the possibilities of the heroic couplet."[18] The "choice of words and Harmony of Numbers" which Dryden considered his chief contribution to English poetry is abundantly illustrated in the lays of shepherds and their loves in the "Pastorals," the glowing descriptions of the pursuits of a country life in the "Georgics," and the stately, dramatic narrative of "the long Glories of Majestic Rome" in the "Aeneis."

Tonson considered that so important a work as Dryden's *Virgil* merited a subscription edition on an unprecedented scale. One hundred first subscribers paid five guineas apiece to have their names, titles, and coats of arms conspicuously printed beneath the elaborate "sculptures" or "cuts." Among the first subscribers were Princess Anne, Prince George of Denmark, and the boy Duke of Gloucester; numerous noblemen; and such high-ranking statesmen as Somers, Lord Chancellor; the Earl of Pembroke, Lord Privy Seal; and Sir William Trumbull, Principal Secretary of State. Second subscribers, who paid two guineas apiece, included Congreve and his friends Joseph Keally and Charles Mein, and the theatrical celebrities Thomas Betterton, Elizabeth Barry, and Anne Bracegirdle.

Tonson found it convenient to use again the "sculptures" that had been used in Ogilby's 1654 edition of *Virgil*. He probably concluded that they were too good to be laid aside and that having new ones made would lessen his profits. Besides, they had been generally admired and had increased the popularity of Ogilby's accurate but uninspired translation. Franz Cleyn, a native of Germany, had designed these illustrations. Cleyn had been employed by Charles I and various members of the nobility and, like other skilled draughtsmen, had sought employment by publishers after the decline of Court patronage. He had designed and manufactured famous tapestries, and his designs have a tapestried effect in their heavy foliaged, side-framing trees with finely shaded leaves.[19] Cleyn's designs for *Virgil* had been engraved mainly by Wenceslaus Hollar, a Czech *émigré*, who had been scenographer to Charles II, and Pierre Lombart, an accomplished French engraver.

The illustrations for the "Pastorals" and "Georgics" have similar but pleasant extensive landscapes, often with hills or classical buildings in the distance, and in the foreground shepherds and other rustic swains. Many scenes are enlivened by animals, faithfully and humorously depicted, an inquiring cow, a smiling dog, charging bulls, or horses joyously tossing their manes. The "Aeneis" had

offered Cleyn such dramatic possibilities as a violent storm and shipwreck; the torment of Laöcoon; the Trojan horse disgorging warriors; Aeneas escaping with his father and son from flaming Troy;
a naval battle; war games (utilized by Tonson to divert the young
Duke of Gloucester); and ghosts and monsters in hell.

Dryden's *Virgil* was printed, as *Juvenal* had been, on paper of the
best quality, with large type, and with generous margins which were
not cluttered, like those in Ogilby's 1654 edition, with notes. Tonson made certain significant changes in the illustrations. A new
frontispiece by Michael Van der Gucht represented Virgil in flow-
ing robes, holding in his hands Dryden's volume, with the Muse about
to place a laurel wreath on the poet's head and a winged cupid, poised
above, bearing a laurel-wreathed medallion conspicuously inscribed:
Dryden's Virgil. Printed for Jacob Tonson. The other changes
were more subtle but unmistakable. In most of the illustrations not
only is the straight nose of Ogilby's Aeneas replaced by a hooked
one, strongly suggestive of the shape of King William's, but long
lines on either side of his face give Virgil's hero an older, sterner
expression.

Ogilby had published five editions of Virgil within a period of
thirty-five years. Tonson published four editions within nineteen
years. His nephew was to publish a fifth and sixth edition, and a
seventh was published by the sons of Jacob junior, Jacob and Richard Tonson, and Samuel Draper. Editions of Dryden's text by other
publishers continued to appear up to 1880.

A still more imposing subscription edition was Tonson's Latin
text, *C. Julii Caesaris Quae Extant* (1712), which had been so
eagerly awaited during the nine years since Tonson began prepara-
tions to publish it. Addison was probably not the only one of Tonson's "eminent hands" who considered that Tonson's *Caesar* might
be "the noblest Volume that ever came from the English press."[20] As
his editor Tonson had chosen a well-known English metaphysician,
Samuel Clarke, rector of St. Benet's in London and one of Queen
Anne's chaplains in ordinary. Clarke's scholarship had attracted attention in his undergraduate days in Cambridge, where he was
known as "the lad of Caius." Tonson was also fortunate in his
printer, John Watts,[21] who was soon to serve him as printing partner
in a series of classical texts.

C. Julii Caesaris Quae Extant is an enormous folio, profusely illustrated. In a double-page frontispiece, engraved by Cornelis Huyberts, against a background of Roman buildings, muscular cupids in mid-air hold a medallion with a bust of Caesar above a seated female figure, attended by a cupid holding a sceptre and the Muse blowing a trumpet. Under the Latin title the publisher's name, "*Jacob Tonson, 1712*," stands out boldly in English. The volume was dedicated to Marlborough, whose portrait by Kneller precedes the Dedication. On each of the double or single page plates appears the name with the coats of arms of the subscriber, with the inscription, *Hac Tabula humillime Diccata est.* Headpieces, tailpieces, and ingeniously decorated initial capitals supply further embellishments. Tonson's *Caesar* was praised by an English bibliographer of the nineteenth century, William Lowndes, as "the most sumptuous classical work which this country has produced."[22]

The eighty-seven engravings were the work of Dutch artists, chiefly: Cornelis Huyberts, Bastiaen Stoopendael, Jan de Leeuw, and Andries Van Buysen, and were suited to the subject-matter of the five Commentaries. The scenes most frequently represented are extensive landscapes, terminated by towering mountains. Rivers wind to the sea through plains where a few walled towns and encampments are located. The foreground provides side-framing trees with luxuriant foliage, shading resting warriors. Everywhere there is precise and exquisite detail: in every leaf of the trees, every curl of a horse's mane, in the foreground; and in the clustered houses of the towns, the ships at sea, and the tiny figures of individual horsemen in the middle ground. The maps display meticulous workmanship.

A unique engraving, which Tonson had taken unusual pains to acquire, is of the bison belonging to Frederick I, King of Prussia. The engraving is dedicated to Frederick William, Prince of Brandenburg, who was soon to succeed his father. The figure of the black, plump animal, with nicely shaded hide and long tail spread against a tree, completely fills two folio pages. In profile the bison's large round eye has a genial expression, and he raises his forefeet obligingly, as if to avoid crushing a small horse and an antlered stag in a pastoral middle ground glimpsed between his legs. One of the most carefully executed engravings is of the city of Alexandria and its harbor. One of the most gruesome represents a giant wooden cage, with large numbers of agonized captives leaning from it to view the fire prepared below to burn them. The final illustrations are Huybert's engravings of the nine famous paintings of "The Triumph of Caesar" by the Italian artist, Andrea Mantegna. The first in the series was dedicated to Somerset, the ninth to Somers.

Eighteenth-century readers became familiar with and presumably admired the many attractive duodecimo volumes of the Greek and Latin texts of Maittaire's Classics, published by Jacob Tonson and John Watts between 1713 and 1719. In 1713 Queen Anne, recognizing the labor and expense involved in such an enterprise, granted "to Michael Maittaire, his executors, administrators and assigns" her royal license for the sole printing and publishing of a collection of all the Greek and Latin authors "in twelves," with complete indexes, "for the Term of Fourteen Years."[23] Again Tonson selected with care an editor who, if somewhat pedestrian, had "a large measure of Scholarship."[24] Maittaire, the son of a French Protestant émigré, had had an exceptionally long apprenticeship in the study of Greek and Latin authors under the formidable Dr. Busby of Westminster School. For the use of Westminster students Maittaire compiled his *Graecae Linguae Dialecti* (1706) and an *English Grammar* (1712), and he was for a time second master at the school. It may be inferred that Maittaire's long-continued services to Tonson were more profitable to Tonson than to his hard-working editor. Maittaire wrote an urgent letter to Tonson in 1717 requesting an advance of money for editions of the Greek poets and Cicero and offering to supply several other texts which were "much in request." "My pressing necessities," wrote Maittaire, "are impatient for an answer. Were I not press'd to it, I would never put my modesty to the wrack in discovering my wants."[25]

Maittaire's "very curious and correct" editions of *Terence, Lucretius, Justin, Phaedrus, Aesop, Salust,* and *Pompey* were printed in 1713. In April, 1714, Tonson announced that "the collection will be made compleat with all convenient speed."[26] *The New Testament* in Greek was printed in 1714; *Horace, Florus, Ovid* in three volumes, *Virgil, Nepos,* and *Catullus* followed in 1715; *Caesar, Rufus, Juvenal and Persius,* and *Martial* in 1716; *Paterculus* in 1718; and *Lucan* in 1719.

The small, gilt-edged books were uniform in format, on good paper but with fine print, with title pages lettered in black and red.

The French artist Louis du Guernier designed and engraved most of the frontispieces, headpieces, and tailpieces. A favorite tailpiece featured Cupid on a cloud blowing a trumpet. A favorite headpiece represented small cupids equipped with bows and arrows, surrounding a fountain. The scholarly indexes were a third as long as the text, or longer.

It is not surprising that Tonson concluded his editions of classical authors with a sumptuous edition of *Ovid's Metamorphoses in Fifteen Books. Translated by the most Eminent Hands.* In 1626 George Sandys had published his translation of this work in a small volume which at once became popular in Court circles, followed in 1632 by a large folio edition, *Ovid's Metamorphosis Englished, Mythologiz'd and Represented in Figures.* The 1632 volume, printed on very fine paper with neat print, large margins, marginal notes, and notes at the end of each book, has been described as "one of the handsome books of English Renaissance printing."[27] Franz Cleyn designed the fifteen copper plate illustrations prefacing the various books and providing a pictorial summary of the subject matter. Ten editions had appeared by the end of the century. Dryden, who had read Sandys's translation in boyhood, was originally critical of Sandys as a poet but ultimately praised him as "the best versifier of the former age."[28]

In 1678, at the beginning of Tonson's publishing career, George Sawbridge, who had sometimes published with Thomas Basset and whom Tonson as a young apprentice had known and admired, brought out the seventh edition of Sandys's *Ovid.* Gradually, as his publishing career advanced, Tonson had printed portions of the *Metamorphoses* translated by his eminent hands.[29] A considerable part of the contents of Tonson's 1717 edition was already available when Tonson chose Garth to find other assistants for the remaining portions and to edit the work as a whole.

Pope satirized Garth's editorial labors in "Sandys' Ghost: Or a Proper New Ballad On the New Ovid's Metamorphosis: As it was intended to be Translated by Persons of Quality." In "dead of night" the ghost of Sandys, "with saucer Eyes of Fire," pays a visit to "a Wit and courtly 'Squire," bringing ominous news:

> I hear the Beat of Jacob's Drums,
>   Poor Ovid finds no Quarter!

> See first the merry P[elham] comes
>> In haste, without his Garter.
>
> Then Lords and Lordings, Squires and Knights,
>> Wits, Witlings, Prigs, and Peers;
> G[ar]th at St. James's, and at White's
>> Beats up for Volunteers.

Fenton, Gay, Congreve, Rowe, and Stanyan have refused to participate in the work, but "any one" *may* contribute to it. The publisher is advised:

> Now, *Tonson* list thy Forces all,
>> Review them, and tell Noses;
> For to poor Ovid shall befal
>> A strange *Metamorphosis*.

The dire consequence of Garth's undertaking will be the change of Ovid into waste paper.[30]

Pope took some satirical liberties in his ballad, for Gay, Congreve, Rowe, and Temple Stanyan all contributed to the new translation. Dryden's share, culled from his previous works, was the most substantial, comprising all of Books I and XII and episodes from six other books. Joseph Addison was represented by Books II and III; Samuel Croxall by Book VI and episodes from four other books; Samuel Garth by Book XIV and one other episode; Arthur Mainwaring by Book V; Laurence Eusden by most of Book IV; Nahum Tate by most of Book VII; John Gay by nine episodes; Thomas Vernon by five; Leonard Welsted by four; Alexander Catcott by two; William Congreve by one and part of another; and Alexander Pope, Nicholas Rowe, Temple Stanyan, Stephen Hervey, William Stonestreet, and John Ozell by one each. Pope would scarcely have thought of himself as among such minor contributors as might properly be considered "any one."

Garth dedicated this volume to Princess Caroline, Princess of Wales, whose interest in literature was one agreeable compensation for the accession of George I. The portrait of the Princess by Kneller appeared as a frontispiece; and as a pleasant innovation the fifteen books were dedicated to fifteen ladies, most of them titled, whose coats of arms were engraved beneath their names. The engravings, by Louis du Guernier, Michael Van der Gucht, Elisha

Kirkall, and R. Smith, presented crowded scenes of the ingeniously contrived transformations of mortals and gods by divine magic. The aim of the translators, announced in the Preface, was to copy the beauties of Ovid and "throw a shade" over his imperfections. So composite a work naturally suffered from the poetical limitations of some of Garth's recruits. But with the advantage of an elaborate format and several famous "hands" among the contributors, Tonson's *Ovid* was well received and had several editions up to 1826.

In publishing monumental editions of the works of classical authors, Tonson was following the example of his most significant precursors in the publishing business. In rescuing from obscurity or oblivion the masterpieces of English authors and publishing them with similar care, he was an innovator. His first and best triumph in this neglected field was the fourth edition of Milton's *Paradise Lost*, which Tonson published with Bentley in 1688. The works of Milton were to bring Tonson more recognition and greater financial returns than any other publishing ventures. Years later, when Tonson was asked what poet he had got most by, he replied unhesitatingly: "Milton."[31]

The sales of earlier editions of the epic had not been reassuring. As is well known, Milton had not fared well with his publisher, Samuel Simmons, to whom in 1667 he sold the copyright of *Paradise Lost* for £5, on the understanding that he would receive £5 more when thirteen hundred copies of the first edition had been sold; £5 more after the sale of the same number of copies of the second edition; and another £5 after the same sale of the third. No edition was to exceed fifteen hundred copies. Simmons published the second edition in 1674, the third in 1678. In 1680 Milton's widow was quite content to resign for a total payment of £8 the £5 due her for the second edition and the £5 not yet due on the third. Soon afterward Simmons was equally willing to sell his copyright to Brabazon Aylmer for £25, but Aylmer showed no interest in attempting another edition. For ten years there was no new edition of the poem.

The first edition of *Paradise Lost*, with the text in ten books, was a modest small quarto which sold for three shillings a copy. The paper is yellowish but good, with the lines close together, the margins narrow. The headpieces and decorative initial capital letters are attractive. The pages are not numbered, but the lines are numbered in tens. A comparison of the text with Milton's manuscript of Book I[32] indicates accuracy in printing. The second edition, a small octavo, with the text arranged in twelve books, is rather less attractive than the first but has a portrait of Milton and commendatory verses, and the pages are numbered. The third edition, another small octavo, was modeled on the second, with poorer paper and type sometimes blurred. In the same year in which the third edition was printed, Thomas Rymer wrote scornfully of "that *Paradise Lost* of Milton's which some are pleased to call a poem."[33] Dryden judged otherwise. He is said to have returned a copy of the poem which Dorset loaned him with the comment: "This man cuts us all out and the Ancients too."[34]

When Tonson acquired the copyright of *Paradise Lost*, Aylmer sent him Milton's manuscript of the poem and also the manuscript of Milton's contract with Simmons. Tonson carefully preserved the manuscript of Book I and the contract, and these documents remained in the possession of his nephew's heirs. The subsequent history of the contract is curious. At the death of Tonson's great-nephew, Jacob Tonson the third, many papers connected with the Tonson publishing firm were stored in the cellars of a house in the Strand which the great-nephew had owned and which became the property of Mr. Hodsoll, a banker. Clerks of the banking house with an interest in literature apparently raided the papers, some were removed, and the remainder were ultimately destroyed. Milton's contract with Simmons and some other documents were left by a lodger, in lieu of rent, with his landlord in Clifford Road, Bond Street, and were sold by the landlord to a bookseller. In 1831 the Milton-Simmons contract was purchased for £50 by Samuel Rogers, the poet, who gave it to the British Museum.[35]

The frontispiece chosen by Tonson and Bentley for the 1688 folio edition of *Paradise Lost* was an engraving of Milton in an oval frame by the mezzotint engraver Robert White, and beneath it was printed (without Dryden's name) Dryden's tribute to Milton:

> Three Poets, in three distant Ages born,
> Greece, Italy, and England did adorn.
> The first in loftiness of thought surpass'd,
> The next in Majesty; in both the Last.
> The force of Nature cou'd no farther goe:
> To make a Third she joynd the former two.

As it seemed advisable to apologize for a poem written in blank verse, rather than in the popular form of heroic couplets, a statement entitled "The Verse" occurs on a separate page after the title page. The reading public is advised that "the neglect of rime is not to be taken as a defect, though it may seem so perhaps to vulgar readers."

The 1688 edition, in the style of all of Tonson's more elaborate books, was distinguished by excellent paper, large, clear type, and ample margins. It was the first illustrated edition of Milton. A Spanish artist, John Baptist Medina, who had recently come to England, designed the "sculptures," eight of which were engraved by Michael Burghers, a Dutch engraver who had settled in Oxford. The illustrations conformed to popular taste for a prettified, pictorial representation of Milton's majestic poem. The most striking scene reveals a grotesque winged Satan rising from the flames of the burning lake, where his followers are confined. In these engravings foreground, middle ground, background, and the heavens above are well occupied, the device of "multiple staging" making possible an array of several episodes at the same time in various portions of the scene. In the engraving for Book XI Michael addresses a distracted Adam and Eve in the foreground; and in the distance Eve is seen asleep, Adam talks with Michael on a hill, a lion pursues a hart and hind, and an eagle swoops from the sky to his prey.

Also in 1688 Randal Taylor published in separate volumes *Paradise Regained* and *Samson Agonistes*. In 1691 Bentley and Tonson brought out a fifth edition of *Paradise Lost,* which was reissued in 1692 under Tonson's name alone. Meanwhile, Tonson had succeeded in acquiring the copyright for Milton's other poems. In 1695 Tonson published *The Poetical Works of Mr. John Milton. Containing Paradise Lost, Paradise Regain'd, Sampson Agonistes, and his Poems on Several Occasions. Together with Explanatory Notes on each Book of the Paradise Lost and a Table never before Printed.* The commentary on *Paradise Lost* in this edition was the first which Milton had received and was the work of "P. H." (Patrick Hume). In 321 pages, this Scottish scholar learnedly annotated Biblical references, noted classical parallels, and clarified obscure words and phrases. It has been claimed that all subsequent editors have been indebted to Hume's commentary, "and often with far too little acknowledgment."[36]

In 1705 and 1707 Tonson published editions of *The Poetical Works* in two volumes. In 1711 he published a pocket edition of *Paradise Lost* only, which he dedicated to Somers with commendable brevity in the following words:

My Lord,

It was Your Lordship's Opinion and Encouragement that occasion'd the first appearing of this Poem in the *Folio* Edition, which from thence has been so well receiv'd, that notwithstanding the Price of it was Four times greater than before, the Sale encreas'd double the Number every Year. The Work is now generally known and esteem'd; and I having the Honour to hear Your Lordship say, that a smaller Edition of it would be grateful to the World, immediately resolv'd upon Printing it in this Volume, of which I most humbly beg your Acceptance, from / My Lord / Your Lordship's / Ever Obliged Servant.[37]

The successful editions of Milton may have encouraged Tonson to launch a much-needed new edition of Shakespeare. Between the fourth edition of Shakespeare's plays, published by Henry Herringman, A. Brewster, and R. Bentley in 1685, and the edition published by Tonson in six volumes in 1709, nearly a quarter of a century had elapsed. The Fourth Folio text was rare and expensive, and it was highly desirable that readers should be able to purchase all of the plays in more convenient volumes and at moderate cost. Again, Tonson succeeded in acquiring an important copyright. As editor of *The Works of Mr. William Shakespear* Tonson wisely chose a capable dramatist, Nicholas Rowe, who was a less prejudiced critic of Shakespeare than many of his contemporaries.

The frontispiece of the first volume of the new edition had an inset of Shakespeare's portrait engraved by Michael Van der Gucht, and each play was preceded by an engraving representing some phase of the action. The illustrations were adapted, as much as possible, to the manners of Rowe's time. Thus, the setting for *A Midsummer Night's Dream* shows two groups of eighteenth-century courtiers meeting by a stream in a moonlit pastoral scene; in the forest of Arden in *As You Like It* the bewigged gentlemen masquerading as courtiers strut about in high-heeled shoes; and the Queen and Hamlet in the ghost scene in *Hamlet* are attired as they would have been at the Court of Queen Anne.

Rowe dedicated "the best of our Poets to the Protection of the best Patron," the Duke of Somerset. He explained in his Dedication that in an endeavor to redeem Shakespeare "from the Injuries of former Impressions," he had compared earlier editions in order to secure "the true Reading" and had supplied many missing lines, as "in Hamlet one whole scene," left out in the last edition. "Such as it is," Rowe remarked modestly, "it is the best Present of *English* Poetry I am capable of making your Grace."[38]

A fairly long essay, "Some Account of the Life, &c of Mr. William Shakespear," preceded the plays. Rowe's was the first biographical account of Shakespeare and was reprinted by all other eighteenth-century editors of the dramatist. Inadequate though it was, it incorporated all that "tradition, then almost expiring, could supply."[39] Johnson included it in his own edition of Shakespeare, commenting, "it relates . . . what is now to be known, and therefore deserves to pass through all succeeding publications."[40] Not only was Rowe's "Account" the first biography of Shakespeare; it was "the standard biography till the time of Malone."[41] As to the chronology of the plays, Rowe candidly confessed that he was in the dark.

Rowe felt the necessity of defending Shakespeare from such "severe remarks" as the strictures of Rymer.[42] With noteworthy enthusiasm, in view of the veneration for classical conventions then prevailing and his adherence to them in his own plays, Rowe acclaimed Shakespeare's irregular genius:

> Whether his Ignorance of the Antients were a disadvantage to him or no, may admit of a Dispute: For tho' the knowledge of 'em might have made him more Correct, yet it is not improbable but that the Regularity and Deference for them, which would have attended that Correctness, might have restrain'd some of that Fire, Impetuosity, and even beautiful Extravagance which we admire in Shakespear: And I believe we are better pleas'd with those Thoughts, altogether New and Uncommon which his own Imagination supply'd him so abundantly with, than if he had given us the most beautiful Passages out of the Greek and Latin Poets, and that in the most agreeable manner that it was possible for a Master of the *English* language to deliver 'em.[43]

Rowe's observations on individual plays reflect his personal taste. He commended *Romeo and Juliet*, *Hamlet*, and *Othello* for having a fable founded on one action. His enjoyment of sentiment led him to pronounce *Romeo and Juliet* "wonderfully Tender and Passionate in the Love-Part, and very Pitiful in the Distress."[44] He had high praise for that "lewd old Fellow,"[45] Falstaff, found Shakespeare's clowns "all very entertaining,"[46] and considered Caliban an example of "wonderful Invention."[47] Rowe concluded that "no Dramatick Writer ever succeeded better in raising *Terror* in the Minds of an Audience than Shakespear has done."[48]

Rowe's was the first serious attempt to edit Shakespeare's plays. He modernized spelling and corrected punctuation. Himself a dramatist, for the first time Rowe provided a list of characters for each play, divided and numbered acts and scenes "on rational principles," and added stage directions. Basing his text on the Fourth Folio, he occasionally consulted the First or Second Folio in order to clarify certain passages. He made emendations, "without the pomp of notes or boasts of criticism,"[49] of which "some are right, some are plausible, some are wrong."[50] Many of his emendations succeeding editors "received without acknowledgment."[51] Unfortunately, Rowe's sixth volume included the six spurious plays which had been retained in the Fourth Folio.[52]

In the same month in which Tonson published Shakespeare's plays, Curll advertised as nearly ready a seventh volume of Shakespeare's works, containing his poems and critical notes on all the plays, and offered "a Gratification from J. Baker at the Black Boy in Pater-Noster-Row" to any gentleman who could contribute anything to improve the notes.[53] A few weeks later, the volume of poems duly appeared, published by E. Curll and E. Sanger, and advertised as "printed exactly as the Plays, and some on large Paper to compleat Sets."[54] For this volume Charles Gildon supplied "An Essay on the . . . Stage" and "Remarks on the Plays of Shakespear," with critical comments considerably less enlightened than Rowe's. Gildon did point out, however, that there was "not the least Ground"[55] to consider the last six plays in Tonson's edition genuine and alleged that the bookseller (Tonson) who printed them had included them "according to the laudable Custom of the Trade to swell the Volume and the Price." Furthermore, that same bookseller, "out of a good-natur'd Principle, agreeable to the Man, . . . thought it not impolitic to lessen the Towns Expectation of these Poems, because he had no hand in their Publication."[56]

It was characteristic of Tonson that he ignored this attack and joined forces with Curll in the complete and improved edition of Shakespeare published in 1714 by J. Tonson, E. Curll, J. Pemberton, and K. Sanger. This edition was in nine duodecimo volumes, consisting of Rowe's Preface and the plays edited by him in eight volumes, and the poems, with Gildon's essays and a glossary, in the ninth. Tonson paid "Mr. Hughes" (John Hughes) £28 7s. for what appears to have been substantial work by him on this edition. It is not known to what extent Rowe shared in the work of revision. Rowe had received from Tonson £36 10s. for his previous editorial labors on Shakespeare.[57]

Jacob Tonson was again successful in obtaining the copyright of Spenser's *Works*, which had not been published since the third edition of 1679. In 1715 Tonson printed in an octavo edition *The Works of Mr. Edmund Spenser. In Six Volumes. With a Glossary Explaining the Old and Obscure Words. Publish'd by Mr. Hughes.* Perhaps Somers, who had urged Tonson to publish Milton, had proposed that Tonson should render a similar service to Spenser. In any case, Hughes dedicated these volumes to Somers, in the last year of Somers's life. "It was your Lordship's encouraging a beautiful Edition of *Paradise Lost*," wrote Hughes, "that first brought that incomparable poem to be generally known and esteem'd." Somers was "one of the greatest Statesmen the Age has produc'd," who had "a more than common Share" in obtaining the Settlement. Now, "even in your greatest Retirement, you can never be wholly hid from the Eyes of a People, to whom you have done so much good."[58]

In the 1715 edition all of Spenser's poems and his treatise, "A View of the State of Ireland," were included. One printing was on royal paper for subscribers, whose names were listed. Spenser's text was in rather small print, the accompanying essays in large print. The pictorial quality of the poems supplied du Guernier, who designed and engraved the illustrations, with varied opportunities for groups of graceful figures against a more-or-less Roman background.

John Hughes, a minor poet, as well as a painter and musician, was well chosen as editor. Hughes was an able, if not scholarly, critic and an admirer of Spenser in an age which had shown little interest in the Elizabethan poet. Hughes had consulted earlier editions, including some early quartos of the minor poems, corrected some errors, followed Spenser's spelling, as he said, "for the most part," and provided a moderately satisfactory glossary. He supplied four very readable essays, "The Life of Mr. Edmund Spenser," "An Essay on Allegorical Poetry," "Remarks on the Fairy Queen," and "Remarks on The Shepherd's Calendar &c."

Hughes could give only a slender account of Spenser's life, but he had been at some pains to secure as much information as possible. He included a pleasant anecdote of Sir Philip Sidney's bounty to Spenser after reading the ninth canto of the first book of *The Faerie Queene* and referred to Congreve's efforts in behalf of a descendant of the poet. In "An Essay on Allegorical Poetry" Hughes praised the "extraordinary native Strength" of both Chaucer and Spenser, which had made it possible for them to take "deep Root, like old *British* Oaks,"[59] despite their archaic language. Since the critics had not been concerned with making rules about allegorical poetry, Hughes made his own and claimed that Spenser fully satisfies the requirements of liveliness, elegance, consistency, and clarity. Hughes was courageous enough to take issue with Sir William Temple, who had declared Spenser's moral "so bare that it lost the Effect." "I do not understand this," confessed Hughes. "A Moral which is not clear, is in my Apprehension next to no Moral at all."[60] In his praise of *The Shepheardes Calender* Hughes reveals his delight in pastoral poetry, a taste which he shared with his contemporaries and for one of the same reasons, that "it is a wonderful Amusement to the Imagination, to be sometimes transported, as it were, out of modern life."[61]

In "Remarks on the Fairy Queen" Hughes offers sound, perceptive, and even romantic criticism of Spenser's masterpiece.

> The chief Merit of this Poem consists in that surprizing Vein of fabulous Invention which runs thro it, and enriches it every where with Imagery and Descriptions more than we meet with in any other modern Poem. The Author seems to be possess'd of a kind of Poetical Magick; and the Figures he calls up to our View rise so thick upon us, that we are at once pleased and distracted by the exhaustless Variety of them; so that his Faults may in a manner be imputed to his Excellencies: His Abundance betrays him into Excess, and his Judgment is overborne by the Torrent of his Imagination.[62]

Hughes noted some defects of the poem and, like his contemporaries, had reservations about the Spenserian stanza, although he found Spenser's diction "for the most part, strong, significant and harmonious." He chose excellent illustrations of the "Beauties" which abound in every canto of each book. In one important respect he was far in advance of contemporary criticism. Admitting that *The Faerie Queene* lacks unity of design, Hughes refused to consider this a fatal blemish. Spenser never intended to design his poem by the rules of Homer and Virgil, and to compare it with the models of antiquity would be like drawing a parallel between Roman and Gothic architecture. "There is a Bent in Nature, which is apt to determine Men the particular way in which they are most capable of excelling; and tho it is certain he [Spenser] might have form'd a better Plan, it is to be question'd whether he cou'd have executed any other so well."[63]

One more de luxe edition was published by Tonson, this time of the *Works* of the popular contemporary poet, Matthew Prior. The enterprise was not initiated by Tonson but was promoted as "a piece of friendship" by a group of Prior's friends to relieve Matt's straitened circumstances after the dismal end of his diplomatic career. Backed by influential supporters and widely advertised, the project attracted unusual attention, with gratifying results.

One evening in January, 1717, Earl Bathurst and Lord Edward Harley, son of the Earl of Oxford, met at the house of Erasmus Lewis, with Prior, Pope, Gay, and Arbuthnot also present. While the others were discussing a subscription edition of Prior's poems, Lewis wrote a letter to Swift, requesting him to solicit Irish subscriptions. It was decided that subscribers should pay one guinea in advance and another on receiving the book.[64] Swift exerted himself and ultimately secured seventy subscriptions, and the task slowly got under way. On one occasion, Prior invited Pope to come to his house to meet Erasmus Lewis there and "confer upon the premises" with Jacob Tonson concerning the proposed publication.[65]

Prior had a grandiose scheme for the new edition, not all of the details of which could be realized. He longed to have his poems printed on vellum and reluctantly accepted the verdict that this would be "impracticable, improbable, impossible." But he was able to assure Lord Harley that "paper imperial, the largest in England," would be used; and Tonson and Adrian Drift, Prior's secretary, managed to arrange for a frontispiece "as big as has been formed since the days of Alexander the Coppersmith."[66] Prior devoted the greater part of 1718 to personal supervision of the edition. He sought the advice of Humfrey Wanley, the Earl of Oxford's "library-keeper," consulting him about the use of capital letters for "Emphatical words" and other matters, and sending him sheets for inspection. Wanley abetted Prior in protesting to the printer about "filthy hooks, meagre letters and unequal lines."[67] Prior wrote to Swift that he employed "two colon and comma men" to help him with corrections, and he designed himself with meticulous care such emblems as "cupids, torches, and hearts" for initial capital letters.[68] Despite his complaints and denials, Prior rejoiced in a labor very close to his heart. "A pretty kind of amusement," he jested, "I have engaged in: commas, semicolons, italics, and capitals, to make nonsense more pompous, and furbelow bad poetry with good printing."[69]

Poems on Several Occasions was published in three sizes in December, 1718, without Prior's name, by Jacob Tonson and John Barber. There were 1,447 subscribers, a list of whose names precedes the poems. Several subscribers ordered ten copies and a considerable number, five. Nearly all of the eminent persons of the time subscribed. Prior was to bequeath one copy of extra large size to St. John's College, Cambridge, of which he had been a fellow.

There is no reason to suppose that the subscribers objected to the massiveness of their purchase. But a small spurious edition of Prior's poems, published by T. Johnson in 1720, was launched with the following artful and double-barrelled attack on Tonson by its publisher:

> Mr. Prior's Poems are generally & most deservedly esteemed; but every one cannot spare a Guiney to buy the folio Edition. beside that its bulk makes it unfit to carry about either in Town or Country; which yet one would be desirous to doe, because many of his pieces are so pretty & diverting. So this Edition will please as well those that have the large Edition [Tonson's], as those that have it not; & the character, besides its beauty & neatness, is large enough to be read by old people as well as young; whereas the pocket Editions we have lately had of *Waller, Milton, Hudibras* & others [Tonson's] are printed on so small a letter, that they cannot be read by any one above forty, without great pain & fatigue to the eyes, which every wise man will shun as much as possible.

The unauthorized publisher concluded with an air of scrupulous veracity: "There has been some more pieces attributed to Mr. *Prior*, but I believe, without reason, since he has given in this Collection all that he has written in this kind worth publishing under his name; & in my opinion, 'tis a great fault to print under a man's name any thing that he disowns, whether good or bad."[70]

Prior included in the 1718 edition all of the poems he had printed thus far[71] which he wished preserved in his name. It was not a large collection, although substantially increased by two long poems, "Solomon," which Prior liked better than his friends did, and "Alma," with which he had beguiled his imprisonment. Although Prior was sometimes at odds with Tonson, he referred good-humoredly to his publisher near the beginning of "Alma":

> Ratts half the manuscript have eat:
> Dire Hunger! which We still regret:
> O! may they ne'er again digest
> The Horrors of so sad a Feast.
> Yet less our Grief, if what remains,
> Dear Jacob, by thy Care and Pains
> Shall be to future Times convey'd.[72]

In the Preface to "Solomon" Prior made a significant and forward-looking, if somewhat hesitant, attack on the heroic couplet, which he had employed *ad nauseam* in that tedious poem:

> If striking out into Blank Verse, as Milton did (and in this kind Mr. Philipps, had He lived, would have excelled) or running the Thought into Alternate and Stanza, which allows a greater Variety, and still preserves the Dignity of the Verse; as Spenser and Fairfax have done; If either of these, I say, be a proper Remedy for my Poetical Complaint, or if any other may be found, I dare not determine: I am only enquiring, in order to be better informed; without presuming to direct the Judgment of Others. . . . But once more; He that writes in Rhimes, dances in Fetters: And as his Chain is more extended, he may certainly take longer steps.[73]

Prior's fastidious and constant supervision contributed to making this perhaps the most attractive of Tonson's illustrated editions. There is a singular charm in Prior's designs for initial capitals, as of a tiny cupid enclosed in the letter Q, or bearing a trumpet and peeping from the letter T. The French artist, Louis Chéron, designed the numerous headpieces and tailpieces. Graceful scrolls frame figures in classical draperies, or kneeling cupids, or boys supporting garlands. Some of the shorter poems have dainty miniature tailpieces. Prior chose to adorn with the most elaborate of the tailpieces his unfinished "An Epistle, Desiring the Queen's Picture. Written at Paris, 1714. But left unfinish'd, by the Sudden News of Her Majesty's Death." The poem breaks off in the middle of a line. With his diplomatic career shattered by the death of the Queen, Prior could only offer to the memory of "my bright Defender" the final tribute of an eloquent silence and a vision of a beautiful Pegasus in flight, looking wistfully back at a seated Muse.

The ostentation upon which Prior insisted, and of which his contemporaries apparently approved, was gently and delightfully ridiculed by Austin Dobson many years later:

> With the small copy of 1718, Johnson might have knocked down Osborne the bookseller; with the same work in its tallest form (for there were three issues), Osborne the bookseller might have laid prostrate "the great Lexicographer" himself. It is, of a surety, one of the vastest volumes of verse in existence. . . . As one turns the pages of the big tome, it is still with a sense of surprise and incongruity. The curious mythological headpieces with their muscular nymphs and dank-haired river-gods, the mixed atmosphere of Dryden and "the Classicks," the unfamiliar look of the lightest trifles in the largest type, the jumble of ode and epigram, of Martial and Spenser, of La Fontaine and the "weary King Ecclesiast"—all tend to heighten the wonderment with which one contemplates these portentous *Poems on Several Occasions*.[74]

The 1718 edition of Prior's poems brought to a fitting end Tonson's most ambitious achievements. Short of publishing on vellum, he could carry elegance no farther. He could, and undoubtedly did, look back with satisfaction on his successive triumphs in a field which he had dominated. Tastes in the format of books inevitably change as the centuries pass, and the modern reader may examine Tonson's more ponderous volumes, if he consults them at all, with more curiosity than enjoyment. The important fact is that more assiduously than any other publisher of his time Tonson kept alive and introduced to an ever-widening reading public the finest works of distinguished authors.

Tonson and
His Public

n Tonson's lifetime there was an aristocracy of taste, as well as an aristocracy of blood. As a man of taste, Tonson was the ever-welcome companion of his social superiors among the Kit-Cats. Himself a gifted man, he gained much from his contacts with gifted and learned men, especially Dryden. His career was his personal and unique triumph. For forty years he gave enlightened and unremitting attention to its multifarious demands.

Like Dryden, Tonson wished to please the age in which he lived. The coterie with which Tonson was most closely associated required an unending supply of classical texts, translations, and "imitations" of classical works. These Tonson readily and regularly produced. In the long span of his publishing career, there were important changes in taste, but the taste for the classics remained constant.

When heroic plays ceased to be popular and his disfavor with the government prevented fresh achievements in political satire, Dryden turned to translations as a never-failing though modest means of support. His services to his contemporaries in this field were very great. A knowledge of classical, especially Latin, literature was the criterion of a well-bred man in the Age of Dryden and also in the Age of Pope. The public schools and universities and the tutors of noblemen supplied this indispensable background of culture. Latin quotations came easily to the lips of statesmen as well as scholars. When Lord Halifax interceded with the Earl of Oxford to continue Congreve in his government post, after a change in ministry, Oxford aptly reassured Halifax by repeating two lines from Virgil's *Aeneid* (I, 567):

> *Non obtusa adeo gestamus pectora Poeni,*
> *Nec tam aversus equos Tyria Sol jungit ab urbe.*[1]

Addison and Steele prefaced each number of *The Spectator* with a "motto" in Latin or Greek. Over one half of these were from Horace and Virgil, roughly a third from Horace.[2] Addison explained: "My Reader is . . . sure to meet with at least one good Line in every Paper, and very often finds his Imagination entertained by a Hint that awakens in his Memory some beautiful Passage of a Classick Author. . . . I must confess the Motto is of little use to an unlearned Reader. For which Reason I consider it only as *a Word to the Wise*. But for my unlearned Friends if they cannot relish the Motto, I take care to make Provision for them in the Body of my Paper." With the characteristic delicate irony which he bestows on his feminine readers, Addison added: "what the more encourages me in the use of Quotations in an unknown Tongue, is, that I hear the Ladies, whose approbation I value more than that of the whole Learned World, declare themselves in a more particular manner pleas'd with my *Greek* Motto's."[3]

According to Swift, whose Tory prejudices must be borne in mind, most of the Kit-Cats were not men of strong intellect. They all belonged, however, to a society which talked more-or-less seriously about literature. As a man of wit, or at least a pretender to wit, one must embark on literary conversation. One must have literary opinions and be able to support them with references to recognized classical authorities. If going directly to Aristotle, or even to Horace, was too much of an effort, Dryden provided "neat little treatises, not too difficult to read."[4] In his prefaces Dryden briefly (if digressively) compared and evaluated the principal classical authors; and he offered in his translations pleasing English versions of them in well-turned, easily memorized, heroic couplets. Swift wrote with a touch of sarcasm:

> Read all the *Prefaces* of *Dryden*,
> For these our Criticks much confide in;
> (Tho' merely writ at first for filling,
> To raise the Volume's Price a Shilling.)[5]

If many of his contemporaries could only lean on Dryden, without realizing the distinction of his literary criticism, he remained free, as most of them did not, from the bondage of "a superstitious regard for the Ancients" and was able "to turn a highly inquisitive and absorbed, but perfectly impartial, eye on all the literature (and it was extensive) that interested him."[6] What Dryden so bountifully contributed to the knowledge of classical literature Tonson had the privilege of conveying to a reading public that was eager for such fare.

Ovid, Virgil, and Horace were popular favorites in Tonson's separate editions and in excerpts in his Miscellanies. Even a fop, as described by Steele, "has read all the Miscellany Poems, a few of our Comedies, and has the Translation of Ovid's Epistles by Heart."[7] Women were mainly more avid readers of French romances than of the classics. But Lady Mary Wortley Montagu in her youth was such a "vast admirer" of Ovid's *Metamorphoses* that she secretly locked herself up for five or six hours a day in her father's library and "stole the Latin language," which at fifteen she understood "perhaps as well as most men." Mr. Wortley encouraged her in this bold venture, "and Mr Congreve was of great use to her after it came to be known."[8]

Translating was an epidemic. Tonson's Miscellanies furnished a convenient amount of space for beginners in the art who could try their hand at odes or episodes. Dryden generously advised disciples who lacked his gifts and sometimes revised their work. When the brilliance of Dryden was not available, the ambitious publisher sought the services of reputable, if not brilliant, scholars for translations and for the more pedestrian editing of the classical texts which came from his press in such profusion.

It was inevitable that Pope should satirize in *The Dunciad* those "good *scholiasts*" who

> with unweary'd pains
> Make *Horace* flat, and humble *Maro's* strains.[9]

It was Pope's original intention to retain from the manuscript of *The Dunciad* the lines:

> On yonder part what fogs of gathered air
> Invest the scene, there museful sits Maittaire.

But Edward Harley, second Earl of Oxford, persuaded the poet to suppress this unkind reference to Tonson's unflagging editor.[10] Pope did not neglect the booksellers who published the labors of the scholiasts. In the manuscript of *The Dunciad* Tonson himself participates in Book II in a foot race with Curll, sponsored by the God-

dess of Dulness, for the prize of an image of Gay. Tonson receives
the epithets of "Fat Tonson," "left-legged Jacob," and "mine host
of Shakespeare's Head." When Curll "slidders" in the mud, Jacob
seems likely to be the victor,

> And *Jacob, Jacob*, rings thro' all the Strand.

But revived at the behest of Cloacina, Curll rises,

> Re-passes Tonson, vindicates the race,
> Nor heeds the brown dishonours of his face.[11]

Pope afterward thought better of subjecting the leading publisher of the day to such indignities, and in all editions of *The Dunciad* Lintot and Curll are the contenders in the foot race, which is
won by "shameless Curl." In the 1728 edition:

> With steps unequal L——t urg'd the race,
> And seem'd to emulate great Jacob's pace.[12]

In the 1729 edition there is a slight alteration in the first line of
the couplet:

> With legs expanded Bernard urg'd the race
> And seem'd to emulate great Jacob's pace.[13]

In the 1741 edition, published after Jacob's death, although Jacob
does not take part in the race, Pope could not resist the temptation to
recover from his manuscript the familiar jest about Jacob's legs:

> With arms expanded Bernard rows his state,
> And left-legg'd Jacob seems to emulate.[14]

In all published versions of *The Dunciad*, Tonson does fare better
than any of the other booksellers, despite the hint that he promotes
dull works. In Book I the Goddess of Dulness

> beholds the Chaos dark and deep,
> Where nameless *somethings* in their causes sleep,
> Till genial Jacob, or a warm *third-day*
> Calls forth each mass, a poem or a play.[15]

Tonson had greater respect than Pope for scholiasts, and they
were very useful to him. But again like Dryden, he wished to persuade English readers that their own literary heritage was as valuable
to them as the masterpieces of classical antiquity. In this wholesome
endeavor Dryden had pointed the way. "It is easy enough for us to
regard Chaucer, Spenser, Shakespeare, Milton, as towering figures;

but it was Dryden who first declared they were so."[16] Among these great writers Tonson early selected Milton as a neglected poet whom he would seek to introduce to a larger circle of readers. The choice was original and also bold at a time when the best that a typical contemporary reader could find to say of Milton was: "A good Author though an ill subject to his Prince."[17] During forty years of publishing, Tonson published Milton as regularly as the classics. His numerous editions of *Paradise Lost* proved the success of the experiment.

In 1720, soon after Tonson's retirement, Jacob junior published in two quarto volumes an elegant subscription edition of the *Poetical Works* of Milton, superintended by Thomas Tickell, with a list of three hundred subscribers. This edition was reprinted in duodecimo size in 1721. To an edition of 1725, also in two volumes, and reprinted in 1727 and 1730, Elijah Fenton contributed a "Life" of Milton. The Tonsons continued to publish editions of Milton until 1759. The death of Jacob Tonson the third brought to an end their long monopoly of Milton's poems.

Tonson was well aware of the effectiveness of advertising in current newspapers and journals. *The Spectator*, largely the work of two of his own "eminent hands," gave Tonson the largest body of readers that any contemporary publisher could command. Of the most popular numbers of *The Spectator* twenty thousand copies, according to contemporary estimates,[18] were sold in a day. Moreover, these essays afforded "a constant Topick for our Morning Conversation at Tea-Tables, and Coffee-Houses."[19] It would be interesting if we could know to what extent the sales of Tonson's 1711 edition of *Paradise Lost* were increased by Addison's twelve much-admired Saturday papers[20] in which he described at length, with appropriate illustrations, the superlative beauties of Milton's epic. Addison concluded the series well pleased with his achievement:

> Had I thought, at my first engaging in this Design, that it would have led me to so great a length, I believe I should never have entered upon it; but the kind Reception which it has met with among those whose Judgments I have a Value for, as well as the uncommon Demands which my Bookseller tells me have been made for these particular Discourses, give me no Reason to repent of the Pains I have been at in composing them.[21]

Nor did Addison confine himself to this popular series in his tributes to Milton. Unhesitatingly he accords Milton "the first place among our English Poets" and confesses: "I have drawn more quotations out of him than from any other."[22] Addison had reservations about blank verse, which he once "made it his business to run down" at Jacob Tonson's.[23] He believed that "others of the Moderns" rivaled Milton "in every other part of Poetry; but in the greatness of his Sentiments he triumphs over all the Poets, both Modern and Ancient, *Homer* only excepted."[24] Sir Roger de Coverly, whose reading in general does not extend beyond Baker's *Chronicle*, is represented[25] as so impressed by one of Adam's speeches to Eve after the Fall that he borrows Will Honeycomb's "Pocket Milton" (Tonson's recently published edition) in order to "read over those Verses again before he went to bed."[26] So frequently does Addison quote long excerpts from the "inimitable" speeches of Adam and Eve that the thousands who read *The Spectator* with their morning tea must have felt nearly as well acquainted with our first parents as with their own hearts.

It was after Tonson's retirement that he suffered the only blow to his prestige as a publisher which, so far as we know, he took seriously. The blow fell, where it pained him most, in a disparagement of his editions of *Paradise Lost*. Jacob junior, John Poulson, and others published in 1732 a text of *Paradise Lost* edited by Dr. Richard Bentley. That learned but erratic critic had declared that the first edition of *Paradise Lost* was "polluted with such monstrous Faults, as are beyond Example in any other printed Book" and that for more than sixty years the poem had had "miserable Deformity by the Press, and not seldom flat Nonsense."[27] These charges stung Tonson to a fury of indignation, which he expressed vigorously in letters to his nephew. Tonson spent "some hours" examining Bentley's and Addison's sentiments on Milton, which were "quite opposite." Bentley had shown his "cowardliness" by not finding much fault with the many lines praised by Addison. Jacob junior should show Bentley, but "keep very carefully tis of valew," the manuscript of Book I of *Paradise Lost*, which would be "enough to knock down ye Drs opinion" of the "nonsensical" corruptions in Milton's text. It must be hoped that Pope would "lash" so insolent a detractor of "the devine milton." The doctor "attacks ye Sense of all the most learned readers, Poetical or otherways," and has "not allowed the least matter to his overlearned mind to praise or seame to commend." Should Tonson vent his wrath "as long as I am angry I should never have done."[28]

Tonson sent his nephew Milton's manuscript of Book I and requested that it should be shown to Pope. With the manuscript Tonson enclosed very detailed comments in confirmation of the fact that the first edition of the poem had been carefully printed from it, and he expressed further protests over "this vultures [Bentley's] falling upon a Poet that is the admiration of England & its greatest credit abroad."[29] It was disappointing, Tonson wrote later, that Pope had decided to ignore Bentley. "The love of milton shoud make him write, Indignation make[s] any one."[30]

Although Pope chose not to "lash" Bentley, others did. Tonson may have taken some satisfaction in one of these lashings, David Mallet's *Of Verbal Criticism*, published in 1733. Mallet assails Bentley as a critic who

> Dares, in the fulness of the Pedant's pride
> Rhime tho no genius, tho no judge decide.
>
> .   .   .   .
>
> To *Milton* lending sense, to *Horace* wit,
> He makes 'em write what never Poet writ:
> The *Roman Muse* arraigns his mangling pen,
> And *Paradise*, by him, is *lost* agen.[31]

Mallet added a footnote, thoroughly in accordance with Tonson's judgment of Bentley:

> This sagacious Scholiast is pleased to create an imaginary Editor of Milton, who, he says, by his blunders, interpolations, and vile alterations, lost Paradise a second time. This is a *postulatum* which surely none of his critics can have the heart to deny him; because otherwise he would have wanted a fair opportunity of calling *Milton* himself, in the person of this phantom, fool, ignorant, ideot, and the like critical compellations, which he plentifully bestows on him.

Dryden would have welcomed a critical edition of Shakespeare, and he may have recommended such a project to Tonson. Although he had debased Shakespeare in unfortunate adaptations, Dryden had achieved a masterpiece in *All for Love* (1677) and had written one

of the best appraisals of Shakespeare's genius. With compelling eloquence, as early as 1684, Dryden defended Shakespeare's commonly deplored lack of learning:

> To begin then with Shakespeare; he was the man who of all mod-
> ern, and perhaps Ancient Poets, had the largest and most compre-
> hensive Soul. All the Images of Nature are still present to him, and
> he drew them not laboriously, but luckily; when he describes any
> thing, you more than see it, you feel it too. Those who accuse him to
> have wanted learning, give him the greater commendation: he was
> naturally learn'd; he needed not the Spectacle of Books to read
> Nature; he look'd inwards, and found her there.[32]

Johnson rightly considered this passage "an epitome of excellence,"
which editors and admirers of Shakespeare could only diffuse and
paraphrase, without being able to improve upon it.[33] Narrow-
minded critics were preoccupied with Shakespeare's total disregard
of the unities, his taste for tragicomedy, and the unrestrained exuberance of his diction. Dryden's praise and his practice of adapting
Shakespeare's plays, if not silencing such critics, outweighed their
influence. In a *Spectator* paper (No. 141) John Hughes reminded
readers that Dryden refused to consider even Beaumont and
Fletcher capable of imitating Shakespeare.

> Shakespeare's *Magick cou'd not copy'd be,*
> *Within that Circle none durst Walk but He.*[34]

And although often in mangled form, Shakespeare continued to
dominate the stage.

The first critical edition of Shakespeare by Nicholas Rowe initiated a tradition of critical editons and served as a challenge to
successive editors to follow Rowe's example. Jacob junior published
Pope's edition of Shakespeare in 1723–1725 and reprinted it in
1728. Pope used Rowe's edition, probably the reprinted one of
1714,[35] as the basis of his text, consulting the quartos more carefully
than Rowe had done, but "preparing" Shakespeare for the press, re-
jecting or altering what he disliked, and putting passages in the
margins which he could not account for except as stage directions.
Pope reprinted Rowe's "Account of Shakespear" but condensed and
rearranged it without indicating that he had done so.[36] The criticism
of Pope's edition by Lewis Theobald, a less gifted but more accurate

commentator,[37] led Pope to depose Cibber in *The Dunciad* as Prince of Dunces and replace him with Theobald.

Two years before the death of Jacob Tonson the third, the 1765 edition of Shakespeare's plays in eight volumes, published by Tonson's great-nephews, Jacob and Richard Tonson, with other "proprietors," marked the climax of eighteenth-century editing of Shakespeare. Samuel Johnson, as the distinguished editor, combined scholarship and good sense. He judiciously appraised the work of all preceding editors, gave due weight to the readings of old editions, and added his own preface and notes. Johnson advised an age addicted to the minutiae of commentary that notes are "necessary evils." They should not deprive readers of the excitement of discovering Shakespeare for themselves "through integrity and corruption." It was Johnson who finally demolished with grandeur the sacred classical unities of time and place, for "the circumscriptions of terrestrial nature" may be despised by "a mind wandering in ecstasy."[38] Johnson's noble preface, albeit the work of a great classicist, has never been surpassed, or even equalled, in Shakespearean criticism.

For obtaining the copyright of Shakespeare, Tonson may have been envied by other publishers. For the copyright of Spenser he may well have had no competition. The publication of a six-volume edition of Spenser in 1715 was one of those risks which from time to time Tonson was prepared to take in view of the value of the work reprinted. Even Dryden qualified his praise of Spenser, concluding that Spenser's verses are "so Numerous, so Various, and so Harmonious, that only *Virgil*, whom he professedly imitated, has surpass'd him among the *Romans*; and only Mr. *Waller* among the *English*."[39] Addison told Pope that he had never read Spenser until fifteen years after he wrote his (disparaging) comment on Spenser in his "Account of the Greatest English Poets."[40] The only essay in *The Spectator* dealing, "in loose Hints," with *The Faerie Queene* was not contributed by Addison.[41]

The attempts of eighteenth-century critics to evaluate *The Faerie Queene* in terms of pseudo-classical rules cast darker than Gothic shadows over Spenser's genius. He was found defective in structure, obscure in language, and crippled by an unfortunate verse form. Alone among these critics, John Upton tried—a hopeless effort—to prove that *The Faerie Queene* does have a kind of structural unity that conforms to Aristotle's rules. "The beginning is, the British Prince saw in a vision the Fairy Queen, and fell in love with her: the middle, his search after her, with the adventures that he underwent: the end, his finding whom he sought."[42] As has been observed, "The case for Spenser is hardly so simple and clear."[43] No eighteenth-century commentator except Tonson's excellent editor, John Hughes, was so free from contemporary prejudice as to commend Spenser, as Hughes did, for having selected the plan of composition best suited to his talents. Many years later, Thomas Warton came closest to Hughes in affirming: "To sum up all in a few words; tho' in the Faerie Queene we are not satisfied as critics, yet we are transported as readers."[44]

Although the critics continued to judge Spenser with some severity, he gradually gained favor with eighteenth-century poets who were influenced by him and who stimulated a greater interest in his poetry. Prior, who ranked "our great Countryman, Spencer," with Horace,[45] chose to be buried in Spenser's grave. Always somewhat irked by the restrictions of the heroic couplet, Prior adapted the Spenserian stanza. Samuel Croxall used the same stanza for a political purpose in *An Original Canto of Spencer*, "design'd as part of his Fairy Queen but never printed" (1713), and in *Another Original Canto* (1714). The Spenserian stanza provided an agreeable pattern for Shenstone's quaintly humorous *The Schoolmistress* (1737, 1742) and was used by James Thomson with something of Spenser's magic in *The Castle of Indolence* (1748). In 1758 Jacob and Richard Tonson published John Upton's carefully annotated text of *The Faerie Queene*.

Dryden praised Spenser's great precursor, Chaucer, unequivocally, well aware that he was expressing a highly unconventional opinion. "The Vulgar Judges," wrote Dryden, "which are Nine Parts in Ten of all Nations, who call Conceits and Jingles wit, who see *Ovid* full of them, and *Chaucer* altogether without them, will think me little less than mad, for preferring the Englishman to the Roman."[46] Much as Dryden admired Chaucer, he believed that a poet so unintelligible to contemporary readers must be modernized in order to be appreciated by them. Chaucer was "a rough Diamond, and must first be polish'd e'er he shines."[47] In the *Fables* Dryden provided a corrective for Addison's youthful and rash strictures on Chaucer, which were representative enough of the general lack of esteem for Chaucer in the late seventeenth century:

> But Age has rusted what the Poet writ,
> Worn out his Language, and obscur'd his Wit:
> In vain he jests in his unpolish'd Strain,
> And tries to make his Readers laugh in vain.[48]

Dryden's recipe was at least moderately successful. A very minor poet, Jabez Hughes, expressed (c. 1707) the usual view that Dryden's imitations in his *Fables* were far superior to Chaucer's own poems:

> cloth'd by Thee, the banish'd Bard appears
> In all his Glory, and new Honours wears.
> Thus *Ennius* was by *Virgil* chang'd of old:
> He found him Rubbish, and he left him Gold.[49]

Samuel Johnson withheld approval of Dryden's selection of Chaucer's tales to modernize, complaining that the tale of "The Cock" "seems hardly worth revival," and the story of "Palamon and Arcite" contains "an action unsuitable to the time in which it is placed."[50] Pope read Chaucer "with as much pleasure as almost any of our poets. He is a master of manners and of description, and the first tale-teller in the true enlivened natural way."[51] Like Dryden, Pope offered Chaucer to eighteenth-century readers in the modern dress in which he was chiefly known to them.

Besides publishing Dryden's adaptations of Chaucer, Tonson published two of Pope's, "January and May," in the Sixth Miscellany, and "The Wife of Bath her Prologue" in Steele's *Poetical Miscellanies*.[52] In an increasingly "moral" age, the latter piece offended some readers, including Joseph Warton, who commented: "One cannot but wonder at his [Pope's] choice, which perhaps nothing but his youth could excuse."[53] It was Lintot who had the dubious distinction of publishing in 1721 an edition of Chaucer which has been described as "from the point of view of the text, the worst ever issued."[54] As late as 1754 Thomas Warton regretfully referred to Chaucer as "a neglected author" who should be more universally and attentively studied. "Chaucer seems to be regarded rather as an old poet, than as a good one, and that he wrote English

verses four hundred years ago seems more frequently to be urged
in his commendation, than that he wrote four hundred years ago
with taste and judgment."⁵⁵ The first "good text"⁵⁶ of *The Canterbury Tales* was Thomas Tyrwhitt's in 1775.

During Tonson's lifetime, Dryden was the most quoted, bor-
rowed from, and imitated of contemporary writers. Addison is said
to have been jealous of Dryden's reputation. According to Tonson,
"Addison was so eager to be the first name that he and his friend,
Sir Richard Steele, used to run down even Dryden's character as far
as they could. Pope and Congreve used to support it."⁵⁷ Is it significant that the first place in Mr. Spectator's list of books in "Leonora's" library is given by Addison to Ogleby's *Virgil* rather than
Dryden's? Perhaps no snub for Dryden was intended. Ogleby's
translation had just been reprinted, but Dryden's was generally recognized as far more distinguished. Leonora's library is humorously
described as an apartment resembling a grotto, in which works of
solid learning which Leonora has heard about are outnumbered by
the ones which she really reads, chiefly French romances. Dryden's
Juvenal has second place in the list of her books.⁵⁸

Although he quotes in *The Spectator* many of Dryden's "celebrated Lines," Addison's comments tend to downgrade Dryden.
Absalom and Achitophel is referred to as "one of the most popular
Poems that ever appeared in *English*. The poetry is indeed very fine,
but had it been much finer it would not have so much pleased, without a Plan which gave the Reader an Opportunity of exerting his
Talents."⁵⁹ After noting that "most of Mr. Dryden's tragedies"
end happily, Addison condemns tragicomedy, "the Product of the
English Theatre," as "one of the most monstrous Inventions that
ever enter'd into a Poet's Thoughts."⁶⁰ He quotes ironically in the
same essay a bad example of ranting, an art which Dryden and Lee
"in several of their Tragedies, have practis'd . . . with good Success."⁶¹ Addison hints that in his translation of Virgil Dryden has
not always maintained Virgil's nobility of sentiments.⁶² He suggests
that if the reader compares Milton's description of Adam leading
Eve to the nuptial bower with Dryden's on the same occasion in *The
State of Innocence and Fall of Man*, "he will be sensible of the
great Care which *Milton* took to avoid all Thoughts on so delicate
a Subject that might be offensive to Religion or Good-manners."⁶³
Such remarks on Dryden, scattered through *The Spectator*, seem

to provide evidence of Addison's ability to "Just Hint a fault, and hesitate dislike."[64]

Addison's tepid homage to Dryden was in marked contrast to Pope's adulation. Pope told Spence: "I learned versification wholly from Dryden's works, who had improved it much beyond any of our former poets, and would probably have brought it to its perfection, had not he been unhappily obliged to write so often in haste."[65] Warburton commented in his edition of Pope's *Works*: "On the first sight of Dryden he [Pope] found he had what he wanted. His Poems were never out of his hands."[66] Pope wrote the most memorable of all tributes to the poetry of "that great man":

> Waller was smooth; but Dryden taught to join
> The varying verse, the full resounding line,
> The long majestic march, and energy divine.[67]

The heroic couplet was perfected by Pope in fields which "copious" Dryden, ranging widely, had made fashionable: argumentative and satiric verse, and translations or imitations of classical models which, as with Dryden, turned out to be original poems.

Of contemporary drama after 1700 Tonson had a poor opinion. In a letter to Vanbrugh in 1722 he lamented that Congreve and Vanbrugh had stopped writing plays.[68] He seems to have been aware that many of the plays and operas he published (his interests were increasingly elsewhere) were inferior productions. Gratifying, however, was the well-deserved popularity of certain plays. Whatever advertising could do to promote the sales of a play, and it could do a good deal, was accomplished in the case of the two most outstanding classical tragedies of the eighteenth century, both of which Tonson published. Ambrose Philips' *The Distrest Mother*, based on Racine's *Andromaque*, was successfully acted at Drury Lane Theatre on March 17, 1712, and was printed by Tonson ten days later. Over a month before the play was acted, Steele had devoted a *Spectator* paper (No. 290) to a lavish account of its merits. The players then rehearsing the play had asked Will Honeycomb to bring the new tragedy to Mr. Spectator to read, and it had given him "a most exquisite Pleasure." The "inimitable" heroine is "one who has behaved her self with heroick Virtue in the most important Circumstances of a female life, those of a Wife, a Widow, and a Mother." In her sufferings spectators might "see Sorrow as they would wish to bear it whenever it arrives."[69] On March 25 Addison offered his readers Sir Roger's "Natural Criticism" of *The Distrest Mother*, when the good old knight, who had not seen a play for twenty years, attended a performance of this tragedy with Mr. Spectator and Captain Sentry and expressed his approval of it in loud, naive comments, to the entertainment of all who heard him.[70]

Addison's *Cato*, the greatest theatrical success of the century, gave rival publishers an opportunity to collect crumbs from Tonson's table and at the same time gave added publicity to Tonson's publication. A few examples must suffice. On April 14, 1713, the day that *Cato* was first acted, Lintot published *The Life and Character of Cato*, soon followed by a second edition. Less than a week after Tonson published *Cato*, Baldwin and Curll published *Observations upon Mr. Addison's Cato* "in Quarto, to bind with the Play."[71] A few days later, J. Pemberton (Curll) published *Cato Examin'd*, "Necessary for the Perusal of not only the Readers of Cato but of all other Tragedies"[72] and dedicated to Joseph Addison. In July Lintot published John Dennis's (satirical) *Remarks upon Cato, A Tragedy*. Meanwhile, *Cato* had reached a seventh edition.

Much of what Tonson published to suit the taste of his age has not retained interest for later generations. The histories over which his "hands" toiled so industriously seem to have been valued in proportion to their scope, however conjectural their accounts of the remote past. Writers "prostituted" their judgment, as Johnson remarked, in long and servile dedications to patrons, who might be expected to respond with more guineas than could be earned from a publisher. Prologues and epilogues were fashionable compositions, often unrelated to the subject matter of the plays which they advertised, and an added source of income to their authors. Short pieces by very minor poets were space fillers in the Miscellanies and contributed to making them the "insipid Hotch-Potch" that Wycherley labeled them.[73] The occasional poems on contemporary events that Tonson produced in separate folio editions in his largest type, on the finest quality of his paper, were usually the most conventional, least inspired, strains of the best poets and the worthless effusions of mere versifiers.

Congratulatory poems to distinguished writers were also fashionable, and Tonson's own early and anonymous "dabblings in Poetry"[74] took this approved form. His two poems "To Mr. Creech on his Translation of Lucretius"[75] were such successful experiments in the style of Dryden and Waller, respectively, that the first was generally taken for Dryden's and the second, much to Tonson's amusement, was inserted by Atterbury in his unauthorized edition of *The Second Part of Mr. Waller's Poems*, published in 1690.[76] Both poems indicate that besides counting lines as a publisher, Tonson scrutinized rather closely the stylistic characteristics of the poets most in vogue. Tonson slipped inconspicuously into his Second Miscellany his pastoral elegy "On the Death of Mr. Oldham,"[77] which has the decorative details, essential to such verse, of blasted oak, neglected sheep, purling streams, and crystal spring. Tonson's tribute to Mrs. Behn, *"To the Lovely Witty* Astraea *on her Excellent Poems"* (1684), is the most personal in tone of these poetical exercises and conveys, in the midst of its platitudes, the genuine enthusiasm which Tonson felt for this "'wonder of thy Sex."[78]

Tonson's critical judgment was appraised by the eccentric bookseller, John Dunton, who remarked: "He [Tonson] was a Bookseller to the *famous Dryden*, and is himself a very good Judge of Persons and Authors, and as there is no Body more competently qualified to give their Opinion of another, so there is none who does it with a more severe Exactness, or with less Partiality; for, to do Mr. Tonson Justice, he speaks his mind, (upon all Occasions) and will Flatter no Body."[79] Dunton's view is supported by what we know of Tonson's observations on authors and their works. Pope seconded Tonson's homage to Congreve with the words: "Aye, Mr. Tonson, he was Ultimus Romanorum!"[80] In his old age Tonson offered his nephew pertinent reflections on the books which he was reading. He believed that "mr Popes poem" addressed to Lord Burlington did not come up to Pope's other poems, though "very far above" Young's *The Universal Passion*. Pope's poem has some fine lines but is much too severe. Inscribed to Lord Burlington, it was "not written (nor is) so much upon his praise as to lash others."[81] In Oldmixon's *History* Tonson found "a great many passages which are false ill mannerd & abusive," although Oldmixon gives Cromwell "fairer play" than Ludlow had done.[82] The author (David Mallet) of *The Excursion* and *Eurydice* writes in Milton's manner "at least as well as Mr. Thompson."[83] Everything that Voltaire wrote interested Tonson, for "His Genius is extraordinary."[84] Whatever Swift wrote must be entertaining. Tonson regarded Pope as the chief English poet of the age and wished England could furnish "such another pen."[85]

Tonson was not the first publisher of most of Dryden's plays; and Pope's most famous works were not published by Tonson, nor by his nephew. In the long view, perhaps Tonson's finest memorial as a publisher is the large amount of distinguished prose which he published. Where in the annals of English literature has a single publisher been host to three authors with such varied mastery of English prose as Dryden, Congreve, and Addison?

Johnson admired Dryden's gift, displayed in his Prefaces, for "expressing with clearness what he thinks with vigour," in a style which is "always equable and always varied."[86] Addison's prose Johnson considered "the model of the middle style."

> His page is always luminous, but never blazes in unexpected splendour. . . . What he attempted, he performed; he is never feeble, and he did not wish to be energetick; he is never rapid, and he never stagnates. His sentences have neither studied amplitude, nor affected brevity; his periods, though not diligently rounded, are voluble and easy. Whoever wishes to attain an English style, familiar but not coarse, and elegant but not ostentatious, must give his days and nights to the volumes of Addison.[87]

As for the flexibility of which English prose is capable, where is this more apparent than in that "most accomplished" of all English comedies, Congreve's *The Way of the World*? There was much excellent contemporary prose which Tonson did not publish, but his was a generous share in the very best of it.

Retirement

onson was sixty-three when his career as a publisher ended rather abruptly. His nephew, who had probably been bearing an increasing responsibility in the Tonson publishing business, now assumed complete charge of it. Tonson's decision to retire had apparently already been made before he left England for a prolonged visit in Paris, extending from the autumn of 1718 to the spring of 1720. Little that is significant can be gleaned of his activities at this time beyond the facts that he was investing heavily and successfully in the stocks of the French Mississippi Company,[1] had a very serious illness, and decided to purchase an estate with his recently acquired wealth and lead henceforth the life of a country squire. For what has survived of Tonson's news from England during this interval we are indebted to a sequence of most delightful letters to Tonson from Vanbrugh.

From Nottingham Castle, "northern seat" of the Duke of Newcastle, which Vanbrugh had undertaken to repair, Vanbrugh wrote on July 1, 1719, to astound Jacob with the news of his marriage, which had recently occurred. Vanbrugh reminded his absent friend that "it was ever agreed, if I fell, you'd tremble." But he could speak reassuringly of the married state, though "fitter to end Our life with, than begin it." He has "very often enquired at Shakespeare head how you did, and what you did, and more than once, have found my Self so far from a Slave, that I have dar'd to own I wish'd my Self with you, for eight and fourty hours: for you must know, whatever evils Marriage may designe me; it has not yet lessen'd one grain of my Affections to an old Friend." Vanbrugh had "talk'd even my Gentlewoman" into an inclination for a trip to Paris "next Spring." He hoped that meanwhile Jacob would return to England for the winter, "and after being a little pleas'd with some folks, and very weary of others," be ready for a fresh expedition. The letter was affectionately signed, "Your faithful Old Friend & Servant / J. Vanbrugh."[2]

With mock concern Vanbrugh not long afterward informed the Duke of Newcastle that "'Friend Jacob" had been seen in Paris "in a Frock,"[3] as a desperate device to escape the contagion of marriage. Although this report proved to be false,[4] it was true that Jacob had had the good fortune to make £10,000 by investing in the stocks of a "New Company" (the Mississippi Company), as a "loving Letter"[5] to Vanbrugh related.

A few months later, in mid-October, 1719, Tonson's friends were stunned by items in several London newspapers[6] announcing his death from a contusion in his head, due to a fall from his horse. In Applebee's *Original Weekly Journal* it was stated that his nephew had at once set out for Paris. Not long afterward, the same papers had to concede that Tonson was not only still alive but sufficiently recovered for his nephew to "return home by the next Pacquet."[7]

Tonson had the unusual satisfaction of being assured by Vanbrugh that on hearing of his death, his friends had drunk to his memory and had shown every indication that he would not have been "dropt as Mainwaring was." Vanbrugh wrote in response to "a very welcome and very kind letter" from Jacob. He congratulated Jacob both on being alive and on his "lucky hit" in the French stocks, and professed to be encouraged by Jacob's opinion that marriage "may possibly do me as much good, as it has mischief to many a one we know."[8]

In his next letter Vanbrugh welcomed Tonson's resolve to spend £500 on a "New Petticoat" for "your Old Mistriss Barnes." To be sure, "Her Charms don't lye in her Beauty, but her good Conditions. She feels better than she looks, and what she wants in her Eyes, she has in her Commodity. And thence it was, I always found a Tate a Tate more pleasing with you there; than I should have done at Blenheim, had the house been my own tho' without my Lady Marlborough for my Wife." Vanbrugh would not wish so drastically to correct Jacob's manners "as to Stifle one of your Jokes upon Matrimony," although "by a sort of Messissippi good fortune" that chain "hangs a little easy about me." His wife is sorry she has not a sister for Jacob, "but she knows them that have" and is ready to provide at least as well for him as for her husband. "She desires I'll tell you farther, that I have said so much to her of you, while you were alive, after you were dead, and Since you are alive again, That she knows you well enough, to desire to know you better." She accepts Tonson's invitation to dinner at Barnes and welcomes his promise to accept hers at Greenwich. At this point Harriet Vanbrugh took up her husband's pen and in her own hand proposed, *"if you will make one at cards as I understand you have often done, with much finer Ladys than I am I give you my word that I will neither cheat nor wrangle."*

Vanbrugh agreed to inquire about estates which were for sale. He could not take Tonson's advice to buy stocks, having no money to dispose of. Besides having the expenses of the Haymarket, he had not been made Surveyor of the Works, and "that wicked Woman," the Duchess of Marlborough, is trying to cheat him of £6,000 due him for the building of Blenheim. "But I have been so long us'd to attacks of fortune of these kinds; and found my Self able to bear up against them, That I think I can do so Still, tho they cost me Some Oathes and Curses, when I think of them: Which to prevent (it being Sunday) I'll say no more of them now."[9]

In answering Tonson's letter of November 14, Vanbrugh sent news of the Duke of Newcastle, who "really has a great regard to you in a Serious, as well as merry way." The "ill tim'd broyles" of Whigs and Tories continue, but are not likely to "disturb you at Barnes, nor your humble Servant at Greenwich. And so let us be easy."[10]

Tonson's next letter to Vanbrugh pleased Newcastle so much that he showed it to his Duchess and others and assured Vanbrugh that he would honor Tonson with a reply. "He has not however found time to do it," wrote Vanbrugh, "but every day says he will." On the eve of Tonson's departure from Paris, Vanbrugh reported briefly on the current excitement in rising South Sea stocks, "a sort of Young Messissippy," on Steele's quarrel with Newcastle, and on the prospect of a good opera season.[11]

Far less pleasing than Vanbrugh's letters, in fact with decidedly disagreeable overtones, is another sequence of letters from Paris to Jacob junior from a certain Robert Clarke, who seems to have been either a self-appointed spy on Tonson during his illness, or the nephew's too-eager agent, employed in prying relentlessly into the uncle's private affairs. After the nephew's return to England, Tonson suffered a relapse and a recurrence of fever. Clarke kept him for three days without food and wine, took up his "old quarters" near him, and determined not to leave him until he was "pretty harty."[12] As the patient convalesced, they drank together (for Tonson could not be restrained from this indiscretion), and Clarke began plying him unceasingly with questions about the new will that Tonson proposed making. The details of the will changed daily, as Tonson reflected favorably or otherwise on Jacob junior, and Clarke dispatched frequent bulletins recording these reactions. Two of the nephew's letters Jacob read to Clarke "over and over" and to himself "I believe twenty times at least." Yet he thought of leaving "at least five thousand pounds" to Dick Tull (the son of his sister Rose), having been touched by Tull's offer to him of £1,000, if he needed it. He planned to leave his cousins in Ireland £100 each, instead of the £500 he had once intended. And he wanted to lay out £2,000 a year in lands, which the nephew was to find for him.[13] It was unfortunate that Jacob junior's use of the word "impertinent" in one of his letters (perhaps with reference to the rash offer of such a poor relation as Tull) rankled with Tonson. He was prepared to cast off Jacob junior and said Cousin Tull "was to be his heir and his fortune made for ever." Then he was diverted from making any will at all and talked only of purchasing land. Jacob junior would do well, Clarke reflected, never to let his uncle leave England again without having made a suitable will.[14]

Jacob junior's success in locating an estate for his uncle to purchase quite obliterated Tonson's pique. He stopped mentioning Tull's name and thought only of selling stocks and sending over £16,000, and more if necessary, for the purchase of the property. All will be well, Clarke affirmed, if the nephew and his family can only flatter the peevish invalid to the last. "He is not nor I believe never [can be][15] ye same man he was six months agoe. his head is quit gon." Clarke will never desert him for others to "make a fine penny of him." Clarke thanks Jacob junior for designing a finer present for him than he ever expected. The two maps and half a dozen books would have sufficed.[16] Jacob junior should say nothing more about the disastrous word "impertinent" and might have his wife or mother send the uncle a kind New Year's letter. The £16,000 should be promptly drawn, for a small matter would at any time make Tonson change his mind.[17]

As the time for Tonson's return to England drew near, the danger of a substantial legacy for Tull and some other legacies loomed again. Tonson also wavered as to whether to sell all, or half, or none of his stocks. But it was a hopeful sign that he intended to buy for his favorite niece Molly a doll costing 100 livres "that will be allmost as big as her self," and he had bought a silver gilt snuff box for Mrs. Tonson.[18]

Whether or not he suspected the motives of his over-attentive inquisitor, Clarke's spry victim eluded the snares set for him. On April 19, 1720, Tonson left Paris by the Calais coach, and to his chagrin, Clarke just missed seeing him once more at St. Denis. Jacob made his escape without a lace suit for Mrs. Tonson and the doll for Molly, and without having made a new will. He did give Clarke 500 livres. Clarke admitted that the task of humoring Tonson would be formidable. Little presents of eatables might help. Somewhat lamely, Clarke offered his future services, if desired.[19]

For reasons which are not known, Tonson decided to relinquish Barn Elms to his nephew and to live alone, independently, on his new estate. When the time came to renew the lease for Barnes, he confessed to Jacob junior: "I do indeed love the place & I doe most cordially assure you that the thoughts it may be healthfull to you & our deare litle ones puts out of my mind any other thoughts in the world that coud possibly make me hesitate uppon it."[20] The nephew took charge of the complicated arrangements for the purchase for his uncle of the Hazels, a desirable piece of property near Ledbury in Herefordshire. While these negotiations were dragging on, much more slowly than had been foreseen, Tonson paid a visit of several months to the Duke of Newcastle at Nottingham Castle.

Jacob was always a welcome guest at the Duke's house and was ready to "wait upon him" whenever his presence was commanded. At Nottingham, at the end of August, he met Vanbrugh, and he discussed with Carpenter, a horticulturist in Newcastle's service, plans for an orchard and vineyard at the Hazels. The Duke, a hospitable bon vivant, was peculiarly susceptible to judiciously administered flattery. He was employing Vanbrugh in the building of Claremont House in Sussex as an agreeable southern country house, suited to his requirements as newly created Duke of Newcastle. Tonson was able to supply just the right ingredients of compliment in the following ditty on Claremont:

When I belonged to Earl of Clare
To call me Claremont was but fair.
But since my Master is raised higher,
All things about him should aspire.
The World must own my fashions new
And that I'm like a Castle too.
To second thoughts let first then bow,
And call me pray New Castle now.[21]

That Jacob was a lively guest is confirmed in one of Newcastle's invitations for a visit at Claremont: "But to make me compleatly happy, Dear Jacob, you must not refuse me your good Company . . . you shall live . . . as you please, Drink Water or Wine, ride or go in ye Coach. Read or Laugh at Any thing in ye World."[22] Tonson urged his nephew to bribe Kneller with the offer of more venison from the Duke if he would speedily finish with his own hand the Duchess of Newcastle's portrait.[23]

Tonson spent the autumn of 1720 in Bath. He invested £2,000 in South Sea stocks and sold out at their highest value his remaining French stocks.[24] He accepted his nephew's invitation to stay at Hollyport, his nephew's country house near Windsor in Berkshire, while waiting for the purchase of the Hazels to be completed, for he was unwilling to go on to Ledbury until he could go "as a confirmed landlord"[25] and legally collect rents from the tenants. Meanwhile, he had energy to spare to criticize his nephew for cutting down trees at Barnes[26] and "ventured" to improve Hollyport with a new parlor door and lock, red hangings, and new furniture.[27]

A clear title to the Hazels was finally secured only with recourse to a suit in Chancery. Jacob's long-suffering nephew, overworked, in poor health, but struggling to complete the purchase, assured him: "I think nothing a trouble, & if I had known the Court of Chancery so well in the beginning of this affair as I do now I shou'd have lead Swift [one of the former owners of the property] a worse life than he has lead us."[28] Jacob established himself at Ledbury in January, 1722. The tenants acknowledged him as their landlord, and his nephew had the necessary documents drawn up.[29]

The new way of life presented problems. "If I had not been used to Live alone," Jacob admitted, "it would be insupportable to stay here, but I beare it pretty well & resolve as much as I can to weather every thing, & tho' I know my incapacity to manage such affairs, yet am resolved to exert my patience to the utmost because it is absolutely necessary."[30] He feared that his tenants, perceiving his ignorance of the functions of a landlord, might "think of being sharp" with him. But it was not his custom to retreat from difficulties, and he "saw noe body that can, I think, help me soe wel as my Self."[31] There was much to be done. His land must be surveyed and a good deal of it cleared, although "it may be best to leave some little garden to every house & some may have a Walnut tree."[32]

It was not long before possession of one estate whetted Jacob's appetite for another and another. He felt an irresistible urge to buy every piece of property near the Hazels that came on the market. Each new estate was such "a pretty thing," ostensibly for the future benefit of the nephew's family, but actually for the joy of possession. Tonson acquired acres with the same zeal and savoir faire as he had once acquired authors. Opposition from some would-be purchaser only made him "goe on more vigorously."[33] The nephew was always instructed to handle the legal transactions and at least once could not suppress a wish that he had "never meddled."[34] At seventy-eight Tonson still bought land with unabated enthusiasm.

His favorite acquisition was the Vineyard, two miles beyond the Hazels, between Ledbury and Gloucester, purchased in 1728. Tonson planned here a "moderate box" of a house, to resemble his nephew's country house, Down Place, of which he requested a plan. He would make bricks and cut down fir trees for timber for the floors. A "pretty nursery"[35] of apple trees would lead to a middle walk among the vines. Although he expressed "a fancy for building," he was diverted from this by his interest in the vineyard itself, where he had two hundred loads of "excellent muck" spread on the best roots of vines that his nephew could buy for him. There could be no more charming place in which to end one's days. In the spring, when the orchards were in bloom, all Herefordshire looked like "a particular garden to the rest of England, & my Vyneard a particular pleasing Spot in that."[36] And each autumn the Vineyard yielded excellent red and white wine and "the best Cyder" that Tonson had ever tasted.[37]

It must be regretted that the strenuous years of Tonson's career as a publisher are not nearly so well documented as the many years of his relatively uneventful retirement. Except for a period of four years (1723–1726), during which letters are mainly or wholly lacking, Tonson's letters to his nephew from his Herefordshire retreat, and a fair sampling of the nephew's replies, have been preserved. A few other significant letters fill certain gaps. The portrait that emerges is that of an old man whose mental faculties remained unimpaired, but whose pursuits assumed a monotonous pattern and whose eccentricities increased as his physical vigor diminished.

Many of the letters are concerned with the necessities of Jacob's bachelor housekeeping, for his nephew was always the chief provider of these numerous items. A multitude of large and trivial requests is oddly jumbled in Jacob's letters. His wagons, laden with hampers of red and white wine and hogsheads of cider, were regularly and frequently sent to London, to be returned groaning with a miscellaneous assortment of supplies. Once Tonson even proposed that baskets from his wagon should stand in Jacob junior's back shop, so that parcels could be sent away "each hour."[38] The nephew's prompt attention to all of Jacob's requirements was taken for granted, although on a rare occasion he received his uncle's thanks for "ordering Soe many things soe very well."[39]

Increasingly parsimonious, Jacob nevertheless did not stint himself in food and drink. Having requested an ox and a chine of mutton from London, he sent his servant along to see them cut up "ye London way."[40] He ordered a buttock of beef salted, a pipe of port and hogshead of muscadine, the best French white wine, whatever the cost, half a tub of the very best salt butter, the best and largest pears, "Dantyish Cates,"[41] if they could be had, "Solid Soope"[42] sold by the pound, two pounds of the very best coffee beans roasted, two pounds of the very best tobacco that could be obtained, a rope of Portuguese onions, and six pounds of Spanish liquorice. In the same sentence in which he asked for a pamphlet on repealing the Sacramental Test, Tonson noted approvingly that "the slabs of Red Herings you sent me were mighty good."[43]

Roots of "extraordinary vines"[44] for the Vineyard were a major purchase. Household utensils, on the other hand, were reduced to the modest minimum of a large iron sieve left at Barnes, Dr. Radcliffe's roaster, "a good kettle to boyl fish,"[45] an earthen pudding pot with a cover, a copper coffee pot, a pair of pewter candlesticks that looked like silver, and "a thing to dry Plates before ye fire."[46] Clothing needs, though carefully specified, were still less important. Six yards of Scotch plaid and six of "small checkered plaid, both red and green,"[47] were required for mending two nightgowns, and strong muslin should be sent for neckcloths.

Jacob's satisfaction in the knowledge that he could afford to buy whatever he wanted was tempered by his painful awareness of the expense which lavish spending imposed. Having concluded that his watch, made by his old friend Thomas Tompion thirty-two years ago, was really worn out, in a moment of exuberance Tonson decided to indulge both his vanity and his curiosity in "a gold repeating watch of the very best and most eminent maker, let it cost what it will." Tompion's watch had cost fifty guineas. Even if watches were now dearer, Tonson advised his nephew, "pray dont let that hinder you from getting me one." At the same time, he must have spectacles, a larger reading glass, a folding stick, another part (if out) of the *History of Printing*, and a dial plate for a post in the garden.[48] A word to the wise from his nephew had the immediate effect of dispelling Jacob's ill-timed interest in gold repeating watches. He hastily countermanded his order for one, convinced that its merits could not amount to the rise in price. "As for ye repeating clock & ye Dyale," he told his nephew, "I will defer my fancy for them until farther time, in ye mean time pray with what conveniency you can buy for me a plain gold watch such as you have for yore Self."[49]

The ever-ready services of his nephew were not matched by the loyalty of Tonson's servants. He discovered that the carriers who went with his wine to London and brought back supplies to Ledbury were "downright exacting careless rogues"[50] and sent servants with them to guard his possessions. The servants also proved to be dishonest. Even the most trusted of them, the faithful Pots, was detected in a plot to rob his master, and Tonson reluctantly turned him off. Successive betrayals of confidence wounded the old man's pride and increased his sense of loneliness.

Tonson was disinclined to give up public life altogether. When the Tory interest seemed likely to prevail in Parliament in 1721, he owned that he "would give a good deal to be in."[51] He acquired an interest in county politics. The duties of sheriff seemed to him too burdensome at his age, and each year he asked influential friends to intervene to spare him such an assignment. But he welcomed the office of justice of the peace as a means of increasing his influence in local affairs. In February, 1722, Tonson wrote to his nephew:

"When the Comission of peace is renewed it will be of use to me to be in for this County for I find they favour one another."[52] For well over a decade he served Hereford in this capacity.

Tonson exerted himself to secure for Ledbury much needed turnpike roads and petitioned against the quartering of dragoons in so small a town, which would cause a rise in the price of food and "be very hard with ye Poor."[53] The plight of the poor seriously concerned him, although not to the extent of supporting a new property tax to assist them. He was gratified to find the whole parish "roused" over this proposed tax, including that "honest man," the new parson.[54]

In his voluntary exile from London, Tonson had the pleasure of correspondence with friends and occasional meetings with them in Ledbury, Bath, London, or at Barnes. Generous gifts of cider for his nephew to convey to Newcastle, "Master Harry" Pelham, Newcastle's brother, Vanbrugh, Wilmington, Cobham, and others brought appreciative letters of thanks. When Newcastle responded with a reciprocal gift of choice wines, Tonson excelled himself in gay and gallant flattery. "Empowred by your Graces Bounty," he declared, "I will launch out into ye Oceans of Port, Claret, & Champaign; in wch Voyage I have for some Years been a Stranger. I have fixed to give my mind and humour a chearfull loose upon the twenty first of next month [Newcastle's birthday], with some hearty admirers of our truly Good and Glorious King, and, by Consequence, honourers of your Grace."[55]

Tonson was visited by Steele on his way to Wales and met Congreve in Bath in the spring of 1728. He instructed his nephew to let Congreve know "ye pleasure I promised my self in having (as I hope) his company, pray let me know if any one, or who, goes with him."[56] Congreve's death in January, 1729, prevented another meeting with him to which Tonson had looked forward. He had "flatterd myself wth seeing him at the Bath this Spring [1729] woud have been a sufficient reason for my going there." He asked his nephew for details of Congreve's circumstances at his death and hoped the Duchess of Marlborough would order a monument for him.[57] There were much desired but infrequent visits from his nephew, and on one of these Tonson fancied his old rival Lintot "would come with you if asked."[58]

Gallantry to socially prominent ladies was always congenial to

Tonson. He particularly wished his nephew to congratulate Temple Stanyan on his marriage, in the late autumn of 1720, to a lady[59] "to whose father I was really more obleidged than to any other of my friends and acquaintances." He added, "I wont pretend to praise a family wch by his long knowledge of he must know better than I can, but I dare say he has the best motherinlaw in ye world."[60] To his neighbor, Lady Scudamore,[61] whose country house was between the Hazels and Hereford, Tonson wished to extend the correct degree of civility. He was at some pains to have his nephew send him for her a little miniature of Sir Kenelm Digby which he had bought some years ago in Rouen. Lady Scudamore had a large and handsome library and could read French and Italian. She was a patroness of literary men and a kind hostess to Gay. Wilmington had thought of courting her. Gay and Pope are "very sensible," commented Tonson, "of this Lady's excelling qualitys."[62] It was reported that her daughter, "a young Lady Esteemed by all ye County," would have £7,000 a year.[63]

The lively letters of Vanbrugh, judging by those which have been preserved, must have been as refreshing to Tonson as his own excellent Herefordshire cider. Vanbrugh missed seeing his dear old friend in town, although he could not blame him for spending his life "I believe much as I wou'd do, had I made a good voyage to the Messissippy." He gave Tonson an account of the Duke of Marlborough's will, the flourishing state of the opera, the dearth of fresh poets, and the pleasures of matrimony. "Have a Care," he jested, "of this retired Country life. We shall hear of some Herefordshire Nymph in your Solitary walks bounce out upon your Heart, from under an Apple Tree and make you one of us."[64]

This last sally inspired a delightful rejoinder, in a letter of which Tonson fortunately kept a copy. Tonson agreed that good poets no longer appeared. "The Immortall King William produced your selfe & mr Congreve, & my own most honoured Lord Somers. Let me live long enough to see such another production." He had many questions to ask about Marlborough's will, when they could meet at Barnes and "talk our minds." On the provocative subject of matrimony Jacob launched forth with all of the sly wit of Kit-Cat days:

> You hint the danger of my heart being trapt by a Bait from an Aple Tree. The first *tete a tete* club was in Paradise, & the minute ye woman (tired with having the onely conversation of her, to be sure,

deare Spouse) took in a spruce Prig (though certainly older than the
first of all our familys) & upon onely saying Countryman, will you
eat a pippen? We have been all—as we are—The Club from *Tete a
Tete* was soon turnd to Corps au Corps—and this if true is certainly a
better excuse for a Herefordshire mistake than for some other Countrys indeed this humour seems to prevail, & as in some poor countrys
they part with Lands without Lawyers conveyances by writings, soe
here to save the charges of an asking & ring—in the Ordinary sort,
there is noe Scruple of taking a liken as children say at trapball without any notice taken otherways than the product be noe charge to the
Parish—and soe much for the Naturall History of Herefordshire.

I do most sincerely wish you true Joy of the encrease of yre Nursery, & hope, notwithstanding ye terrible consequence, you will goe
on & get Boys and Girls til you come to have used soe many of your
freinds as to accept mee for a godfather without any fear of having
if a Boy an old Testament name tacked to the being a godfather.[65]

Vanbrugh described in detail to Tonson an expedition to various
country houses which he and his wife made with Lord Carlisle and
his daughters. Their stay in Oxford "in a Whig Inn" and in Wood-
stock, where the Duchess of Marlborough excluded the Vanbrughs
from Blenheim, recalled a similar pilgrimage made with Lord Essex
when Tonson was of the party. "And had the same Master of
Rowsham,[66] been at Rowsham now, We shou'd have pleas'd him
and our Selves in dining with him, as We did then."[67]

Only a few months before his death,[68] Vanbrugh again mentioned to Tonson for a second time his hope for a meeting of former
Kit-Cats on some "day of Happy Remembrance." Newcastle favored such a gathering *"one day,* or one hundred, if God so pleases."
In this last letter Vanbrugh shared with his "'old and intimate Acquaintance" the good news that Walpole had helped him finally to
secure payment for his services at Blenheim, in spite of the teeth of
that "B. B. B. B. Old B. the Dutchess of Marlbh."[69]

A late friendship which Jacob greatly valued blossomed between
him and Pope, whom he had introduced to the literary world a
quarter of a century ago. Pope had found it more profitable to employ Lintot as his publisher, had at least two disagreements with
Jacob junior,[70] and shot a few bolts at Tonson's publications. Nevertheless, and particularly in his intrepid old age, Jacob won Pope's
admiration and proved be quite worth cultivating, as one might
cherish a frost-resisting December rose.[71]

According to Spence, Tonson gossiped with Pope about the Kit-Cat Club and many other matters. Tonson and Pope were agreed in disliking Addison's personality and in considering Congreve, as Pope put it, "ultimus Romanorum."[72] In February, 1731, Pope tried to arrange a dinner at his villa with Lord Bathhurst and the Earl of Oxford, with Tonson as the *pièce de résistance.* "To entertain you," Pope tempted Oxford, "I will show you . . . a Phaenomenon worth seeing & hearing, old Jacob Tonson, who is the perfect Image and Likeness of Bayle's Dictionary; so full of Matter, Secret History, & Wit and Spirit; att almost fourscore."[73] The dinner was postponed and took place a little later at Barnes. In a letter to Swift on March 20 Gay wrote: "Lord Oxford, Lord Bathurst, He [Pope] & I din'd yesterday at Barnes with old Jacob Tonson where we drank your Health."[74]

Pope wrote to Tonson on November 14, 1731, begging him to use his influence with his nephew to prevent any slander on Pope's personal character from being included in the forthcoming edition of Shakespeare by Lewis Theobald[75] which, to Pope's regret, Jacob junior was publishing with other sharers in the copyright. Pope would like to discuss with Tonson proposals for other editions of Shakespeare and of the best English classics. He sent news of mutual friends and commented: "My Mother[76] is pretty well & remembers [you]." Pope had a "very pretty Poem" to show Tonson on the gardens of Stowe.[77] The letter ended with the urgent request: "You live not far from Ross. I desire you to get me an Exact information of the Man of Ross,[78] what was his Xtian & Surname? what year he dyed, & about what age? and to transcribe his Epitaph, if he has one. And any Particulars you can procure about him. I intend to make him an Example in a Poem of mine."[79]

In a letter of June 7, 1732, Pope thanked Tonson for "the great diligence (or let me give it a higher title, zeal)" which Tonson had shown in sending "so many particulars of the Man of Ross." Of these he had selected "the most affecting" for his poem. He was not sorry that worthy man had no monument and would mention this in a note or in the body of the poem, "unless you entreat the contrary in your own favor, by your zeal to erect one." The poem might not be printed for some time[80] but with other pieces could be inspected by Tonson "on these quiet banks of the Thames." Pope was having his portrait by Dahl copied for Tonson and acknowledged Jacob's gift of a copy of Garth's portrait. He considered Milton *above* and Dr. Bentley *below* all criticism. And so, "Adieu, and health, and peace, and fair weather attend you."[81] The hint about a monument for the Man of Ross was not lost on Tonson, who decided to spend twenty pounds for one, with Pope's tribute inscribed on it.[82]

Reluctant to inflict his elderly scrawl on his friends, Tonson sent them messages by his nephew. The last of these was for Pope in the following postscript to a letter written on August 22, 1735, not long before the nephew's death:

> pray find some way to let mr Pope know I am most Sensible of his favour & ye great honor of his very valuable present. I wish you could let mee know how I coud any way please mr Pope—ne[v]our any one in my opinion has soe fine & just notions as him And I think his Prose excels all others as his verse—He has noe equal or any other pen near his—my hand is lame, & yet I can nevour be weary in writing my Sinceer thoughts about Such a miracle of general knowledge—I may be tedious but I think my hand mends and far from being tired.[83]

As the years passed and Tonson gave up riding and other active pursuits, his "almost onely pleasure" was in reading, "& that makes me keep at home & in my night gown mostly."[84] He scanned advertisements in the London newspapers and expected his nephew to send him anything new "that has a character."[85] Intermixed indiscriminately with his orders for food, wine, and clothing were regular orders for books. His tastes were catholic. Among his requests were: a new edition of Bayle's *French Dictionary*; a French dictionary printed in Holland; Thomas Powell's *Repertorie of Records*, whatever the cost; the *Votes* of the House of Commons; Ben Jonson's *Works*; *Horace* in Latin and English "in two volumes the best paper & neatly bound";[86] Sir John Perrot's *Life*, printed by Curll, "if good for anything";[87] Voltaire's *Hendriade* and *Epic Poetry of the European Nations* in French or English; "any new plays that are tolerable";[88] Daniel's *History of France*; his own copy of Montaigne's *Essays*, printed by Abel Angelier; "the *Dunciad* or any other such poetical Squabble";[89] Rabutin's *Letters*; Oldmixon's *History*; Swift's *Drapier's Letters*; Thomson's *Sophonisba*; the *History of Printing*; the *Life* of Father Paris in French; and Richardson's "silly notes"[90] on Milton.

Tonson kept a watchful eye on his nephew's business activities and made comments as they occurred to him. It would be "500 guineas very well laid out" to get Dr. Waterland to translate *Josephus*. Tonson had once tried to persuade Clarke to improve on L'Estrange's "sad" version.[91] For a new translation of *Lucretius* by the author of *The Excursion* and *Eurydice* "a good parcel of guyneas" might very profitably be expended.[92] In a new edition of *Virgil* it would be important to correct "a very great Errour"—"Aristotle" for "Ariosto" in the Dedication of the *Aeneid*.[93] Tonson's occasional suggestions were cautiously offered, and in the correspondence of uncle and nephew there are no indications that Jacob junior sought his uncle's advice.[94]

It is not surprising that Tonson took a strong proprietary interest in Congreve's posthumous reputation. Nor is it surprising that his concern was affectionate and businesslike at the same time. He wished Jacob junior would consider Congreve's library "worth your buying," for Congreve's collection of books was "very genteel and wel chosen," with notes and corrections of his own, and "every thing from him will be very valuable."[95] A new edition of Congreve should be speedily published. "Let a man's worth be nevour soe great after Death it gets strangely out of ye minds of his Surviving acquaintance." Whom would Jacob junior choose for an editor? The quarto edition of 1710 would be "ye best coppy to follow."[96] The frontispiece should be engraved by Virtue from the Kit-Cat portrait, since in Smith's mezzotint there was "a stiffness about the mouth which is not in the painting."[97]

Jacob junior's increasing ill health gave him no respite from his uncle's staggering demands. Although Tonson worried about his nephew, his own elderly ailments were a more immediate problem. But his love for his nephew, however selfish, was the deepest, most engrossing attachment of his life. It was a grief not easily borne that they could meet "but very seldome."[98] Tonson missed Barnes but was pleased that such surroundings would be healthful for his nephew's children—a better tonic than any medicine. He had thought of borrowing the Kit-Cat portraits for his life. "But since I find their remaining with you is soe much to your satisfaction I will nevour desire or think of their being remov'd & this you may depend on shal nevour be asked of you." Copies could be made and sent at the nephew's leisure, for "as my eyes prove weaker a coppy wil please me as wel as an Original, & ye best of our Gentlemen is such as to like a signpost as wel as vandyke, & any sad poem wth Rime as wel as Paradise Lost."[99] With old-fashioned courtesy Tonson begged Jacob junior to accept his chaise: "allow me to say it is no longer mine."[100] On another occasion he bought for his nephew "a pretty little farm."[101] It must be remembered that Tonson's generous gifts (and they could be very generous) were never lightly made.

Tonson was keenly interested in the welfare of his nephew's children. "I am next to you," he wrote, "the most in the world pleased with our Childrens coming on."[102] Their frequent illnesses distressed him, and he took pride in their achievements. Jacob and Dick were trained for the publishing business. Young Jacob attended Eton[103] and a writing school and at twenty-one was assisting his father. In 1735 he was invited to visit Tonson at the Hazels, in order to be introduced to "ye knowledg of a Country estate."[104] To Sam, who bade fair to be the literary member of the family, Tonson designed to leave his "not inconsiderable" library. "Your intention of breeding up Sam to the law," he assured his nephew, "is indeed wonderful pleasing to mee." Tonson had noted with satisfaction the lad's "quick capacity and compliable duty."[105]

In a long and interesting letter to his nephew, Tonson stated his very practical reasons for preferring Westminster School to Eton for his youngest great-nephew. Eton, he objected, "is very much filled by the Sons of Quality & who are not to be much pressd to study." Westminster made "manly Orators & the very air of London brings on the Improvement of Youth for any business of ye world beyond any other parts of ye Nation. It is the same thing in Amsterdam & Paris, & in ye last place the University being there is a vast advantage, in Amsterdam they come early into business, & in Paris there are very rarely any pedantick learned men wch we abound with very much in Oxford & Cambridge."[106] Despite these forceful arguments, Eton[107] was the school chosen for Sam. With equal conviction, Tonson made further proposals for the boy's future. Might not Sam have at Eton the services of one of the older boys, as was once the custom at the Charterhouse?[108] Might not Sam get a scholarship and come to be a fellow of King's College, as both the Walpoles were?[109] And he should see Herefordshire, "where he might live some time as councillor."[110]

Tonson's interest in schools is indicated in a gift of £50 which he made in July, 1733, to Dr. Richard Newton, Principal of Hart Hall in Oxford, for the purchase of valuable books for the school library. The donation was conveyed to the grateful recipient by "Three well-behav'd young gentlemen," two of them sons of Jacob junior. Dr. Newton selected the books in consultation with Jacob junior.[111]

A naturally sanguine temperament and long and shrewd observation of human affairs reconciled Tonson to "inconveniences yt are tacked to life."[112] From the Vineyard, which pleased him more and more, he wrote to his nephew, "I am I thank God mighty well & in the best humour in the world."[113] After eight years of retirement in Herefordshire, he remarked: "I really doe not desire to come again to London for I find the natural effects of age come on but not faster than any thankful man must acknowledge & to rest satisfied with."[114] If at seventy-four his health was indifferent, he had "noe reason to complain when I think how old I am."[115] He drank wine liberally and fell asleep over it, but kept regular hours and used simple remedies for minor ailments. His deafness increased, and he required glasses, "but I would not have them for an elder's sight."[116] At eighty he had the satisfaction of noting that in praise of Pope his lame hand was far from being tired. He was never bored. There were endless possibilities in store for improving his property, and there was always an unfailing supply of "pretty" estates for which he could bargain.

With age and solitude Jacob's eccentricities became accentuated, to the delight, or exasperation, or both, of those who were subjected to them. One blustery March morning in 1733 his neighbor, Samuel Croxall, rode over from Hereford to the Vineyard to see Tonson and regaled Jacob junior with a most amusing description of the extraordinary visit. At a distance of some yards from the house, Croxall could hear Jacob's servant "with the utmost exercise of his Lungs" trying to make Jacob hear the name of his caller. This feat accomplished, Jacob came down, received his guest "'very graciously," and "'lugg'd me up stairs" to drink a glass of his nephew's "excellent sack." Throwing open a pair of folding doors, he led Croxall over an arch into the vineyard.

> Tho' the Morning was pretty cold & some snow had fall'n not long before, he had nothing on his head but a thin cotton cap, nor over his shirt but a poor old unwadded Gown: He made me shiver to see him,

so I forc'd him into the house again as soon as I could. There, with no little pleasure, he shew'd me his famous Bed, & askd me if it was not very pretty. Then I was carried into another room, which I will call his Museum; where there was a fire, and he had been making improvements and alterations in Pope's Imitation of Horace.[117]

The Museum had bare brick walls and only two or three pictures. The bedchamber had no hangings, folding doors, and two door places which afforded "a comfortable thoroughfare for the Wind."

The purpose of Croxall's visit seems to have been to beg Tonson's assistance for an account of the members of the Kit-Cat Club which Croxall thought of undertaking.

Tho' I roar'd like a Bull, I could hardly make him comprehend me; but when he did he came into it at once, said, no body could tell better what to say of them than him self for, to tell the truth, he had been drunk with every one of them. He designs to be very exact in doing it, & will take some time for it. He talk'd of coming to Hereford assizes next Week; I press'd him, if he did, to bring the Characters along with him; he said it would be impossible to finish them as they ought to be done in that time.

Croxall made his escape before dinner, although Jacob urged him to share with him a stuffed fillet of veal already spitted in the kitchen. It could not be denied that Jacob showed "the same Life and Spirits" that he always had, but he was "a good deal emaciated."[118]

From Bath, two years later, Dr. William Oliver, a well-known physician and friend of Jacob junior, reported to the latter that Tonson "is grown extreamly deaf and feeble" and seemed resolved to "decamp" and "take to his bed for the Remainder of his days, that He may have the Pleasure of knowing how much the World will regret his Loss before He dies."[119] To another friend, Dr. Alexander Small, Dr. Oliver described Tonson as "the most Singular Peice I ever met with amongst the human Species." To be heard by him, one must apply one's nose too near and too long to a very dirty nightcap. "He describes himself to me as weak, and feeble as Volpone could do to his expecting Executor; but the next hour I Spy him (when He thinks nobody sees him,) walking about as Stoutly as if He thought every-body He met wisht him dead, and He had a Mind to give them the Spleen." He begrudged the faggots which "a confounded cold Summer" had cost him but was loud in praise of a veal pie that would remain edible for a fortnight in cool weather. It was Oliver's hope that an account of "all this nonsense" would serve to cheer Jacob junior, who was then seriously ill.[120]

Tonson lingered on in Bath, and "the good old Sardanapalus's Company" was not to be shaken off so soon as Oliver had hoped. Unable to hear, commented Oliver, "He wants to see a good deal. He has the same Pleasure in Seeing people play for large Sums as a *good-natured* Man has to see a Shipwreck from the Shoar, and hugs himself to think that He never ventured upon that boisterous, and uncertain Element. I spent an hour with him yesterday, when He talked the whole time and Said a great many very good, Strong Things, which Shewd his Understanding to be better than his Heart."[121]

An authentic history of the Kit-Cat Club has never been written and cannot now be hoped for. We can only speculate as to what valuable document on the subject Croxall and Tonson between them might have produced before the memories faded. Tonson lived long enough to see in print John Faber's handsome collection of mezzotints of Kneller's Kit-Cat portraits, published by Jacob junior in 1735, the year before Tonson's death. Faber had been at work on the plates for five years, receiving at intervals three pounds a plate as the publisher's share in the expense of each engraving.[122] The Duke of Somerset, who had originally sponsored the painting of the portraits, contributed to the cost of the publication and received Faber's graceful tribute of thanks in the Dedication:

> As this Collection of Prints owes it's very Being to Your Graces Liberality, in setting the Example to the other Members of the Kit-Cat Club of honouring Mr Tonson with their Pictures; and as Your Grace has ever been Eminently Distinguished by that Noble Principle, for the Support of which that Association was known to have been form'd, the Love of your Country, and the Constitutional Liberty thereof, But more especially as the Arts and Sciences have always found in Your Grace a Most Illustrious & Indulgent Patron, This Work is humbly Inscrib'd to Your Grace.[123]

The title page, engraved by Faber, is adorned with a medallion, supported by martial figures, a proud Pegasus, with wings outspread, and decorative scrolls, flowers, grapes, and musical instruments. The series of forty-eight engravings begins with Kneller's self-portrait,[124] followed by the portraits of Somerset and the other members of the peerage in the order of their rank, the baronets, and the untitled members of the club, ending with Jacob Tonson. The dates when Kneller painted ten of the portraits are recorded: in 1702 Dartiquenave's; in 1705 Essex's; in 1707 Mohun's; in 1709 Montagu's, Kingston's, and Congreve's; in 1715 Thomas Hopkins's; in 1716 Burlington's; in 1717 Scarborough's and Pulteney's. Faber included seven portraits which apparently were not hung at Barnes: Marlborough's, Burlington's, Huntingdon's, Shannon's, Dunch's, Edward Hopkins's, and Dartiquenave's.

In the last year of the nephew's life, Tonson and Jacob junior had a serious misunderstanding, the cause of which remains obscure. Tonson had continued to express in his letters to Jacob junior his concern over the financial problems of Dick Tull, and he may have announced an increased legacy for Tull in a new will. He seems also to have made critical remarks regarding his nephew's indulgent treatment of his eldest daughter and eldest son. It was Dr. Small, acting as intermediary in the crisis, who effected a reconciliation which was as important to Tonson as life itself. With infinite relief Tonson thanked Small for this vital service in restoring a relationship which had gone on "soe many Yeares" to the mutual interest of himself and his nephew. "I am truly grieved," Tonson wrote, "yt I ever said & I can say upon my Soul I nevour thought any thing disobleiging to or of any one of ye family who I naturally must love & do admire."[125]

Jacob junior died at Barnes at the age of fifty-two on November 25, 1735, leaving a large estate of £100,000.[126] In his will, consisting of twenty-seven pages in his own hand, he made careful provision for his six orphaned children, whose ages were between fourteen and twenty-two. He left fifty guineas to his uncle, "and considering his Age and his Love of Retirement from this Town and Business I hope he will forgive me that I have not laid so great a Load upon him as the Care of my Family and Affairs would necessarily have given him." He took "this last Opportunity" of requesting his uncle's friendship for his children and for those who befriended them. "So God bless you" was his final solicitous message to the young family whose guidance must now be undertaken by others. For the Kit-Cat portraits, which his uncle had assigned to him, he made no less careful provision. They, "with the frames . . . in which they are fixed," were to remain at Barnes, where he had "lately at some Expense" erected a building for them, and were to be enjoyed there by his uncle and his family during the remainder of the lease. After his uncle's death, the paintings were to be the property for life of his three sons in turn, then of their male heirs in turn, and for lack of male heirs, of his eldest daughter Mary.[127]

How did the shock of his nephew's death affect Tonson at eighty? We have no means of knowing. One last glimpse of Tonson, and a pleasant one, is in a letter of condolence Pope wrote to him on December 4, 1735. Pope assumed that Jacob junior's death might have brought Tonson to London once more and hoped that they might meet again. The fact that Tonson could hear nothing, wrote Pope, would not be an obstacle between old friends.

> Whether your Deafness will permit our Conversation to be on Equal terms, or whether I can only hear you, That will be a great Pleasure to me, & I shall only be sorry to give you none on my part. Yet I think you love me well enough to find it some meerly to be face to face. As soon as you can, pray write me a line, when, & where we shall pass a day & a night together. I can show you papers, if you can't hear me talk, & I can ask you Questions, at least in writing, & I don't care how prolix you are in answering.
>
> I've often thought of writing to you, but I believe you may have read too many of my Letters of late, which is a favour you owe to Curll. I took very kindly the Paragraph in yours which your Nephew communicated to me.[128] I am glad if any of my Writings please you who have been used to so much better, and I am glad if the Writer pleases you, who have known so many better. Let me be what I will, I assure you I am very sincerely / Dear Sir / Your Affectionate / Friend & humble / Servant / A Pope.[129]

Had the crabbedness of Tonson, which Croxall and Oliver described so vividly, not without a touch of malice, abated? More often than not, Pope's pen was venomous, but he preferred, in this instance, to be tender. From Pope's solicitude for his aged mother may have stemmed a special tolerance for the infirmities of all very elderly people. It seems appropriate that this last softened portrait of old Jacob was painted by the first poet of the age, whom he so greatly admired.

Tonson died at the Vineyard on March 17, 1736. His estate, estimated at £40,000, was probably very much larger.[130] A funeral hearse conveyed his body to London, the expenses of the journey of eight days and of his funeral amounting to £124 5s 4d.[131]

Tonson was buried on April 1 in the church of St. Mary Le Strand.[132] The following account of his funeral appeared in *The London Evening Post*:

> Thursday Night about Ten o'Clock, the Corpse of Jacob Tonson Esq; one of his Majesty's Justices of the Peace for the County of Hereford, who died at his seat of the Vineyard near Ledbury in that County, the 17th of last month in the 82d Year of his Age, was carry'd from his Great Nephew's Dwellinghouse in the Strand, and interr'd in a Vault in St. Mary Le Strand, in a very handsome Manner, and the following Genlemen [*sic*] supported the Pall, viz. Th. Spence, Esq; Temple Stanyan, Esq; Peter Forbes, Esq; Mr. Round, Mr. Knaplock, and Mr. Wilson.[133]

Tonson's last will was witnessed on December 2, 1735, and it was proved the day after his burial. His great-nephew, Jacob Tonson the third, was made his sole executor and residuary legatee. Tonson left what he finally considered a reasonable legacy to his nephew Richard Tull, who was to receive "the summe of eighty pounds a year during his life to be paid him quarterly," the first payment to commence the day of Tonson's decease.[134] Always worried over the future of this relative who had not "made good," Tonson had felt that some further provision for Tull might, after all, be necessary. He therefore directed:

> I do most earnestly recommend my said Nephew Richard Tull to the friendship of my Executor herein named not in the least doubting the humanity and good nature of my said Executor towards him in giving him any further assistance which my said Executor shall judge necessary for his service. But nevertheless it is my Will and meaning that my said Nephew Richard Tull shall not have any Claime either in Law or Equity upon my Estate or my said Executor further than for the said eighty pounds per annum so bequeathed to him as aforesaid for his life.

Young Jacob was to give to each of Tonson's servants "such Benefaction as he shall judge they may have deserved in proportion to their services towards me." For two years after his death, five pounds a year were to be "distributed to such poor persons of the parish of Ledbury as are not allowed in the poors books anything from the said parish." His property in Herefordshire and Gloucestershire and all the rest of his personal estate Tonson left to this eldest great-nephew. In a single codicil he specifically transferred to his young executor the unexpired lease of Barn Elms and his right to and interest in the Kit-Cat portraits there.[135]

The publishing house of Tonson continued in a flourishing state until the death of the last Tonson, Jacob junior's son Richard, in 1772, when the Tonson copyrights passed into the hands of the Rivingtons. Jacob junior's family was reduced by the early deaths of his daughter Elizabeth[136] and his youngest son Samuel.[137] His eldest daughter Mary married in 1742 William Baker, son of John Baker, a London draper, and her sister Anne married Philip Lemprière. Jacob the third, who died unmarried in 1767, was commended by Samuel Johnson as "a man who is to be praised as often as he is named."[138] Richard Tonson also died unmarried. After the death of his brother Jacob, he moved the Kit-Cat portraits to a room that he had built for them at his "elegant villa" at Water Oakley, near Windsor.[139] It was after Mary Tonson's death (in 1753) that her husband, knighted in 1760, "invested in Hertfordshire acres" part of the money he had made as a merchant in London and built Bayfordbury House, completed in 1763.[140] At Richard Tonson's death, the Kit-Cat portraits passed into the hands of the Baker family, and another special room was made for them at Bayfordbury.

For many years the Tonson MSS remained undisturbed at Bayfordbury in the possession of Mary Tonson Baker's descendants. In 1904 Henry Clinton Baker offered to Sotheby for £5,000 Milton's manuscript of Book I of *Paradise Lost*, which Tonson had probably considered his most precious treasure. The manuscript was later purchased by Mr. Pierpont Morgan. From 1924 onward some of the more valuable Tonson letters were sold at intervals to London dealers and were fairly widely dispersed. Masses of Tonson letters were a casualty of World War II and "went for pulp" when in May, 1940, Lady Rosa Clinton Baker vacated Bayfordbury at short notice.[141] At a sale in 1945 a tin box of Tonson wills and letters was acquired by the National Portrait Gallery in London, and a portion of the papers from the same sale went to the Folger Shakespeare Library in Washington, D. C.

Kneller's Kit-Cat portraits, sold from Bayfordbury in 1945, were purchased by the National Art-Collections Fund and presented to the National Portrait Gallery in London. Forty-four portraits, of "Kit-Cat size,"[142] now make up the collection, if the conversation piece of Newcastle and Lincoln is counted as two and the self-portrait of Kneller is also counted. Dartiquenave's portrait is a copy. Shannon's is an unfinished sketch.[143] From their carved and gilt wood frames the noblemen and gentlemen who were members of the club look down at visitors to the gallery with expressions of dignified aloofness. Most of the Kit-Cats were distinguished men, and they all took pride in belonging to "the best Club that ever met." They were expensively dressed, with elaborately curled periwigs, in graceful poses, affecting an agreeable nonchalance.

The dynamic figure among them is that of Jacob Tonson, their founder, presiding competently and acceptably over them, as he did in life. He had had the skill and energy to mold these divergent personalities into a harmonious union of kindred spirits, sociable, gay, witty, argumentative, passionately concerned with national crises. Seated in his secretary's chair, Tonson is wearing a red turban and a plain cravat, loosely tied; and the ample folds of a green gown betray his corpulence. His gaze is shrewd and penetrating. He has a determined, vigilant, appraising air. In his hand he holds conspicuously a handsomely bound copy of the fourth edition of *Paradise Lost*, as evidence of the vocation which had brought him wealth and fame.

The Tonson Pedigree

Tonson {

John (d. ca. 1652)
m. Anne Griffin { Richard (d.s.p. by 1666)

Richard (d. 1643)
m. Margaret
[Nicholson?]
(d. 1655)
{

Jacob (1620–1668)
m. Elizabeth Walbancke
(b. 1631)
da. Matthew Walbancke
{

Elizabeth (b. 1651)
m. Jeremiah Lewin

Richard (1653–1690)
m. 1679
Mary Draper
da. Capt. Draper
of Wandsworth, Surrey

Rose (b. 1654)
m. 1690
Samuel Tull.

Jacob Tonson [the Elder] (1655–17.
d.s.p.

Tabitha (b. 1665)

Maj. Richard (1621–1693)
m. Elizabeth Becher
In regiment of
Col. Richard Lawrence, 1656.
Received grant of land in
Co. Cork from Chas. II.
d. at Spanish Island, Co. Cork.
{

Henry
of Spanish Island
(d. 1703)
m. 1692
Elizabeth Hull

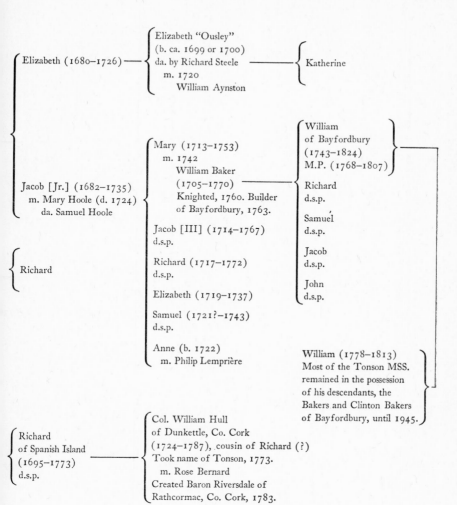

Elizabeth (1680–1726) —

Elizabeth "Ousley"
(b. ca. 1699 or 1700)
da. by Richard Steele ——— Katherine
m. 1720
William Aynston

Jacob [Jr.] (1682–1735)
m. Mary Hoole (d. 1724)
da. Samuel Hoole

Mary (1713–1753)
m. 1742
William Baker
(1705–1770)
Knighted, 1760. Builder
of Bayfordbury, 1763.

William
of Bayfordbury
(1743–1824)
M.P. (1768–1807)

Richard
d.s.p.

Samuel
d.s.p.

Jacob
d.s.p.

John
d.s.p.

Jacob [III] (1714–1767)
d.s.p.

Richard (1717–1772)
d.s.p.

Elizabeth (1719–1737)

Samuel (1721?–1743)
d.s.p.

Anne (b. 1722)
m. Philip Lemprière

Richard

William (1778–1813)
Most of the Tonson MSS.
remained in the possession
of his descendants, the
Bakers and Clinton Bakers
of Bayfordbury, until 1945.

Richard
of Spanish Island
(1695–1773)
d.s.p.

Col. William Hull
of Dunkettle, Co. Cork
(1724–1787), cousin of Richard (?)
Took name of Tonson, 1773.
m. Rose Bernard
Created Baron Riversdale of
Rathcormac, Co. Cork, 1783.

Notes

The following abbreviations have been used: Add. MSS. (Additional Manuscripts, British Museum, London); ASO (All Souls, Oxford); Bodl. (Bodleian Library, Oxford); DUL (Durham University Library); *EHR* (*English Historical Review*); FSL (Folger Shakespeare Library); GL (Guildhall Library, London); HL (Huntington Library); HMC (Reports of the Royal Historical Manuscripts Commission); *MP* (*Modern Philology*); NPG (National Portrait Gallery, London); NUL (Nottingham University Library); PCC (Prerogative Court of Canterbury Will Book or Administration Act Book, Somerset House, London); *PMLA* (*Publications of the Modern Language Association*); PRO (Public Record Office, London); RFL (Rosenbach Foundation Library); SH (Stationers' Hall, London); SP (State Papers, Domestic).

CHAPTER 1: *Heritage*

1. GL MS. 6673/3.
2. E[lijah] Williams, *Early Holborn and the Legal Quarter of London* (London, 1927), II, 1232, 1233. Middle Row was demolished and the site thrown into the roadway in 1867.
3. NPG Tonson MSS.
4. PCC 1655, A.A., f. 255.
5. GL MS. 6667/1.
6. GL MS. 5265/1.
7. For a discussion of these matters, see J. F. V. Woodman, *The Freedom of the City of London* (London, 1960). An assumption which cannot be supported by the facts has persisted that Tonson's father was a barber surgeon. See G. F. Papali, *Jacob Tonson, Publisher, His Life and Work (1656–1736)* ([Auckland], New Zealand, 1968), pp. 2–4, and Harry M. Geduld, *Prince of Publishers, A Study of the Work and Career of Jacob Tonson* (Bloomington and London, 1969), p. 5. In the parish registers of St. Andrew, Holborn (Guildhall Library), Tonson's father appears always as "shoemaker."

8. Elizabeth Walbancke was baptized May 30, 1631. See GL MS. 6667/2. Papali, p. 4, and Geduld, p. 5, both assume incorrectly that Elizabeth Walbancke Tonson was the sister of Matthew Walbancke.

9. See SH "Apprentices Register Book 1605 To 1666." A misleading account of the Walbanckes appears in two books by Henry R. Plomer, *A Dictionary of the Booksellers and Printers Who were at Work in England, Scotland and Ireland From 1641 to 1667* (London, 1907), p. 186, and *A Dictionary of the Printers and Booksellers Who were at Work in England, Scotland and Ireland From 1668 to 1725* (London, 1922), p. 298. Plomer assumes that Matthew Walbancke died in 1667. It is evident, however, that his death occurred before March, 1662, for on March 3 of that year Samuel Heyrick, an apprentice of "Mr Math Walbancke decd," became a freeman of the Stationers' Company. See SH "Freemen's Register Beginning 1605 To 1703." Walbancke's latest publications seem to have been three brief tributes to Charles II printed in 1660. Plomer further conjectures that Elizabeth Walbanck, bookseller, was "perhaps" the widow of George Walbanck, and that the latter was "possibly" son and successor of Matthew Walbanck. I suggest that "G. Walbancke" was probably Gilbert Walbancke, who had been an apprentice (1649–1658) of Matthew Walbancke, and who appears to have remained at the shop in Gray's Inn Gate, Holborn, possibly in partnership with Samuel Heyrick, after Matthew Walbancke's death. Indispensable guides to the publications of seventeenth-century publishers are: Donald Wing's *Short-Title Catalogue of Books Printed in England, Scotland, Ireland, Wales, and British America And of English Books Printed in Other Countries 1641–1700*, 3 vols. (New York, 1948), and Paul G. Morrison's *Index of Printers, Publishers and Booksellers in Donald Wing's Short-Title Catalogue*, etc. (Charlottesville, Va., 1955).

10. *Annalia Dubrensia* . . . (London, 1636), "To my worthy Friend Mr. Robert Dover."

11. See *A Diary*, May 24 to May 31, 1644, and August 28 to September 4, 1645.

12. The shop under the old gatehouse of Gray's Inn was used as a bookshop by Walbancke's widow and then by his grandsons until 1710 and was afterward leased to other booksellers. The shop under the new (Holborn) gatehouse of Gray's Inn was the last Gray's Inn shop to be torn down, in 1892. A sketch, with a brief account of the shop's history, was published in the *Pall Mall Budget* on March 31, 1892. The shop was first occupied by Henry Tomes, a bookseller who published in 1607 *The Commendation of Cockes and Cock-Fighting*, a work which may well have attracted the attention of frequenters of a cockpit a few doors away. It was in this shop that Matthew Walbancke served his apprenticeship to Robert

Wilson. He acquired the lease of the shop in 1614. Samuel Heyrick apparently leased the shop after Walbancke's death and in 1684 took Richard Sare into partnership with him. Richard Williamson succeeded Sare. See *The Pension Book of Gray's Inn, 1569–1669*, ed. Reginald J. Fletcher (London, 1901), and Ralph Douthwaite, *Gray's Inn; Its History and Associations* (London, 1886).

13. NPG Tonson MSS.

14. In 1638 "Mr. Taunson" paid his annual rent of £8 for his house in the High St. Precinct, near Kings Alley, in the parish of St. Botolph without Aldgate. See T. C. Dale, *The Inhabitants of London in 1638* (London, 1931), p. 194.

15. PRO Reynardson C.9.371/41, *Tonson vs. Tonson*.

16. GL MS. 6667/3 and MS. 6667/4. Failure to consult the parish registers of St. Andrew, Holborn, has led to the common assumption that Jacob Tonson the Elder was born in 1656.

17. Elizabeth married Jeremiah Lewin, and Rose married Samuel Tull in 1690 and became the mother of Richard Tull, for whom Jacob Tonson the Elder made cautious provision in his will.

18. The term "cordwainer" was derived from Cordova in Spain. A pair of well-tanned and waxed boots cost 14s 10d per pair.

19. C. H. Waterland Mander, *A Descriptive and Historical Account of the Guild of Cordwainers of the City of London* (London, 1931), p. 111.

20. Bodl. MS. English letters c. 129, f. 118. For accounts of teaching methods in London schools, see Charles Hoole, *A New Discovery of the old Art of Teaching School, in Four small Treatises*, ed. E. T. Campagnac (London, 1913); *A Cyclopedia of Education*, ed. Paul Monroe (New York, 1913), V, 821 f.; and Foster Watson, *The English Grammar Schools to 1660; their Curriculum and Practice* (Cambridge, 1908).

21. Samuel Pepys, *Diary*, ed. Henry B. Wheatley (London, 1894), IV, 213.

22. Williams, II, 1247.

23. For a graphic, though fictionalized, account of the Plague see Daniel Defoe, *A Journal of the Plague Year* (London, 1722). In 1665 Defoe was a child of five. For a more authoritative account see Walter George Bell, *The Great Plague in London in 1665* (London, 1924).

24. See Walter George Bell, *The Great Fire of London in 1666* (London, 1920).

25. *The Diary of John Evelyn*, ed. E. S. De Beer (Oxford, 1955), III, 459.

26. PCC 1668, 147 Hene. Papali, p. 2, has misread "William Jolly" as another brother "of the deceased."

27. GL MS. 6673/4.

28. Sir Charles Firth, *The Regimental History of Cromwell's Army* (Oxford, 1940), I, 357 and 358. See also Add. MSS. 35,102, f. 55.

29. See *Indexes to Irish Wills*, ed. W. P. W. Phillimore (London, 1910), II, 108.

30. See Add. MSS. 28,275, f. 284 and 351.

31. Major Richard Tonson married Elizabeth Becher. His son Henry of Spanish Island married in 1692 Elizabeth, second daughter of Sir Richard Hull, and died in 1703. He was succeeded by his son Richard (1695–1773). At Richard's death a cousin (?), Colonel William Hull, took the name of Tonson, and ten years later he was elevated to the peerage as Baron Riversdale of Rathcormac, county Cork. These relationships are briefly traced in Sir Bernard Burke's *Dormant, Abeyant, Forfeited and Extinct Peerages of the British Empire* (London, 1883), p. 534.

32. See *A Transcript of the Registers of the Worshipful Company of Stationers, From 1640–1708 A.D.* (London, 1913), II, 481–483. On June 29, 1674, Elizabeth Walbancke, widow, "the relict and administratrix of the goods of Matthew Walbancke, late citizen and staconer of London deced," assigned eighteen copyrights and parts of others to Samuel Heyrick.

33. *The Term Catalogues, 1668–1709*, ed. Edward Arber (London, 1903), I, 165.

34. SH "Apprentices Register Book From 1666–1727."

35. SH "Freemen's Register Beginning 1605 To 1703."

36. SH "Apprentices Register Book From 1666–1727."

37. See Cyprian Blagden, *The Stationers' Company, a History, 1403–1959* (London [1960]), p. 79.

38. See William Roberts, *The Earlier History of English Book-Selling* (London, 1889), p. 93.

39. Joseph E. Tucker, "John Davies of Kidwelly," in *The Papers of the Bibliographical Society of America*, XLIV (1950), 119.

40. J. D. [John Davies], *Epictetus Junior* (London, 1670), p. 125.

41. *Ibid.*, p. 13.

42. *Term Catalogues*, I, 202.

43. *Ibid.*, p. 229.

44. *Ibid.*, pp. 25–300, *passim*.

45. *The Life and Errors of John Dunton* (London, 1705), p. 280.

46. This was the fifth edition of Sir Richard Baker's *Chronicle of the Kings of England*, which Sawbridge and Thomas Williams published in 1670. Sawbridge published his next edition in 1674.

47. Bodl. MS. Eng. letters c. 129, f. 105.

48. See T. B. [Thomas Blount], *Animadversions Upon Sr Richard Baker's Chronicle, And It's Continuation* (London, 1672), Preface.

49. This manuscript letter is in the Pierpont Morgan Library in New York City. It is quoted in *The Manuscript of Milton's Paradise Lost Book I*, ed. Helen Darbishire (Oxford, 1931), p. xiv.

50. [John Toland], *The Life of John Milton* (London, 1699), p. 148.

51. W. D. [William D'Avenant], *Notitia Historicorum Selectorum, or Animadversions upon the Antient and Famous Greek and Latin Historians* (Oxford, 1678), Preface.

52. SH "Freemen's Register Beginning 1605 To 1703."

53. See *Term Catalogues*, I, 255–350, *passim*.

54. John Downes, *Roscius Anglicanus*, ed. Joseph Knight (London, 1886), p. 36.

55. See Samuel Johnson, *Lives of the English Poets*, ed. George Birkbeck Hill (Oxford, 1905), I, "Dryden," 475.

56. See *Term Catalogues*, I, 300–370, *passim*.

57. See *The Critical and Miscellaneous Prose Works of John Dryden*, ed. Edmund Malone (London, 1800), I, Part I, 502–503. Malone repeats but questions this anecdote, doubting whether Tonson needed to borrow £20, since he "was sufficiently rich to purchase some of the plays of Otway and Tate." However, it was Richard Tonson who purchased the plays of Otway; and Tate's first play would not have commanded the price of a play by Dryden.

58. See Joseph Spence, *Observations, Anecdotes, and Characters of Books and Men*, ed. James M. Osborne (Oxford, 1966), I, 274–275.

CHAPTER II: *Dryden and Tonson*

1. Johnson, I, "Dryden," 372.

2. *Ovid's Epistles* (London, 1680), Preface. Mrs. Behn's "imitation" was Epistle 11, "Oenone to Paris."

3. These editions appeared in 1681, 1683, 1693, 1701, 1705, and 1712.

4. See Hugh Macdonald, *John Dryden, A Bibliography of Early Editions and of Drydeniana* (Oxford, 1939), p. 220.

5. Downes, p. 37.

6. Macdonald, p. 20.

7. Johnson, I, "Dryden," 373.

8. [John Dryden], *Absalom and Achitophel. A Poem* (London, 1681), "To the Reader."

9. Johnson, I, "Dryden," 436.

10. Spence, I, 28.

11. John Dryden, *The Medall, A Satyre Against Sedition* (London, 1682), "Epistle to the Whigs."

12. Charles E. Ward, *The Life of John Dryden* (Chapel Hill, N. C., 1961), p. 187.

13. See Macdonald, p. 30.

14. *Prose Works of Dryden*, ed. Malone, II, 330–331n.

15. *Plutarchs Lives. Translated From the Greek by Several Hands* (London, 1683), "The Publisher to the Reader."

16. *The Letters of John Dryden, With Letters Addressed to Him*, ed. Charles E. Ward (Durham, N. C., 1942), p. 22.

17. Macdonald, p. 67.

18. *Miscellany Poems* (London, 1684), p. 90. After the first reference to each, the six volumes of Tonson's Miscellanies will be referred to briefly by the numbers of the volumes.

19. Dryden, *Letters*, p. 23.

20. *Sylvae: or The Second Part of Poetical Miscellanies* (London, 1685), Preface.

21. *Ibid.*, p. 473.

22. John Dryden, *Threnodia Augustalis* (London, 1685), p. 22.

23. John Dryden, *Albion and Albanius* (London, 1685), Preface.

24. [John Dryden], *The Hind and the Panther* (London, 1687), "To the Reader."

25. Johnson, I, "Dryden," 380.

26. *The Hind and the Panther Transvers'd To the Story of The Country-Mouse and the City-Mouse* (London, 1687), Preface.

27. Spence, I, 278. But see *Prose Works of Dryden*, ed. Malone, I, 1, 199, and Johnson, II, "Halifax," 43.

28. *The Works of John Dryden*, ed. Walter Scott (London, 1808), I, 331n.

29. John Dryden, *Britannia Rediviva* (London, 1688), p. 7.

30. John Dryden, *The Satires of Decimus Junius Juvenalis . . . Together with the Satires of Aulus Persius Flaccus* (London, 1693), p. xiii.

31. Richard Tonson was buried in the church of St. Andrew, Holborn, on September 25, 1690. See GL MS. 6673/6.

32. Two other daughters, Mary, born in 1684, and Martha, born in 1686, did not survive childhood. The death of Martha in 1688 is noted in NPG Tonson MSS.

33. John Dryden, *Amphitryon* (London, 1690), "To the Honourable Sir William Levison Gower."

34. John Dryden, *King Arthur: or, The British Worthy* (London, 1691), "To the Marquis of Halifax."

35. See Ward, *Dryden*, pp. 250–251.

36. Johnson, I, "Dryden," 407.

37. Dryden, *Letters*, p. 49.
38. *Ibid.*, pp. 51–52.
39. Add. MSS. 36,933. See also William Congreve, *William Congreve, Letters and Documents*, ed. John C. Hodges (New York, 1964), pp. 96–97.
40. See Dryden, *Letters*, p. 172, and *William Congreve*, ed. Hodges, pp. 99–100.
41. Ward, *Dryden*, p. 273.
42. Dryden, *Letters*, p. 77. For details of payments and receipts see Henry B. Wheatley, *Dryden's Publishers* (London, 1912), pp. 22–24, Charles E. Ward, "The Publication and Profits of Dryden's *Virgil*," *PMLA*, LIII (1938), 807–812, and John Barnard, "Dryden, Tonson, and Subscriptions for the 1697 *Virgil*," *The Papers of the Bibliographical Society of America*, LVII (1963), 129–151.
43. Dryden, *Letters*, p. 78.
44. *Ibid.*, pp. 80–81.
45. *Ibid.*, p. 85.
46. Johnson, I, "Dryden," 407.
47. *Prose Works of Dryden*, ed. Malone, I, 1, 525–528. See Richard Powys to Matthew Prior, HMC *Bath* MSS. (Hereford, 1908), III, 238–239, for a different, less probable, version of this episode.
48. Dryden, *Letters*, p. 59.
49. Dryden, *Works*, ed. Scott, I, 391.
50. John Dryden, Jr., *The Husband His Own Cuckold* (London, 1696), Preface.
51. John Dryden, *The Works of Virgil* (London, 1697), "Aeneis," Dedication.
52. *Ibid.*, "The Pastorals," Dedication.
53. *Ibid.*, "Aeneis," Dedication.
54. Dryden, *Letters*, p. 93.
55. *Ibid.*, p. 96.
56. *Ibid.*, p. 98.
57. Dryden paraphrased three of *The Canterbury Tales* ("The Knight's Tale," "The Nun's Priest's Tale," and "The Wife of Bath's Tale"), imitated and enlarged the description of "A good Parson" in the "Prologue," and included a paraphrase of "The Flower and the Leaf," then attributed to Chaucer. He paraphrased one whole book of Ovid's *Metamorphoses* and included excerpts from three others.
58. John Dryden, *Fables Ancient and Modern; Translated into Verse, from Homer, Ovid, Boccace, & Chaucer* (London, 1700), Preface.
59. *Ibid.*

60. Ward, *Dryden*, p. 304.
61. See *Prose Works of Dryden*, ed. Malone, I, 1, 561, and Dryden, *Works*, ed. Scott, XVIII, 191.
62. This is known as the Bayfordbury portrait of Dryden and is now in Trinity College, Cambridge.
63. See Dryden, *Letters*, pp. 98–99, for Dryden's comment to Tonson: "I know my translation [of Ovid's *de Arte Amandi*] is very uncorrect: but at the same time I know no body else can do it better, with all their pains."
64. *The Works of Mr. Francis Beaumont, and Mr. John Fletcher* (London, 1711), I, Preface, xii–xxvi. Johnson later reprinted a portion of these notes in *Lives*, I, "Dryden," 471–479.
65. Spence, I, 277.
66. See Dryden's verses to Congreve prefixed to William Congreve's *The Double-Dealer* (London, 1694).
67. *The Dramatick Works of John Dryden, Esq.* (London, 1717), I, "To His Grace the Duke of Newcastle."
68. Johnson, I, "Dryden," 395.

CHAPTER III: *Among the Kit-Cats*

1. Horace Walpole, *Anecdotes of Painting in England* (London, 1849), II, 591.
2. See the useful account of the club in Robert J. Allen, *The Clubs of Augustan London* (Cambridge, Mass., 1933), pp. 35–54 and 232–239.
3. Edward Ward, *The Secret History of Clubs* (London, 1709), p. 363.
4. John Oldmixon, *The History of England During the Reigns of King William and Mary, Queen Anne, King George I* (London, 1735), p. 479.
5. Tonson had very cordial relations with Kneller and is said to have obtained pictures on reasonable terms from the famous portrait painter by combined flattery and gifts of claret and venison. Kneller once commented with satisfaction: "How old Jacob loves me; he is a very good man; you see how he loves me, he sends me good things and the venison was fat." See [Michael Morris] Lord Killanin, *Sir Godfrey Kneller and His Times* (London, 1948), p. 26.
6. John Macky, *A Journey Through England* (London, 1714), I, 188.
7. Tonson's "two left legs" were the subject of much contemporary jesting. In a letter to Spencer Compton, Charles Boyle, and Christopher Codrington, Prior wrote: "My services to the Fish [Tonson] against he prints a new miscellany." Quoted from Longleat MSS. III, f. 275, by Francis Bickley, *The Life of Matthew Prior* (London, 1914), p. 89.

8. Edward Ward, pp. 360–367.

9. Sir Richard Blackmore, *The Kit-Cats. A Poem* (London, 1708), pp. 104–123.

10. Among the many contemporary references to Jacob's "two left legs" perhaps the most amusing anecdote is of a conversation between Lady Wharton and Tonson. Tonson was inspecting Vandyke's painting of Charles I in whole length armor in the Wharton collection and objected to Lady Wharton that oddly enough the two gauntlets worn by the King had been drawn for the right hand. Whereupon Lady Wharton rejoined: "Mr. Tonson, why might not one man have two right hands, as well as another two left legs!" See *The Gentleman's Magazine*, LXXVII, Part II (1807), 738.

11. See above, p. 32.

12. William Shippen, *Faction Display'd. A Poem* (London, 1704), pp. 13–17.

13. *The Spectator*, ed. Donald F. Bond (Oxford, 1965), I, No. 9 (1711), 42.

14. *Notes and Queries*, 5th ser. III (1875), 259–260.

15. *Ibid.*, 2nd ser. III (1857), 205.

16. There is no indication elsewhere that Grantham may have been a member of the club. Henry D'Auverquerque had been created Earl of Grantham in 1698. He was Keeper of the Privy Purse from 1700 to 1702.

17. NPG Tonson MSS. It is possible (Rae Blanchard questions this) that Steele refers to a meeting of the Kit-Cats at the Upper Flask in a letter to Ambrose Philips (June, 1712?). See *The Correspondence of Richard Steele*, ed. Rae Blanchard (London, 1941), p. 57. Steele was living near Hampstead in the summer of 1712.

18. Sir John Vanbrugh, *The Complete Works of Sir John Vanbrugh*, ed. Bonamy Dobrée and Geoffrey Webb (London, 1927), IV, 7.

19. *A Biographical History of England, From the Revolution to the End of George I's Reign: Being a Continuation of the Rev. S. Granger's Work*, ed. Mark Noble (London, 1806), III, 430.

20. Abel Boyer, *The History of the Life and Reign of Queen Anne* (London, 1722), p. 524n.

21. John Faber, *The Kit-Cat Club Done From the Original Paintings of Sr Godfrey Kneller* (London, 1735).

22. Norton's expulsion was noted in *A Kit-Cat C—b Described* (London, 1705).

23. On March 13, 1707, Richard Topham, M.P. for Windsor, was made Keeper of the Records at the Tower. See Narcissus Luttrell, *A Brief Historical Relation of State Affairs, 1674–1714* (London, 1857), VI, 148. Topham was one of the translators of *Several Orations of Demosthe-*

nes, published by Tonson in 1702. For Topham's contribution to a Kit-Cat poem see below, pp. 54–55.

24. Oldmixon, p. 479.

25. Brice Harris, *Charles Sackville, Sixth Earl of Dorset* (Urbana, Ill., 1940), p. 178.

26. Horace Walpole, *A Catalogue of the Royal and Noble Authors* (London, 1806), IV, 13.

27. *Bishop Burnet's History of His Own Time* (London, 1724), I, 792. Gilbert Burnet was rewarded for his services to William with the bishopric of Salisbury. His most important work was his *History*, not published until after his death.

28. Johnson, I, "Dorset," 308.

29. Edward Ward, p. 370.

30. The other two members were Charles Spencer, third Earl of Sunderland, and Edward Russell, second Earl of Orford.

31. John Carswell, *The Old Cause* (London, 1954), p. 76.

32. Sir John Dalrymple, *Memoirs of Great Britain and Ireland*, II (London, 1773), 86.

33. Geoffrey Holmes, *British Politics in the Age of Anne* (London, 1967), p. 240.

34. The provisions of the two Partition treaties for the division of the empire of Charles II of Spain were unpopular in England.

35. In 1682 Somerset married Elizabeth Percy, Lady Ogle, who became a Lady of the Bedchamber to Queen Anne and in 1710 replaced Sarah, Duchess of Marlborough, as Groom of the Stole.

36. Jonathan Swift, *The History of the Four Last Years of the Queen* (London, 1758), p. 30.

37. Holmes, p. 226.

38. *Memoirs of the Secret Services of John Macky, Esq.* (London, 1733), p. 142.

39. *The Gentleman's Magazine*, N.S. VIII (1837), 364.

40. The Kit-Cat Dormer has been wrongly identified as: Lieutenant-Colonel Charles Dormer (d. 1707); Lieutenant-General James Dormer (d. 1741); and John Dormer, Baron Dormer of Wyng (d. 1785).

41. J. H. Plumb, *Sir Robert Walpole* (London, 1956), p. 115.

42. See George Colman the Elder, *The Jealous Wife* (London, 1761), "To the Right Honourable The Earl of Bath."

43. HMC *Portland* MSS. IV (London, 1897), 493.

44. Luttrell noted in his Diary under the date of Nov. 3, 1709, that Edward Hopkins, M. P. for Coventry, had been appointed to go as envoy to the Court of Hanover. See Luttrell, VI, 509.

45. HMC *Portland* MSS. II (London, 1893), 209.

46. Vanbrugh, *Works*, IV, 59.

47. Ralph Delavall was a distinguished naval officer.

48. See *The Muses Mercury* (1707), pp. 74–76, and *The Poetical Works of Nicholas Rowe, Esq.* (London, 1715), pp. 13–15.

49. Spence, I, 50.

50. Harvey Cushing, *Dr. Garth The Kit-Cat Poet, 1661–1718* (Baltimore, 1906), p. 27.

51. Spence, I, 51.

52. Walpole had defended the Admiralty against the Junto but returned to the support of his Whig friends.

53. HMC *Portland* MSS. IV, 493.

54. *The Literary Works of Matthew Prior*, ed. H. Bunker Wright and Monroe K. Spears (Oxford, 1959), I, 301.

55. Blackmore, p. 109.

56. Lansdowne MSS. 852, f. 17.

57. Add. MSS. 40,060. "A Letter" is dated "1698" at the beginning of the poem and "1697" at the end.

58. Pope made this marginal identification in his neat handwriting in his copy of *A New Collection of Poems Relating to State Affairs* (London, 1705), p. 477, where "A Letter" is included.

59. Add. MSS. 40,060. The "Ballad" is dated "1698."

60. See Steele's account of toasting in *The Tatler* (London, 1728), I, No. 24 (1709), 160–161.

61. HMC *Bath* MSS. III, 394.

62. *The Patentee* (London, 1700).

63. Add. MSS. 40,060, f. 89. Anne Churchill was the second daughter of John Churchill, first Duke of Marlborough, and wife of Charles Spencer, third Earl of Sunderland. Beautiful but short in stature, she was affectionately called by the Kit-Cats "the little Whig."

64. HMC *Rutland* MSS. II (London, 1889), 177.

65. *The Letters and Works of Lady Mary Wortley Montagu*, ed. Lord Wharncliffe (London, 1893), I, 52–53.

66. Lady Carlisle was Anne Capell, daughter of Arthur Capell, first Earl of Essex, and wife of Charles Howard, third Earl of Carlisle. The Duchess of Bolton was Henrietta Crofts, illegitimate youngest daughter of the Duke of Monmouth, and wife of Charles Pawlet, second Duke of Bolton. Mrs. Dunch was Elizabeth Godfrey, daughter of Colonel Charles Godfrey, niece of Marlborough and wife of Edmund Dunch. Lady Wharton was Lucy Loftus, daughter of Adam Loftus, Viscount Lisburne, and second wife of Thomas Wharton, Baron Wharton.

67. Holmes, p. 298.

68. Some of these entries, with variant readings, were printed, or are to be found in other manuscript collections.

69. The Duchess of St. Albans was Diana de Vere, daughter of Aubrey de Vere, and wife of Charles Beauclerk, first Duke of St. Albans. Lady Manchester was Dodington Greville, daughter of Robert Greville, fourth Baron Brooke, and wife of Charles Montagu, fourth Earl of Manchester. Lady Essex was Mary Bentinck, daughter of the first Earl of Portland and wife of Algernon Capell, second Earl of Essex. Diana Kirke was the daughter of Lieutenant-General Percy Kirke, and afterward wife of John Dormer. Lady Mary Sackville was the daughter of Charles Sackville, sixth Earl of Dorset, and afterward wife of Henry Somerset, Duke of Beaufort.

70. Add. MSS. 40,060, ff. 6–7.

71. Lady Mary Sackville married the Duke of Beaufort in 1702, both being minors. She died in childbirth in 1705.

72. *The Fifth Part of Miscellany Poems* (2nd ed.; 1716), p. 60.

73. In 1713, seduced and blackmailed by her butler, Diana Dormer was the subject of contemporary gossip. See *The Wentworth Papers*, ed. James J. Cartwright (London, 1883), p. 329. John Dormer divorced his wife in 1715 and disinherited their daughter Diana, a child of five. See *Cases of Divorce for Several Causes*, published by Edmund Curll (London, 1715), pp. 41–60.

74. Fifth Miscellany (1716 ed.), p. 67.

75. Add. MSS. 40,060, f. 39. Lady Rialton, afterward Duchess of Marlborough, was Henrietta Churchill, eldest daughter of the Duke of Marlborough, and the wife of Francis Godolphin, Lord Rialton, afterward second Earl of Godolphin. She was the mother of Congreve's daughter, Lady Mary Godolphin, afterward Duchess of Leeds. Lady Monthermer was Mary Churchill, Marlborough's youngest daughter, and the wife of John Montagu, who became successively Lord Monthermer and second Duke of Montagu. Lady Scudamore was Frances Digby, only daughter of Simon Digby, fourth Baron Digby of Geashill, and wife of James Scudamore, third Viscount Scudamore.

76. Steele, *Correspondence*, p. 110.

77. Lady Elizabeth Cromwell was the only daughter and heiress of Vere Essex (Cromwell), fourth Earl of Ardglass. In 1704 she married the Rt. Hon. Edward Southwell.

78. Walsh was the speaker.

79. Add. MSS. 40,060, f. 8.

80. [John Oldmixon], *The Life and Posthumous Works of Arthur Mainwaring, Esq.* (London, 1715), p. 53.

81. Add. MSS. 40,060, ff. 74–75. The printed version in Mainwaring's *Life and Works*, pp. 53–55, has some variations.

82. Add. MSS. 40,060, ff. 20–23, 59–60, and 32–33.

83. Allen, p. 251.

84. See John Loftis, *The Politics of Drama in Augustan England* (Oxford, 1963).

85. Add. MSS. 40,060, f. 41. Pope made the marginal note for this poem in his copy (now in the British Museum) of *A New Collection of Poems*, p. 557, "Certainly written by Mr Congreve."

86. Add. MSS. 40,060, ff. 71–73. See also *The Sixth Part of Miscellany Poems* (2nd ed.; 1716), pp. 250–255.

87. Add. MSS. 40,060, f. 88. In the spring of 1711 Robert Harley had been created Earl of Oxford and appointed Lord Treasurer. After a Whig triumph in the House of Lords in Dec., 1711, he persuaded the Queen to create twelve new (Tory) peers to assist in securing peace terms. Henry St. John, Secretary of State for the North, was created Viscount Bolingbroke in July, 1712.

88. HMC *Fifth Report*, Part I (London, 1876), 359–360.

89. Cushing, p. 18.

90. [Thomas Brown], *A Description of Mr. D——n's Funeral* (London, 1700), p. 4. This account distorts the facts.

91. HMC *Bath* MSS. III, p. 394.

92. *Wit and Mirth: or Pills to Purge Melancholy*, ed. Henry Playford (London, 1700), The Second Part, "Prologue, By Sir John Falstaff," p. 313. Congreve may have written the disparaging comment on modern theatergoers as "washy rogues." "What a washy rogue art thou!" says Foible to her spouse in *The Way of the World*.

93. Thomas Brown, *Amusements Serious and Comical* (London, 1702), p. 50.

94. William Burnaby, *The Reform'd Wife* (London, 1700), Prologue.

95. Thomas D'Urfey, *Wonders in the Sun* (London, 1706), Dedication.

96. NUL Portland (Holles) MSS. Pw 2.571, f. 64.

97. Allen, p. 236.

98. Charles Leslie, *The Rehearsal of Observator, &c*, No. 41 (1705).

99. Spence, I, 51.

100. *An Apology for the Life of Colley Cibber* (London, 1756), I, 244.

101. David Green, *Blenheim Palace* (London, 1951), p. 74.

102. See Vanbrugh, IV, 166–167. Sarah, Duchess of Marlborough, was perhaps interested in Tonson's modest building operations at Barn Elms.

She once made a journey from London to Barnes by barge (summer, 1715?), bringing with her "Two Ladys besides her Self, Ld Carlisle, Ld Clare, Horace Walpole Dr. Samll Garth & Mr. Benson." See Vanbrugh, IV, 63.

103. *The Examiner*, No. 6 (1710). It is not known that Sir Henry F[urnes]e was a member of the Kit-Cat Club. He was a rich alderman and a director of the Bank of England, which was a Whig institution. In 1708 the Bank had assisted the government in its financial difficulties, and its charter was renewed and extended by the Act of 1709. The "Child" is probably Sir Francis Child, the goldsmith banker. H[arle]y was at this date Tory Chancellor of the Exchequer. I cannot accept the suggestion of Allen (p. 50) that Lady H——t is "Lady Harcourt," but in spite of persistent efforts, I have been unable to identify the lady. Possibly, she is Lady Harriet Rialton, afterward Duchess of Marlborough, one of the Kit-Cat toasts, who was "in Pickell for her sins" in 1711 (see *The Wentworth Papers*, p. 214). Tonson may have saved some lady of quality from Grub Street libellers. One of Curll's hack writers, Charles Gildon, went blind from constant writing by candlelight.

104. DUL Clavering MSS., quoted by Holmes, p. 503.

105. HL Stowe MSS. 57, iii, 204, quoted by Holmes, p. 298.

106. Vanbrugh, IV, 8.

107. "The Golden Age Revers'd," in *A New Collection of Poems*, p. 506.

108. Alexander Cunningham, *The History of Great Britain* (London, 1787), I, 280.

109. Bryant Lillywhite, *London Coffee Houses* (London, 1963), p. 288.

110. Holmes, p. 84.

111. George Macaulay Trevelyan, *England under Queen Anne* (London, New York, Toronto, 1948), II, 263.

112. Luttrell, VI, 35.

113. HMC *Downshire* MSS. I, Part II (London, 1924), 885.

114. Burnet, *History*, II, 524.

115. Jonathan Swift, *Journal to Stella*, ed. Harold Williams (Oxford, 1948), II, 415.

116. Oldmixon, *History*, p. 478.

117. [Arthur Mainwaring], *An Excellent New Song, Called Mat's Peace* (London, 1711).

118. HMC *Portland* MSS. V (Norwich, 1899), 338.

119. *Archives du Ministère des Affaires Étrangères, Correspondence Politique d'Angleterre*, Vol. 262, *Supplement*. Quoted by Charles Ken-

neth Eves, *Matthew Prior, Poet and Diplomatist* (New York, 1913), p. 309n.

120. Add. MSS. 28,276, f. 18.

121. Paul J. Dottin in *Notes and Queries*, 12th ser. IX (1921), 482–483.

122. Later on, the Committee of Secrecy (1715) never did have any precise evidence against Prior, although he was tried and kept in custody for some time for having been "an agent and instrument of evil and traitorous Counsellors," and his name was never cleared.

123. See L. G. Wickham Legg, "Extracts from Jacobite Correspondence, 1712–1714," in *EHR*, XXX (1915), 501–518, and by the same author, *Matthew Prior* (Cambridge, 1915).

124. *Letters and Correspondence, Public and Private, of the Right Honourable Henry St. John Lord Visc. Bolingbroke,* ed. Gilbert Parke (London, 1798), IV, 376.

125. *Ibid.,* IV, 544.

126. Steele, *Correspondence,* p. 292.

127. *Ibid.,* p. 293.

128. *Ibid.,* p. 302.

129. Boyer, p. 681.

130. John Campbell, second Duke of Argyll, who had served in the wars under Marlborough, was the leader of the Scottish Presbyterians. In 1715 he defeated in Scotland the adherents of the exiled House of Stuart.

131. *The Wentworth Papers,* p. 414.

132. Not long after the accession of the King, Halifax was made First Lord of the Treasury, to be succeeded in this office by Walpole, and was also created an earl. Wharton was made Lord Privy Seal and was created a marquess. Stanhope was made Secretary of State for the South, later for the North, and was created a baron, later an earl. Walpole was made Paymaster General of the Forces, Pulteney Secretary at War, Somerset once more Master of the Horse, Berkeley First Lord of the Admiralty, Newcastle Lord Chamberlain. Temple was made a baron, later a viscount, and Vanbrugh and Steele were knighted.

133. Steele, *Correspondence,* p. 236.

134. Add. MSS. 28,275, f. 82.

135. Blackmore, p. 122.

136. Vanbrugh, IV, 8.

137. FSL C.c.1 (42).

138. FSL C.c.1 (18).

139. Half of the members had died by 1725. Vanbrugh's death occurred in 1726.

140. Vanbrugh, IV, 167.

CHAPTER IV: *Jacob's Ladder to Fame*

1. On a blank page of the manuscript of the "Pastorals," Pope listed the names of those who had seen the poem. Among the Kit-Cats, besides Walsh and Congreve, were Mainwaring, Garth, Halifax, and Wharton.

2. *The Correspondence of Alexander Pope*, ed. George Sherburn (Oxford, 1956), I, 17.

3. *Ibid.*, p. 50n.

4. *Ibid.*, p. 50.

5. Pope to Henry Cromwell, Nov. 1, 1708, *ibid.*, pp. 51–52.

6. *Ibid.*, p. 59.

7. *Ibid.*, pp. 60–61.

8. *Ibid.*, p. 62.

9. Spence, I, 208.

10. *Examen Poeticum: Being the Third Part of Miscellany Poems* (London, 1693), Dedication.

11. Dryden, *Juvenal and Persius*, "To Mr. Dryden, on His Translation of Persius."

12. Edmund Gosse, *Life of William Congreve* (London, 1888), p. 56.

13. *The Annual Miscellany For the Year 1694* (London, 1694), p. 180.

14. *Diary of Mary Countess Cowper, 1714–1720* (London, 1864), pp. 23–24. As Mary Clavering, Lady Cowper had been one of Congreve's Kit-Cat toasts in 1703.

15. Allen, p. 234. *Luctus Britannici* was edited by Henry Playford and Abel Roper.

16. First printed in Charles Gildon's *A New Miscellany of Original Poems* (London, 1701).

17. Richard Steele, *Poetical Miscellanies* (London, 1714), Dedication.

18. William Congreve, *A Pindarique Ode . . . to the King* (London, 1695), p. 4.

19. William Congreve, *A Pindarique Ode . . . to the Queen* (London, 1706), p. 5.

20. Johnson, II, "Congreve," 232.

21. *Diary and Correspondence of John Evelyn, F. R. S.*, ed. William Bray (London, 1891), III, 369.

22. *William Congreve*, ed. Hodges, p. 21.

23. *Ibid.*, pp. 16–17 and 104–105.

24. *Ibid.*, p. 98

25. *Ibid.*, p. 108.
26. Pope, *Correspondence*, II, 133.
27. *William Congreve*, ed. Hodges, p. 136.
28. Dryden, *Dramatick Works*, ed. Congreve, I, Dedication.
29. See *The Poetical Works of John Gay*, ed. G. C. Faber (London, 1926), p. 166.
30. William Congreve, *The Tears of Amaryllis for Amyntas* (London, 1703), "To the Reader."
31. William Congreve, *Five Plays* (London [1710]), printed by H. Hills.
32. *The Works of Mr. William Congreve* (London, 1710), I, Preface.
33. Prior, *Literary Works*, II, 831–832.
34. *The Gentleman's Journal*, Feb., 1692, p. 5.
35. *Miscellany Poems Upon Several Occasions*, ed. Charles Gildon (London, 1692), p. 7.
36. Prior, *Literary Works*, II, 827.
37. *Ibid.*, I, 85.
38. *Ibid.*, II, 853.
39. HMC *Downshire* MSS. I, Part I, 465.
40. Matthew Prior, *To the King, An Ode on His Majesty's Arrival in Holland* (London, 1695), p. 11.
41. *The Gentleman's Magazine*, N.Ser. II (1834), 464.
42. HMC *Downshire* MSS. I, Part II, 551.
43. Prior, *Literary Works*, II, 896.
44. *The Complete Works of Algernon Charles Swinburne*, ed. Sir Edmund Gosse and Thomas James Wise, *Prose Works*, IV (London and New York, 1926), 140.
45. Add. MSS. 40,060, ff. 59–60.
46. See Ralph Straus, *The Unspeakable Curll* (London, 1927).
47. *The Daily Courant*, No. 1491 (1707).
48. *Ibid.*, No. 1497 (1707).
49. *Ibid.*, No. 1502 (1707).
50. *Ibid.*, No. 1597 (1707).
51. [Matthew Prior], *Poems on Several Occasions* (London, 1707), "Advertisement, From the Publisher."
52. Prior to Halifax, Feb. 4, 1707, Add. MSS. 7121, ff. 49–50.
53. [Matthew Prior], *Poems on Several Occasions* (London, 1709), Preface.
54. For example, in "The Ladle" "Fate's Commands" becomes "Tate's Commands," in the badly mangled "An English Padlock" "Staple" becomes "Steeple," and in "A Simile" "Pindar" becomes "Pindus."
55. Prior, *Literary Works*, II, 887.

56. *The London Gazette*, No. 5418 (1716).

57. Curll published with Gosling and Pemberton *The Carpenter of Oxford, or, The Miller's Tale, From Chaucer . . . To which are added, Two Imitations of Chaucer, I. Susannah and the Two Elders. II. Earl Robert's Mice. By Matthew Prior, Esq.* (London, 1712).

58. *The Works of the Right Honourable Joseph Addison, Esq.*, ed. Thomas Tickell (London, 1721), I, Preface.

59. Third Miscellany, p. 248.

60. Fourth Miscellany, pp. 318–322.

61. *The Letters of Joseph Addison*, ed. Walter Graham (Oxford, 1941), p. 3.

62. Joseph Addison, *A Poem to His Majesty. Presented to the Lord Keeper* (London, 1695), p. 3.

63. Dryden, *Virgil*, "Postscript to the Reader," p. 624.

64. FSL Tonson MSS. C.c.1 (42).

65. Addison, *Works*, I, Preface.

66. Joseph Addison, *The Campaign* (London, 1705), p. 14.

67. Joseph Addison, *Remarks on Several Parts of Italy* (London, 1705), Dedication and Preface.

68. Addison, *Works*, I, Preface.

69. Peter Smithers, *Joseph Addison* (Oxford, 1954), p. 103.

70. Donald F. Bond, "The First Printing of the *Spectator*," in *MP*, XLVII (1950), 165.

71. *The Lucubrations of Isaac Bickerstaff Esq.* (London, 1711), IV, Preface.

72. For a valuable review of the probable procedure followed in printing *The Spectator*, see *The Spectator*, ed. Bond, I, xxvii–xxix.

73. Steele, *Correspondence*, p. 461n.

74. HL MS. H. M. 20052.

75. *The Spectator*, I, No. 1 (1711), 5.

76. *Ibid.*, I, No. 10 (1711), 44.

77. *Ibid.*, p. xxvi.

78. For the vogue of *The Spectator* see Alexandre Beljame, *Men of Letters and The English Public in the Eighteenth Century 1660–1744*, trans. E. O. Lorimer, ed. Bonamy Dobrée (London, 1948), pp. 311–314.

79. *The Guardian* (London, 1714), I, "The Publisher to the Reader."

80. *Ibid.*, No. 59 (1713).

81. HMC *Seventh Report* (London, 1879), Part I, Appendix, 239.

82. [Giles Jacob?], *Memoirs of the Life of the Right Honourable Joseph Addison, Esq.* (London, 1719), p. 40.

83. Pope, *Correspondence*, I, 175.

84. Smithers, p. 260.
85. *Ibid.*, p. 253.
86. See Spence, I, 79, for Tonson's comment on this subject.
87. Elizabeth "Ousley" may have had as a nurse in infancy a certain Dorothea Ousley, who managed secret confinements as an agent for Richard Savage, fourth Earl Rivers, and perhaps for others. See Johnson, II, "Savage," p. 325n and p. 439.
88. See Add. MSS. 28,276, ff. 1–2 for receipts signed by Elizabeth Tonson for quarterly payments of £6 from her brother in 1706, 1707, and 1708.
89. Elizabeth Tonson was buried on March 6 in the church of St. Mary Le Strand, which had become the parish church of the Tonsons. The registers of this church are kept in the Archives Department, Westminster Public Library.
90. Elizabeth "Ousley" was married in St. Paul's Cathedral on May 14, 1720. See *Publications of the Harleian Society*, XXVI (1899), 55.
91. *The Epistolary Correspondence of Sir Richard Steele*, ed. John Nichols (London, 1787), pp. 261–264. Mrs. Aynston's eldest grandson received Steele's family papers from Steele's legitimate daughter Elizabeth, Lady Trevor.
92. *Mr. Steele's Apology for Himself and His Writings* (London, 1714), p. 80.
93. *Ibid.*
94. *Ibid.*, p. 48.
95. Richard Steele, *The Tender Husband* (London, 1705), Dedication.
96. [John Gay], *The Present State of Wit* (London, 1711), p. 12.
97. *Ibid.*, p. 21.
98. Addison, *Letters*, p. 280.
99. Steele, *Apology*, p. xiv.
100. Colley Cibber, *Ximena* (London, 1719), "To Sir Richard Steele," pp. xi–xii.
101. Thomas Somerville, *The History of Great Britain during the Reign of Queen Anne* (London, 1798), Appendix, No. XXXVI.
102. Steele, *Correspondence*, p. 251.
103. Steele's *Apology* had been advertised in *The Daily Courant* (No. 3975) on July 21, 1714, as to be printed "within a few days."
104. Steele, *Apology*, p. 88.
105. See Steele, *Correspondence*, p. 236n.
106. Pope, *Correspondence*, I, 193.
107. Steele, *Correspondence*, p. 47.

108. Add. MSS. 28,275, f. 57.

109. Joseph Addison, *The Drummer* (London, 1722), "To Mr. Congreve."

CHAPTER V: *The Routine of Publishing*

1. For the more conservative estimate see the excellent unpublished dissertation (Yale, 1936) of Hale Sturges, "The Publishing Career of Jacob Tonson, the Elder, 1678–1720," p. 1. The larger estimate is that of Logan O. Cowgill of Washington, D. C., a Tonson collector.

2. See Sturges (microfilmed dissertation), pp. 41–293, and Papali, pp. 144–193.

3. See Macdonald, *Dryden*, and Wright and Spears, *Prior*.

4. For this and subsequent legislation see Marjorie Plant, *The English Book Trade* (London, 1939) and P. M. Handover, *Printing in London from 1476 to Modern Times* (Cambridge, Mass., 1960).

5. See Lawrence Hanson, *Government and the Press, 1695–1763* (Oxford and London, 1936).

6. This act secured to present owners the copyright of works already printed for a further twenty-one years from April 1, 1710. The authors of books not yet printed were to have sole printing rights (which they might assign to another) for fourteen years. After this period the copyright was to return to the author, if living, for another fourteen years.

7. PRO Hamilton 284/283, *Tonson vs. Dickinson*.

8. Add. MSS. 28,276, f. 34.

9. ASO Luttrell MSS. CLXXXL, ff. 117–119. I am indebted to Mr. Esmond S. de Beer for calling these newsletters to my attention.

10. London was in a state of panic over the Popish Plot, fabricated for his own gain by Titus Oates, who produced false evidence, widely believed (but not by the King), of a plot to assassinate Charles II and establish a Roman Catholic government with the Duke of York as King.

11. Thomas Blood, known as Colonel Blood, was an Irish adventurer who had committed daring crimes, including an unsuccessful attempt to steal the Crown jewels. He died Aug. 24 and was buried Aug. 26, 1680. After a sham funeral had been alleged, his body was exhumed, identified, and reburied.

12. Elizabeth Cellier, a noted midwife, had already been tried for treason for alleged complicity in the Popish Plot. She had been acquitted but had written a vindication of herself which led to a second trial for libel. She was found guilty, fined, and required to stand three times in the pillory.

13. Luttrell, I, 54–55.

14. ASO Luttrell MSS. CLXXXI, f. 119.

15. *The Works of Mr. Thomas Otway* (London, 1712), II, 394. See Roswell Gray Ham, *Otway and Lee: Biography from a Baroque Age* (New Haven, 1931), pp. 208–209. Ham supports Otway's authorship of the Prologue.

16. Quoted by Ham, p. 204.

17. *The Works of Aphra Behn,* ed. Montague Summers (London, 1915), I, lvii.

18. The play for which Mrs. Behn wrote the Epilogue was the anonymous *Romulus and Hersilia,* acted in Aug., 1682. See George Woodcock, *The Incomparable Aphra* (London [1948]), pp. 161–162.

19. "A Voyage to the Isle of Love," the long poem with which this volume closes, paraphrased from the Abbé Tallement's French text.

20. *The Gentleman's Magazine,* N.Ser. V (1836), 482.

21. *Ibid.,* p. 483.

22. See Jacob Tonson, *Jacob Tonson, In Ten Letters by and about Him,* ed. Sarah Lewis Carol Clapp (Austin, Texas, 1948), p. 12.

23. Aphra Behn, *Poems Upon Several Occasions: With a Voyage to the Island of Love* (London, 1684).

24. Tonson, *Ten Letters,* p. 11.

25. *Sylvae,* pp. 468–474. John Oldham, famous in his own time for his *Satires upon the Jesuits* (1681), died at the country seat of his patron, the Earl of Kingston, in 1683.

26. Tonson, *Ten Letters,* p. 12.

27. Prior's matchless "To a Child of Quality," published in Tonson's Fifth Miscellany and never collected by Prior, is a case in point.

28. *Examen Poeticum,* "The Bookseller to the Reader."

29. Thomas Newton, "The Life of John Milton," in *Paradise Lost* (London, 1759), p. xlvi.

30. Tonson's other subscription editions were: Dryden's *Virgil* (1697); four volumes of Cambridge Editions of Latin classics (1699–1702); Saint-Évremond's *Oeuvres* (1705), 2 vols.; *Caesar,* ed. Samuel Clarke (1712); Addison and Steele's *The Spectator* (1712–1715), 8 vols.; *Opera et Fragmenta Veterum Poetarum Latinorum,* ed. Michael Maittaire (1713), 2 vols. (published with others); *Spenser,* ed. John Hughes (1715), 6 vols.; *The English Works of . . . Dr. Isaac Barrow,* ed. Archbishop Tillotson (1716), 2 vols.; Joseph Trapp's *Aeneis* (1718–1720), 2 vols.; Laurence Echard's *The History of England* (1718), Vols. II and III; and Prior's *Poems on Several Occasions* (1718).

31. FSL Tonson MSS. C.c.1 (3).

32. Martin Lister's *A Journey to Paris in the Year 1698,* dedicated to Somers, ran to three editions by 1699. Pleased by the book's sale, Tonson

wrote to Lister on March 16, 1699: "I own my self indebted to you, & you shall have what satisfaction you please." See Bodl. MSS. Lister, III, f. 191.

33. Luttrell, IV, 379. The entry is for May 12, 1698.

34. [Daniel Defoe], *The Pacificator, A Poem* (London, 1700), p. 6.

35. Tonson published Blackmore's *King Arthur* (1697) and with Robert Gibson *Tully's Five Books De Finibus*, with a "Recommendatory Preface" by Jeremy Collier (1702).

36. George Stepney, *A Poem Dedicated to the Blessed Memory of Her Late Gracious Majesty Queen Mary* (London, 1695).

37. *The Gentleman's Magazine*, N.Ser. VIII (1837), 362–364.

38. NPG Tonson MSS.

39. FSL Tonson MSS., C.c.1 (8).

40. See the title page of *The Annual Miscellany For the Year 1694.*

41. See the title page of the first edition of Lister's *A Journey to Paris* (London, 1698).

42. *William Congreve*, ed. Hodges, p. 14.

43. *Ibid.*, p. 54.

44. *Ibid.*, pp. 104–105 and 106–107.

45. NPG Tonson MSS.

46. See C. J. Barrett, *The History of Barn Elms and the Kit-Cat Club* (London, 1889).

47. SP 44. 167. 424.

48. FSL Tonson MSS. C.c.1 (43).

49. Vanbrugh, IV, 7.

50. *Ibid.*, p. 11.

51. FSL Tonson MSS. C.c.1 (38).

52. Addison, *Letters*, pp. 43–44.

53. *Ibid.*, p. 40.

54. FSL Tonson MSS. C.c.1 (38).

55. *Ibid.*, C.c.1 (35) (36) (37).

56. *Ibid.*, C.c.1 (11).

57. *Ibid.*, C.c.1 (47) (48).

58. See I. H. Van Eeghen, *Die Amsterdamse Boekhandel 1680–1725,* I (Amsterdam, 1960), 124.

59. See Talbot Baines Reed, *A History of the Old English Letter Foundaries*, rev. A. F. Johnson (London [1952]), p. 209.

60. It was Lintot, who probably offered a higher price for them, who published Rowe's last plays, *The Tragedy of Jane Shore* (1714) and *Lady Jane Grey* (1715).

61. See above, p. 92.

62. See P. M. Handover, *A History of The London Gazette* (London, 1965), p. 50.

63. PRO Patent Rolls, 6 George I. Part 3, No. 17. On Oct. 12, 1722, Tonson the Elder assigned to his nephew his half share in this patent for £1,235 9s. and the yearly sum of £200 during the remainder of his life. See FSL Tonson MSS. C.c.1 (60).

64. See Septimus Rivington, *The Publishing Family of Rivington* (London, 1919), p. 57.

65. FSL MS. S.a.160.

66. On Oct. 14, 1710, the following advertisement appeared in *The Tatler*: "The shop in the Possession of Jacob Tonson at Gray's Inn Gate is to be lett." Tonson's new shop was at the corner of Dutchy Lane and the Strand (south side), a few doors from Somerset House, then an old, privately owned building. Tonson also had a house in Dutchy Lane at the back of the house that faced the Strand. See *The Gentleman's Magazine*, 12th ser. VII (1920), 321–322.

67. Essex died in 1710 at the age of forty.

68. In spite of his mammoth labors, Echard was sunk in debt by 1717. At Tonson's request, William Wake, Archbishop of Canterbury, interceded at Court in 1717 for aid for "this Good man." See Add. MSS. 28,275, f. 31.

69. Van Eeghen, I, 124.

70. Temple Stanyan was the younger brother of Abraham Stanyan.

71. Straus, p. 10.

72. *Ibid.*, p. 21.

73. *The London Gazette* (from June 10 to June 13, 1710).

74. George Seton, fifth Earl of Winton, had been impeached for his share in the Jacobite Rebellion of 1715. When tried, he was found guilty, but he subsequently escaped from the Tower.

75. Straus, pp. 65–67. Curll finally stood in the pillory in 1728 for publishing obscene books, on which occasion he received an ovation from the mob. His feud with Pope gave him considerable satisfaction.

76. See below, pp. 123–124.

77. Tickell's *A Poem to His Excellency The Lord Privy-Seal, on the Prospect of Peace* (1712), published by Tonson, had sold well and had six editions.

78. For the Tickell-Tonson agreement and the subsequent rift between Pope and Addison see Richard Eustace Tickell, *Thomas Tickell and the Eighteenth Century Poets* (London, 1931), pp. 36–49.

79. See RFL MS. 417/10. On Sept. 17, 1718, Tonson assigned to his nephew all of the copyrights or parts of copyrights which he owned sep-

arately. The legal document lists works by twenty-three authors and includes all of the Miscellanies and Tonson's half shares in copyrights formerly owned by Henry Herringman and by George and Mary Wells.

80. It was Samuel Buckley who published *The Universal History of the World*, translated from the Latin text of Jacques Auguste De Thou in 1733, in seven volumes.

81. HMC *Bath* MSS. III, 469.

CHAPTER VI: *Eminent Publisher*

1. Pope, *Correspondence*, I, 373–374.
2. See *The Gentleman's Journal*, May, 1692, p. 25.
3. Dryden, *Juvenal and Persius*, pp. li–lii.
4. *Ibid.*, p. lii.
5. *Ibid.*, p. xxxix.
6. *Ibid.*, p. 191.
7. *Ibid.*, p. 204.
8. *Ibid.* (*Persius*), p. 70.
9. *Ibid.*, p. xxxi.
10. *Ibid.*, p. xxxiii.
11. *Ibid.*, p. xxxvii.
12. *Ibid.*, pp. xxxvii–xxxviii.
13. *Virgil*, "Aeneis," Dedication.
14. *Ibid.*, "Postscript to the Reader," p. 621.
15. FSL Tonson MSS. C.c.1 (22).
16. Dryden, *Letters*, p. 94.
17. Mark Van Doren, *John Dryden* (a reissue, Bloomington, 1960), p. 255.
18. Elizabeth Nitchie, *Vergil and The English Poets* (New York, 1919), p. 152.
19. See Henry V. S. Ogden and Margaret S. Ogden, *English Taste in Landscape in the Seventeenth Century* (Ann Arbor, 1955).
20. Addison, *Letters*, p. 43.
21. John Watts (c. 1700–1763) had an important printing house in Little Queen Street, Lincoln's Inn Fields.
22. William Thomas Lowndes, *The Bibliographer's Manual of English Literature* (London, 1885), I, 344.
23. See *Lucretii Cari De Rerum Natura* (London, 1713) for statement of this license.
24. For Johnson's comment see *Boswell's Life of Johnson*, ed. George Birkbeck Hill, rev. L. F. Powell (Oxford, 1934), IV, 2.
25. Bodl. MS. Montagu d. 18, f. 4.
26. *The London Gazette*, No. 5217 (1714).

27. Richard Beale Davis, *George Sandys, Poet-Adventurer* (London [1955]), p. 204.

28. *Ibid.*, p. 224.

29. For Dryden's previously printed translations from the *Metamorphoses* see the Third Miscellany, the Fifth Miscellany, and *Fables*; for Addison's, Tate's, and Stonestreet's see the Fifth Miscellany.

30. [Jonathan Swift and Alexander Pope], *Miscellanies in Prose and Verse* (London, 1727), IV, 122–127.

31. Spence, I, 333.

32. This manuscript, long in the possession of the Tonsons of Bayfordbury, is now in the Pierpont Morgan Library in New York.

33. Thomas Rymer, *Tragedies of the Last Age Considered* (London, 1678), p. 143.

34. Newton, "Life of Milton," p. xlviii.

35. See Samuel Leigh Sotheby, *Ramblings in the Elucidation of the Autograph of Milton* (London, 1861), pp. 196–204.

36. David Masson, *The Life of John Milton* (London, 1880), VI, 786.

37. John Milton, *Paradise Lost* (London, 1711), Dedication.

38. *The Works of Mr. William Shakespear*, ed. Nicholas Rowe (London, 1709), I, Dedication.

39. Johnson, II, "Rowe," 71.

40. *The Plays of William Shakespeare*, ed. Samuel Johnson (London, 1765), I, Preface.

41. David Nichol Smith, *Shakespeare in the Eighteenth Century* (Oxford, 1928), p. 33.

42. See Thomas Rymer, *A Short View of Tragedy* (London, 1693), pp. 86f.

43. *Works of Shakespear*, ed. Rowe, I, "Some Account," iii.

44. *Ibid.*, p. xxxi.

45. *Ibid.*, p. xviii.

46. *Ibid.*, p. xix.

47. *Ibid.*, p. xxiv.

48. *Ibid.*, p. xxxiii.

49. Johnson, II, "Rowe," 71.

50. Smith, p. 31.

51. Shakespeare, *Plays*, ed. Johnson, I, Preface. See the account of Rowe in Samuel Schoenbaum, *Shakespeare's Lives* (Oxford, 1970), pp. 129–135.

52. The six plays were: *The London Prodigal, The Life and Death of Thomas Lord Cromwell, Sir John Oldcastle, The Puritan, The Tragedy of Locrine*, and *A Yorkshire Tragedy*. Pope rejected these plays as spurious,

but also questioned Shakespeare's authorship of *Pericles* and parts of certain other plays.

53. *The Daily Courant*, No. 2392 (1709).

54. *The Tatler*, No. 57 (1709).

55. "Remarks on the Plays of Shakespear," in *The Works of Mr. William Shakespear*, "Volume the Seventh" (London, 1710), p. 43.

56. "An Essay on the . . . Stage," *ibid.*, p. 2.

57. FSL MS. S.a.163. This manuscript is a quarto sheet, written about 1740, headed, "Paid the Editors of Shakespear."

58. *The Works of Mr. Edmund Spenser* (London, 1715), I, Dedication.

59. *Ibid.*, p. xxvi.

60. *Ibid.*, p. liii.

61. *Ibid.*, pp. ci–cii.

62. *Ibid.*, pp. lviii–lix.

63. *Ibid.*, p. lxi.

64. *The Correspondence of Jonathan Swift*, ed. F. Elrington Ball (London, 1910–1914), II, 360.

65. Pope, *Correspondence*, I, 521.

66. HMC *Bath* MSS., III, 450.

67. Harleian MSS. 3780, f. 342 and 344.

68. Swift, *Correspondence*, III, 8.

69. *Ibid.*, p. 4.

70. Matthew Prior, *Poems on Several Occasions. A New Edition With some Additions which are not in the folio Edition* (London, 1720), pp. 449–451. Many pieces, *all* of which are in the 1718 edition, were marked with an asterisk in the table of contents as "not printed in the former Editions."

71. *The Conversation* was printed by Jacob junior in 1720. *Down-Hall* was one of Curll's happier (unauthorized) grabs, published in 1723, after Prior's death. According to the title page, this whimsical ballad was "Printed for J. Roberts" (one of Curll's "sleeping" partners).

72. *Poems on Several Occasions* (1718 edition), p. 319.

73. *Ibid.*, Preface to "Solomon," p. 390.

74. *Selected Poems of Matthew Prior*, ed. Austin Dobson (London, 1889), Preface, pp. xi–xiii.

CHAPTER VII: *Tonson and His Public*

1. Swift, *Correspondence*, III, 117–118. Dryden translated these lines ("Aeneis," I, 796) as: "We Tyrians are not so devoid of sense / Nor so remote from Phoebus' influence."

2. *The Spectator*, V, Appendix IV, 225.

3. *Ibid.*, II, No. 221 (1711), 359–360.

4. Beljame, p. 120.

5. *The Poems of Jonathan Swift*, ed. Harold Williams (Oxford, 1937), II, "On Poetry," 648.

6. "A Note on Dryden's Criticism," by E. M. W. Tillyard, in Richard Foster Jones et al., *The Seventeenth Century* (Stanford, 1951), p. 334.

7. *The Spectator*, II, No. 150 (1711), 113.

8. Spence, I, 303–304.

9. *The Dunciad. An Heroic Poem* (Dublin, 1728), p. 9.

10. See *The Works of Alexander Pope*, ed. Whitwell Elwin and William John Courthope (New York, 1967), VIII, 235 and 285n.

11. *Ibid.*, IV, 279–281n. These excerpts are quoted from "The Progress of Dulness," Pope's first manuscript (not extant) of *The Dunciad*. Jonathan Richardson the Younger added the quotations as marginalia in a copy of the 1728 edition of *The Dunciad* which is now in the Berg Collection in the New York Public Library. See George Sherburn, *The Early Career of Alexander Pope* (New York, 1963), p. 304, for conjectures as to the date (c. 1725 or earlier?) of Pope's manuscript.

12. *The Dunciad* (1728 edition), p. 18.

13. *Alexander Pope, The Dunciad Variorum*, ed. Robert Kilburn Root (Princeton, N. J., 1929), p. 28.

14. *The Works of Alexander Pope* (London, 1741), V, 130.

15. *The Dunciad* (1728), p. 3.

16. Bonamy Dobrée, *John Dryden* (London, New York, Toronto, 1956), p. 36.

17. Quoted by William Riley Parker, *Milton's Contemporary Reputation* (Columbus, Ohio, 1940), p. 52.

18. Thomas Tyers, *An Historical Essay on Mr. Addison* (London, 1783), p. 42.

19. Gay, *The Present State of Wit*, p. 20.

20. These papers appeared once a week from Feb. to May, 1712, beginning with No. 303 and ending with No. 369.

21. *The Spectator*, III, No. 369 (1712), 392.

22. *Ibid.*, II, No. 261 (1711), 520.

23. Spence, I, 333.

24. *The Spectator*, II, No. 279 (1712), 587.

25. By Eustace Budgell as Mr. Spectator.

26. *The Spectator*, III, No. 359 (1712), 345.

27. *Milton's Paradise Lost*, ed. Richard Bentley (London, 1732), Preface.

28. Bodl. MS. Eng. letters c. 129, ff. 118-119.

29. This letter includes also Tonson's account of his frustrated attempt, as a young apprentice, to call on Milton. See above, p. 13.
30. Bodl. MS. Eng. letters c. 129, f. 123.
31. [David Mallet], *Of Verbal Criticism. An Epistle to Mr. Pope* (London, 1733), p. 10.
32. John Dryden, *Of Dramatick Poesie, An Essay* (London, 1684), p. 33.
33. Johnson, I, "Dryden," 412.
34. *The Spectator*, II, No. 141 (1711), 58. The quotation is from the Prologue to Dryden and D'Avenant's *The Tempest*.
35. Smith, *Shakespeare in the Eighteenth Century*, p. 35.
36. *Eighteenth Century Essays on Shakespeare*, ed. D. Nichol Smith (2nd ed.; Oxford, 1963), p. xxxviii.
37. Lewis Theobald, *Shakespeare Restored* (London, 1726).
38. Shakespeare, *Plays*, ed. Johnson, I, Preface.
39. *Juvenal and Persius*, ed. Dryden, "Discourse concerning Satire," p. viii.
40. Spence, I, 74.
41. *The Spectator*, IV, No. 540 (1712), 428–431. Bond (428n) suggests Steele or Hughes as the author.
42. Spenser's *Faerie Queene*, ed. John Upton (London, 1758), I, Preface, xxi.
43. William Randolph Mueller, *Spenser's Critics* ([New York], 1959), p. 6.
44. Thomas Warton, *Observations on the Faerie Queene of Spenser* (London, 1754), p. 13.
45. Matthew Prior, *An Ode Humbly Inscrib'd to the Queen* (London, 1706), Preface.
46. *Fables*, Preface.
47. *Ibid.*
48. "An Account of the Greatest English Poets," in the Fourth Miscellany, p. 318.
49. See Caroline F. E. Spurgeon, *Five Hundred Years of Chaucer Criticism and Allusion (1357–1900)*, Chaucer Society, 2nd ser. LV (London [1924]), I, xliv.
50. Johnson, I, "Dryden," 455.
51. Spence, I, 179.
52. Pope also wrote *The Temple of Fame. A Vision* (1711), based on Chaucer's *Hous of Fame*.
53. Joseph Warton, *An Essay on the Genius and Writings of Pope* (London, 1782), II, 7.

54. Spurgeon, I, 353n. This edition was John Urry's *The Works of Geoffrey Chaucer* (London, 1721).

55. *Observations on the Faerie Queene*, p. 141.

56. Spurgeon, I, liv.

57. Spence, I, 331.

58. *The Spectator*, I, No. 37 (1711), 154.

59. *Ibid.*, IV, No. 512 (1712), 318. Johnson took exception to such faint praise. "There is no need to inquire," he remonstrated, "why these verses were read, which to all the attractions of wit, elegance, and harmony added the cooperation of all the factious passions, and filled every mind with triumph or resentment." Johnson, I, "Dryden," 374.

60. *The Spectator*, I, No. 40 (1711), 170.

61. *Ibid.*, p. 172.

62. *Ibid.*, II, No. 279 (1712), 588.

63. *Ibid.*, III, No. 345 (1712), 285–286.

64. *Alexander Pope*, Twickenham Edition, IV, ed. John Butt (London [1939]), "An Epistle to Dr. Arbuthnot," 110.

65. Spence, I, 24.

66. *The Works of Pope*, ed. William Warburton (London, 1751), IV, 18n.

67. *Alexander Pope*, IV, "The First Epistle of the Second Book of Horace," 217.

68. FSL Tonson MSS. C.c.1 (74).

69. *The Spectator*, III, No. 290 (1712), 31–33.

70. *Ibid.*, No. 335 (1712), 239–242.

71. *The Post Boy*, No. 2805 (1713) and *The Guardian*, No. 44 (1713).

72. *Pax, Pax, Pax; or a Pacific Post Boy*, No. 2808 (1713).

73. Pope, *Correspondence*, I, 62.

74. See Tonson, *Ten Letters*, pp. 9–12. The manuscript of Tonson's letter to his nephew on this subject is in the Rare Books Collection of the University of Texas, where four other letters from Tonson to his nephew are preserved.

75. See *T. Lucretius Carus* (2nd ed.; London, 1683). The imitation of Dryden, beginning "How happy had our English tongue been made," is the second of the nine congratulatory poems prefixed to the translation; the imitation of Waller, "What all men wisht tho few cou'd hope to see," is the eighth.

76. See *The Second Part of Mr. Waller's Poems* (London, 1690), pp. 54–56. Tonson, who had acquired a share in the copyright of Waller's poems, hastened to publish, also in 1690, Waller's *The Maid's Tragedy*

Altered. With some other Pieces, with a publisher's note protesting the pirated edition.

77. Second Miscellany, pp. 468–476.

78. See *Poems Upon Several Occasions.* Tonson's is the fifth of the nine congratulatory poems prefixed to Mrs. Behn's poems.

79. Dunton, p. 293.

80. Spence, I, 208.

81. Tonson to his nephew, Dec. 17, 1727, Bodl. MS. Eng. letters, c. 129, f. 15. Since *An Epistle to . . . Richard Earl of Burlington* was not published until 1731, Tonson must have read a manuscript version of it. In the 1735 edition of Pope's *Works* the poem was published as "Epistle IV, Of the Use of Riches." Edward Young's *The Universal Passion* was published anonymously in 1725.

82. Bodl. MS. Eng. letters, c. 129, f. 104. John Oldmixon's *The History of England During the Reigns of the Royal House of Stuart* was published in 1730.

83. Bodl. MS. Eng. letters, c. 129, f. 118. Mallet's *Eurydice* was a theatrical success in 1731 and was published in that year. James Thomson's *The Seasons* was published in 1730, having been preceded by *Winter* (1726), *Summer* (1727), and *Spring* (1728).

84. Bodl. MS. Eng. letters, c. 129, f. 22.

85. *Ibid.,* f. 105.

86. Johnson, I, "Dryden," 418.

87. *Ibid.,* II, "Addison," 149–150.

CHAPTER VIII: *Retirement*

1. The Mississippi Scheme was a new stock company, with headquarters in Paris, manipulated by John Law, a Scottish financier. Large fortunes were made by investors before the scheme collapsed in 1720.

2. Vanbrugh, *Works,* IV, 111–112. On Jan. 14, 1719, Vanbrugh had married Henrietta Maria Yarburgh, daughter of Colonel James Yarburgh.

3. *Ibid.,* p. 113.

4. *Ibid.,* p. 114.

5. *Ibid.* This letter and three subsequent letters which Tonson wrote to Vanbrugh have not been preserved.

6. See *The Thursday's Journal,* No. 11 (1719); *The Weekly Packet,* No. 380 (1719); and *The Original Weekly Journal* (Oct. 17, 1719).

7. See *The White-hall Evening Post,* No. 174 (1719), and *The Orphan Reviv'd,* No. 50 (1719).

8. Vanbrugh, IV, 120.

9. *Ibid.,* pp. 121–123.

10. *Ibid.,* pp. 124–125.

11. *Ibid.*, pp. 125–126.
12. Add. MSS. 28,275, f. 502.
13. *Ibid.*, f. 72.
14. *Ibid.*, f. 74.
15. The manuscript is defective.
16. Add. MSS. 28,275, ff. 256–257.
17. *Ibid.*, f. 152.
18. *Ibid.*, f. 97.
19. *Ibid.*, f. 99. In a later, undated letter (*ibid.*, f. 471) to Jacob junior, Clarke begged the favor of a line or two to inform him whether Tonson was living in town or in the country.
20. Bodl. MS. Eng. letters c. 129, f. 21.
21. FSL Tonson MSS. C.c.1 (62).
22. *Ibid.*, C.c.1 (40).
23. Add. MSS. 28,275, f. 110. The Duke of Newcastle had married in 1717 Lady Henrietta Godolphin, daughter of Francis Godolphin, second Earl of Godolphin.
24. *Ibid.*, f. 110 and f. 197.
25. *Ibid.*, f. 129.
26. *Ibid.*, f. 197.
27. *Ibid.*, f. 146.
28. *Ibid.*, f. 170.
29. *Ibid.*, f. 182.
30. *Ibid.*, f. 258.
31. *Ibid.*, f. 158.
32. *Ibid.*, f. 190.
33. Bodl. MS. Eng. letters c. 129, f. 29.
34. *Ibid.*, f. 65.
35. *Ibid.*, ff. 25–26 and 29–30.
36. *Ibid.*, f. 110.
37. *Ibid.*, f. 30.
38. *Ibid.*, f. 39.
39. *Ibid.*, f. 43.
40. Tonson, *Ten Letters*, p. 14.
41. *Ibid.*, p. 15.
42. Bodl. MS. Eng. letters c. 129, f. 23.
43. *Ibid.*, f. 125.
44. *Ibid.*, f. 22.
45. Tonson, *Ten Letters*, p. 12.
46. Bodl. MS. Eng. letters c. 129, f. 36.
47. *Ibid.*, f. 79.
48. *Ibid.*, f. 103.

49. *Ibid.*, f. 106.

50. *Ibid.*, f. 33.

51. Add. MSS. 28,275, f. 122.

52. *Ibid.*, f. 162. Tonson was still a justice of the peace at eighty-one.

53. Bodl. MS. Eng. letters c. 129, f. 35.

54. *Ibid.*, f. 124.

55. Add. MSS. 32,992, f. 340.

56. Bodl. MS. Eng. letters c. 129, ff. 27–28.

57. *Ibid.*, ff. 89–90. Henrietta, Duchess of Marlborough, did provide an elaborate monument for Congreve in Westminster Abbey.

58. Tonson, *Ten Letters*, p. 18.

59. The Christian name of Temple Stanyan's first wife was Susanna. I have been unable to discover her surname. She died on March 23, 1725, and was buried on March 24 at Checkendon, Oxfordshire.

60. Add. MSS. 28,275, f. 259.

61. Lady Scudamore, the widow of Viscount Scudamore, had been a toast of the Kit-Cats in 1708. She died of smallpox in 1729 at the age of forty-four.

62. Bodl. MS. Eng. letters c. 129, f. 87.

63. Tonson, *Ten Letters*, p. 18.

64. Vanbrugh, IV, 145–146.

65. FSL Tonson MSS. C.c.1 (74). This letter was probably written in June, 1722.

66. John Dormer of the Kit-Cat Club, who had died in 1719.

67. Vanbrugh, IV, 166–167.

68. Vanbrugh died on March 26, 1726.

69. Vanbrugh, IV, 170–171.

70. See FSL Tonson MSS. C.c.1 (33).

71. Geduld, pp. 139–140, makes the unjustified assumption that Tonson gave Pope substantial editorial assistance in the latter's edition of Shakespeare, commenting: "Pope directed his instructions to Ledbury and received copious advice in return." Geduld bases his argument on nine manuscript letters from Pope to Tonson in the British Museum (Add. MSS. 28,275, ff. 229–242). These letters, however, were not addressed to Tonson the Elder at Ledbury but to Jacob junior at his bookshop in the Strand. Except for the ninth letter, which is rather cool, the letters are pleasant enough business communications, but are very different in tone from Pope's deferential letters to his elderly friend in Ledbury.

72. Spence, I, 51, 82, 208.

73. Pope, *Correspondence*, III, 176.

74. *The Letters of John Gay*, ed. C. F. Burgess (Oxford, 1966), p. 104.

75. Theobald's edition of *The Works of Shakespeare* was printed in 1733 by Jacob Tonson and five others.

76. Pope's domestic preoccupation was the tender care of Mrs. Pope, then eighty-nine and bedridden. She died at ninety-one in June, 1733.

77. Gilbert West's *The Gardens of the . . . Viscount Cobham,* published in 1732.

78. The "Man of Ross" was an unpretentious philanthropist, John Kyrle, who died at Ross in Herefordshire in 1724.

79. Pope, *Correspondence,* III, 243–244.

80. *Of the Use of Riches, an Epistle To the Right Honourable Allen Lord Bathurst,* was published in Jan., 1733.

81. Pope, *Correspondence,* III, 290–291.

82. Tonson, *Ten Letters,* p. 20.

83. *Ibid.,* p. 31.

84. Bodl. MS. Eng. letters c. 129, f. 79.

85. Tonson, *Ten Letters,* p. 31.

86. Add. MSS. 28,275, f. 164.

87. Bodl. MS. Eng. letters c. 129, f. 9.

88. *Ibid.,* f. 22.

89. *Ibid.,* f. 56.

90. Tonson, *Ten Letters,* p. 31. See Jonathan Richardson's *Explanatory Notes and Remarks on Milton's Paradise Lost* (London, 1734).

91. Bodl. MS. Eng. letters c. 129, f. 118.

92. *Ibid.,* f. 120.

93. Tonson, *Ten Letters,* p. 14.

94. In conjecturing, without evidence, that Jacob junior continued to depend on his uncle's "inspiration and supervision," Geduld, p. 21, discounts the younger publisher's initiative and ability. The nephew's hand at the helm was a firm one, and he maintained the high standards of the Tonson press.

95. Bodl. MS. Eng. letters c. 129, ff. 89–90. Congreve's library was bequeathed, with almost all of his estate, to Henrietta, Duchess of Marlborough.

96. Tonson, *Ten Letters,* p. 16. The new edition was published in 1730.

97. Bodl. MS. Eng. letters c. 129, f. 127.

98. *Ibid.,* f. 110.

99. *Ibid.,* f. 75.

100. *Ibid.,* f. 45.

101. Tonson, *Ten Letters,* p. 22.

102. Bodl. MS. Eng. letters c. 129, f. 87.

103. Jacob entered Eton in 1725 at the age of eleven. See *The Eton*

College Register 1698–1752, ed. Richard A. Austen Leigh (Eton, 1927), p. 339.

104. FSL Tonson MSS. C.c.1 (56).
105. Bodl. MS. Eng. letters c. 129, f. 116.
106. *Ibid.*, ff. 116–117.
107. Sam entered Eton in 1732, probably at the age of eleven. See *The Eton College Register*, p. 339.
108. Bodl. MS. Eng. letters c. 129, f. 118.
109. *Ibid.*, f. 120.
110. Tonson, *Ten Letters*, p. 22.
111. FSL Tonson MSS. C.c.1 (31) and (32).
112. Bodl. MS. Eng. letters c. 129, f. 75.
113. *Ibid.*, f. 46.
114. *Ibid.*, f. 87.
115. *Ibid.*, f. 90.
116. *Ibid.*, f. 105.
117. Pope had published in Feb., 1733, *The First Satire of the Second Book of Horace*.
118. Add. MSS. 28,275, ff. 491–492.
119. *Ibid.*, f. 356.
120. *Ibid.*, ff. 358–359.
121. *Ibid.*, f. 360.
122. NPG Tonson MSS.
123. Faber, *The Kit-Cat Club*, Dedication.
124. Kneller's portrait was hung at Barnes with the portraits of the club members.
125. FSL Tonson MSS. C.c.1 (56).
126. *The Gentleman's Magazine*, V (1735), 682.
127. PCC 1735, 257 Ducie.
128. See above, p. 167.
129. This letter is in the Collection of Arthur A. Houghton, Jr., of New York City. See also Pope, *Correspondence*, III, 513–514.
130. *The Gentleman's Magazine*, VI (1736), 168.
131. FSL Tonson MSS. C.c.1 (69).
132. See the parish registers of St. Mary Le Strand for this entry and entries concerning the family of Tonson's nephew. The baptism of Samuel Tonson is not recorded.
133. *The London Evening Post* (April 1–3, 1736). Appropriately, two of the pallbearers, Robert Knaplock and James Round, were prominent publishers. Temple Stanyan, whose older brother Abraham had been a Kit-Cat, was one of Tonson's intimate friends of long standing.
134. See FSL Tonson MSS. C.c.1 (58) and (59) for wills which Ton-

son made on March 19, 1731, and Jan. 27, 1734. In both of these wills Richard Tull was left a legacy of £60 a year during his life, with provision that he should receive further assistance, if necessary, from Tonson's heir and executor, Jacob junior.

135. PCC 1736, 91 Derby.

136. Elizabeth Tonson died in 1737 at the age of eighteen.

137. The career of Samuel Tonson, "late of Lincoln's Inn," ended with his early death in 1743 at about the age of twenty-two. See PCC 1743, A. A. Boycott.

138. Johnson, I, "Milton," 160.

139. Richard Tonson sat for Windsor in the House of Commons.

140. See Baker Papers (1761–1823) in the Hertfordshire County Record Office in Hertford.

141. See Baker Papers. Williams Lewis Clinton Baker now lives in Tupurupuru, Masterton, New Zealand.

142. Because the ceiling at Barnes was rather low, the size of each portrait had to be limited to thirty-six inches in height by twenty-eight in breadth, a size afterward known as the Kit-Cat size. Each half-length portrait shows one hand.

143. The portrait of Huntingdon, also an unfinished sketch, disappeared some time after 1735.

Bibliography

MANUSCRIPT SOURCES

All Souls Library, Oxford: Luttrell MSS. CLXXXI.
Bodleian Library, Oxford:
  MS. Eng. letters, c. 129, Tonson letters (1727–1731).
  MS. Eng. letters, d. 11, f. 140.
  Lister MSS. III, f. 191.
  MS. Montagu d. 18, f. 4.
  MS. Tanner 305, f. 111.
British Museum, London:
  Add. MSS 4807; 5853; 7121; 28,275–28,276, Tonson letters and
    documents; 28,887; 28,893; 32,992; 35,102; 36,933; 40,060.
  Harleian MSS. 3780.
  Lansdowne MSS. 852.
Durham University Library: Clavering letters.
Folger Shakespeare Library, Washington, D. C.:
  Tonson MSS. C.c.1 (1–83).
  MS. S.a.160.
  MS. S.a.163.
Guildhall Library, London:
  MSS. 5265/1; 6667/2; 6667/3; 6667/4; 6673/3; 6673/4;
    6673/6.
Hertfordshire County Record Office, Hertford: Baker Papers.
Henry E. Huntington Library, San Marino, Cal.:
  MS. H. M. 20052.
  Stowe MSS. 57,iii, 204.
National Portrait Gallery, London: Tonson MSS.
Nottingham University Library: Portland ((Holles) MSS. Pw 2.571.
Pierpont Morgan Library, New York City: letter (n.d.) by Jacob Tonson.
Public Record Office, London:
  Cases in Chancery: Reynardson C.9.371/41, *Tonson vs. Tonson*; Ham-
    ilton 284/283, *Tonson vs. Dickinson.*
  Patent Rolls. 6 George I. Part 3, No. 17.
  SP. 44.167.424.

Philip H. and A. S. W. Rosenbach Foundation Library, Philadelphia, Pa.: MS. 417/10.
Somerset House, London: PCC 1655, A.A. (Margaret Tonson); 1668, 147 Hene (Jacob Tonson, father of Jacob Tonson the Elder); 1690, A.A. (Richard Tonson); 1735, 257 Ducie (Jacob Tonson junior); 1736, 91 Derby (Jacob Tonson the Elder); 1743, A.A. Boycott (Samuel Tonson); 1767, 155 Legard (Jacob Tonson the third); 1772, 461 Taverner (Richard Tonson).
Stationers' Hall, London:
"Apprentices Register Book 1605 To 1666."
"Apprentices Register Book From 1666–1727."
"Freemen's Register Beginning 1605 To 1703."
University of Texas Library, Austin, Texas: five letters (1728, 1729, 1734, 1735) by Jacob Tonson.
Westminster Public Library, London: Parish registers, vol. 4, no. 5 (St. Mary Le Strand).

SELECTED REFERENCES
(Publications since 1900)

Addison, Joseph. *The Letters of Joseph Addison*, ed. Walter Graham. Oxford, 1941.
Allen, Robert J. *The Clubs of Augustan London*. Cambridge, Mass., 1933.
Barnard, John. "Dryden, Tonson, and Subscriptions for the 1697 *Virgil*," *The Papers of the Bibliographical Society of America*, LVII (1963), 129–151.
Behn, Aphra. *The Works of Aphra Behn*, ed. Montague Summers. 6 vols. London, 1915.
Beljame, Alexandre. *Men of Letters and The English Public in the Eighteenth Century, 1660–1744*, trans. E. O. Lorimer, ed. Bonamy Dobrée. London, 1948.
Bell, Walter George. *The Great Fire of London in 1666*. London, 1920.
———. *The Great Plague in London in 1665*. London, 1924.
Bickley, Francis. *The Life of Matthew Prior*. London, 1914.
Blagden, Cyprian. *The Stationers' Company, a History, 1403–1959*. London, [1960].
Bond, Donald F. "The First Printing of the *Spectator*," *Modern Philology*, XLVII (1950), 164–177.
Boswell, James. *Boswell's Life of Johnson*, ed. George Birkbeck Hill, rev. L. F. Powell, Vol. IV. Oxford, 1934.
Carswell, John. *The Old Cause*. London, 1954.
Congreve, William. *William Congreve: Letters and Documents*, ed. John C. Hodges. New York, 1964.

Cushing, Harvey. *Dr. Garth The Kit-Cat Poet, 1661–1718.* Baltimore, Md., 1906.

A Cyclopedia of Education, ed. Paul Monroe. New York, 1913.

Dale, T[homas] C[yril]. *The Inhabitants of London in 1638.* London, 1931.

Davis, Richard Beale. *George Sandys, Poet-Adventurer.* London, [1955].

Dobrée, Bonamy. *John Dryden.* London, New York, Toronto, 1956.

Dottin, Paul J. "Jacob Tonson Sent to France as a Spy on Prior," *Notes and Queries,* 12th Ser. IX ((1921), 482–483.

Dryden, John. *The Letters of John Dryden,* ed. Charles E. Ward. [Durham, N. C.], 1942.

The Eaton College Register 1698–1752, ed. Richard A. Austen Leigh. Eton, 1927.

Eighteenth Century Essays on Shakespeare, ed. David Nichol Smith. Second (revised) edition. Oxford, 1963.

Evelyn, John. *The Diary of John Evelyn,* ed. E. S. De Beer, Vol. III. Oxford, 1955.

Eves, Charles Kenneth. *Matthew Prior, Poet and Diplomatist.* Columbia University Studies in English and Comparative Literature, no. 144. New York, 1939.

Firth, Sir Charles. *The Regimental History of Cromwell's Army,* Vol. I. Oxford, 1940.

Gay, John. *The Letters of John Gay,* ed. C. F. Burgess. Oxford, 1966.
———. *The Poetical Works of John Gay,* ed. G. C. Faber. London, 1926.

Geduld, Harry M. *Prince of Publishers. A Study of the Work and Career of Jacob Tonson.* Bloomington, Ind., and London, 1969.

Green, David. *Blenheim Palace.* London, 1951.

Ham, Roswell Gray. *Otway and Lee: Biography from a Baroque Age.* New Haven, Conn., 1931.

Handover, P[hyllis] M[argaret]. *A History of the London Gazette.* London, 1965.

———. *Printing in London from 1476 to Modern Times.* Cambridge, Mass., 1960.

Hanson, Lawrence. *Government and the Press, 1695–1763.* Oxford and London, 1936.

Harris, Brice. *Charles Sackville, Sixth Earl of Dorset, Patron and Poet of the Restoration.* Illinois Studies in Language and Literature, XXVI, Nos. 3–4. Urbana, Ill., 1940.

Holmes, Geoffrey. *British Politics in the Age of Anne.* London, 1967.

Indexes to Irish Wills, ed. W. P. W. Phillimore, Vol. II. London, 1910.

Johnson, Samuel. *Lives of the English Poets*, ed. George Birkbeck Hill, Vols. I and II. Oxford, 1905.

Jones, Richard Foster, et al. *The Seventeenth Century*. Stanford, Cal., 1951.

Killanin, [Michael Morris] Lord. *Sir Godfrey Kneller and His Times*. London, 1948.

Legg, L. G. Wickham. "Extracts from Jacobite Correspondence, 1712–1714," *English Historical Review*, XXX (1915), 501–518.

————. *Matthew Prior*. Cambridge, 1915.

Lillywhite, Bryant. *London Coffee Houses*. London, 1963.

Loftis, John. *The Politics of Drama in Augustan England*. Oxford, 1963.

Macdonald, Hugh. *John Dryden, A Bibliography of Early Editions and of Drydeniana*. Oxford, 1939.

Mander, C. H. Waterland. *A Descriptive and Historical Account of the Guild of Cordwainers of the City of London*. London, 1931.

Milton, John. *The Manuscript of Milton's Paradise Lost, Book I*, ed. Helen Darbishire. Oxford, 1931.

Morrison, Paul G. *Index of Printers, Publishers, and Booksellers in Donald Wing's Short-Title Catalogue . . . 1641–1700*. Charlottesville, Va., 1955.

Mueller, William Randolph. *Spenser's Critics*. [New York], 1959.

Nitchie, Elizabeth. *Vergil and the English Poets*. New York, 1919.

Ogden, Henry V. S. and Margaret S. *English Taste in Landscape in the Seventeenth Century*. Ann Arbor, Mich., 1955.

Papali, G. F. *Jacob Tonson, Publisher. His Life and Work (1656–1736)*. [Auckland], New Zealand, 1968.

Parker, William Riley. *Milton's Contemporary Reputation*. Columbus, Ohio, 1940.

The Pension Book of Gray's Inn, 1569–1669, ed. Reginald F. Fletcher. London, 1901.

Plant, Marjorie. *The English Book Trade*. London, 1939.

Plomer, Henry R. *A Dictionary of the Booksellers and Printers Who were at Work in England, Scotland and Ireland From 1641 to 1667*. London, 1907.

————. *A Dictionary of the Printers and Booksellers Who were at Work in England, Scotland and Ireland From 1668 to 1725*. Oxford, 1922.

Plumb, J. H. *Sir Robert Walpole*. London, 1956.

Pope, Alexander. *Alexander Pope*. Twickenham Edition, Vol. IV, ed. John Butt. London, 1939.

————. *Alexander Pope, The Dunciad Variorum*, ed. Robert Kilburn Root. Princeton, N. J., 1929.

Bibliography

————. *The Correspondence of Alexander Pope*, ed. George Sherburn. 5 vols. Oxford, 1956.

————. *The Works of Alexander Pope*, ed. Whitwell Elwin and William John Courthope, Vol. VIII. New York, 1967.

Prior, Matthew. *The Literary Works of Matthew Prior*, ed. H. Bunker Wright and Monroe K. Spears. 2 vols. Oxford, 1959.

Reed, Talbot Baines. *A History of the Old English Letter Foundries*, rev. A. F. Johnson. London [1952].

Rivington, Septimus. *The Publishing Family of Rivington*. London, 1919.

Schoenbaum, Samuel. *Shakespeare's Lives*. Oxford, 1970.

Sherburn, George. *The Early Career of Alexander Pope*. New York, 1963.

Short-Title Catalogue of Books Printed in England, Scotland, Ireland, Wales, and British America and of English Books Printed in Other Countries 1641–1700, comp. Donald Wing. 3 vols. New York, 1945–1951.

Smith, David Nichol. *Shakespeare in the Eighteenth Century*. Oxford, 1928.

Smithers, Peter. *Joseph Addison*. Oxford, 1954.

The Spectator, ed. Donald F. Bond. 5 vols. Oxford, 1965.

Spence, Joseph. *Observations, Anecdotes, and Characters of Books and Men*, ed. James M. Osborne. 2 vols. Oxford, 1966.

Spurgeon, Caroline F. E. *Five Hundred Years of Chaucer Criticism and Allusion (1357–1900)*. Chaucer Society, Second Ser. 55. London [1924].

Steele, Sir Richard. *The Correspondence of Richard Steele*, ed. Rae Blanchard. London, 1941.

Straus, Ralph. *The Unspeakable Curll*. London, 1927.

Swift, Jonathan. *The Correspondence of Jonathan Swift*, ed. F. Elrington Ball. 6 vols. London, 1910–1914.

————. *Journal to Stella*, ed. Harold Williams. 2 vols. Oxford, 1948.

————. *The Poems of Jonathan Swift*, ed. Harold Williams, Vol. II. Oxford, 1937.

Swinburne, Algernon Charles. *The Complete Works of Algernon Charles Swinburne*, ed. Sir Edmund Gosse and Thomas James Wise, *Prose Works*, Vol. IV. London and New York, 1926.

The Term Catalogues, 1668–1711, ed. Edward Arber. 3 vols. London, 1903–1906.

Tickell, Richard Eustace. *Thomas Tickell and the Eighteenth Century Poets*. London, 1931.

Tonson, Jacob. *Jacob Tonson, In Ten Letters by and about Him*, ed. Sarah Lewis Carol Clapp. Austin, Texas, 1948.

A Transcript of the Registers of the Worshipful Company of Stationers, From 1640–1708 A.D. 3 vols. London, 1913–1914.

Trevellyan, George Macaulay. *England under Queen Anne.* 3 vols. London, 1930–1934.

Tucker, Joseph E. "John Davies of Kidwelly," *The Papers of the Bibliographical Society of America*, XLIV (1950), 119–151.

Van Doren, Mark. *John Dryden.* [A reissue.] Bloomington, Ind., 1960.

Van Eeghen, I. H. *Die Amsterdamse Boekhandel 1680–1725*, Vol. I. Amsterdam, 1960.

Vanbrugh, Sir John. *The Complete Works of Sir John Vanbrugh*, ed. Bonamy Dobrée and Geoffrey Webb, Vol. IV. London, 1927.

Ward, Charles E. *The Life of John Dryden.* Chapel Hill, N. C. [1961].

————. "The Publication and Profits of Dryden's Virgil," *PMLA*, LIII (1938), 807–812.

Watson, Foster. *The English Grammar Schools to 1660; Their Curriculum and Practice.* Cambridge, 1908.

Wheatley, Henry B. *Dryden's Publishers.* London, 1912.

Williams, E[lijah]. *Early Holborn and the Legal Quarter of London.* 2 vols. London, 1927.

Woodcock, George. *The Incomparable Aphra.* London [1948].

Woodman, J. F. V. *The Freedom of the City of London.* London, 1960.

Index

Daniel, le P. Gabriel, 167
Darby, J., 93
Dartiquenave, Charles, 42, 44, 45, 173, 177
D'Avenant, Charles, 14–15
D'Avenant, Henry, 110
D'Avenant, Sir William, 11, 13
D'Avenant, William, son of Sir William D'Avenant, 13–14, 15
Davies, John, 10, 16
Davis, Walter, 25
de Leeuw, Jan, 122
Defoe, Daniel, 106, 116
Denham, Sir John, 112
Dennis, John, 56, 106
Devonshire, William Cavendish, Marquis of Hartington, afterwards second Duke of, K. G., 41, 46, 57, 59, 61
A Diary, or an Exact Journal (Walbancke), 4
Dickinson, Henry, 96
Dictionnaire historique et critique (Bayle), 74, 109
Digby, Sir Kenelm, 164
The Dispensary (Garth), 43
The Distrest Mother (Philips), 111, 150
The Diverting Post, 78
Dobson, Austin, 137
Dolben, Gilbert, 32
Don Carlos (Otway), 14
Don Sebastian (Dryden), 26
Donne, John, 111
Dormer, Diana (Kirke), daughter of Lieutenant General Percy Kirke, and wife of John Dormer, 51, 52
Dormer, John, 41, 44, 45, 48, 51, 52
Dorset, Charles Sackville, sixth Earl of, K. G.: patron of Tate, 16; introduces Montague to William, 25; befriends Dryden, 26; early member of Kit-Cat Club, 38, 42; considered Augustan Horace of his day, 42; welcomes William of Orange, 43; as poet, 43; at the theater, 56–57; befriends Prior, 74
Dorset, Lionel Cranfield Sackville, seventh Earl and first Duke of, K. G., 47
Dorset, Mary (Compton), Countess

Dorset, Mary (*cont.*)
of, second wife of Charles Sackville, sixth Earl of, 43
Dorset Garden, 24, 49
Dottin, Paul J., 63
The Double-Dealer (Congreve), 69, 106
Dover, Robert, 3
Down Place, 160
The Dramatick Works of John Dryden, Esq., 35–36, 72–73, 112
Draper, Samuel, 121
Drapier's Letters (Swift), 167
Drift, Adrian, 134
The Drummer (Addison), 88, 93
Drummond, John, 63, 108
Drury Lane Theatre, 87, 93, 150
Dryden, Charles, 117
Dryden, John: plays printed by Herringman, 11; Tonson becomes his publisher, 16; works published by Tonson, 16 *seq.*, 116–121, 125; nature of relations with Tonson, 17, 27, 28–29, 30–32, 33, 35; his prefaces, 18, 28, 33, 34; services to Charles II, 18–19, 21, 27; services to James II, 20, 23, 24, 25; collaborates with Tonson in Miscellanies, 21–23, 29, 102; Dorset his patron, 26; sponsors son's play, 32; praises Congreve, 32; on Chaucer, 34, 147–148; death of, 35, 107; funeral, 56; praises Addison, 83; services to reading public, 138, 139–140, 141; services to young writers, 140; on Shakespeare, 145; on Spenser, 146; Addison qualifies praise of, 149–150; influences Pope, 150; prose style, 153
Dryden, John, Jr., 32, 117
du Guernier, Louis, 124, 125, 132
Duke, Richard, 22, 102, 117
Duke of York. *See* James II
The Duke of Guise (Dryden and Lee), 20, 98
Dunch, Edmund, 43, 53, 57, 173
Dunch, Elizabeth (Godfrey), daughter of Colonel Charles Godfrey, and wife of Edmund Dunch, 51, 52
The Dunciad (Pope), 140–141, 146

Gilliflower, Matthew, 105
Gloucester, William Henry, Duke of, son of Princess Anne and Prince George of Denmark, 120, 121
Godolphin, Francis, second Earl of, 46, 59
Godolphin, Sidney, first Earl of, 84
Gosse, Edmund, 70
Gouldman, Francis, 10
Graecae Linguae Dialecti (Maittaire), 123
Grafton, Charles Fitzroy, second Duke of, K. G., 41, 46, 57, 66, 109
Grantham, Henry D'Auverquerque, Earl of, 41
Granville (or Grenville), George, afterwards Baron Lansdowne, 59
Gray's Inn, 3, 8, 15
Gray's Inn Gate, Gray's Inn Lane, 4, 8, 14, 27, 58
Gray's Inn Gate, Holborn, 4, 8
The Great Fire, 6, 7
The Great Plague, 6–7
The Grecian History (Stanyan), 113
Green, David, 20
Grimsthorpe, 59
The Guardian (Steele), 86–87, 90, 91, 92
Guildhall, 7

Halifax, Charles Montague, first Baron, afterwards third Earl of, K. G.: joint author with Prior of *The Hind and the Panther Transversed*, 24–25, 45, 74–75; political career, 44; writes verses for Kit-Cat Club, 51, 54–55; at the theater, 57; subscribes to building of Haymarket Theatre, 57; subscribes to fund to encourage acting of good comedies, 58; confers with Tonson, 61; conveys copy of Regency Act to Elector of Hanover, 61; Prior addresses poem to, 75; Prior's letter of apology to, 80; patronage of Addison, 84; relations with Congreve, 138
Halifax, George Savile, first Marquess of, 27
Hamilton, James Hamilton, fourth Duke of, 46
Hamlet (Shakespeare), 129
Hampstead Heath, 40, 41–42

Handel, George Frederick, 33
Harley, Edward. *See* Oxford, second Earl of
Harley, Robert. *See* Oxford, first Earl of
Harper, Charles, 101
Harrison, John, 42
Hart Hall, Oxford, 170
Hartington, Marquess of. *See* Devonshire, Earl of
Hawksmoor, Nicholas, 59
Haymarket Theatre, 57, 58, 59, 156
The Hazels, 158, 159, 160, 169
Henley, Anthony, 42
Hereford, 170
The Heroine Musqueteer, 15
Herringman, Henry, 11, 16, 112
Hertford, Algernon Seymour, Earl of, 83, 109
Hervey, Stephen, 125
Heveningham, Henry, 49
Hewson, Colonel John, 5
Heylin, Peter, 10
Heyrick, Samuel, 8
Heywood, Thomas, 3
The Hind and the Panther (Dryden), 24–25, 74
The Hind and the Panther Transvers'd To the Story of The Country-Mouse and the City-Mouse (Prior and Montague), 24–25, 45, 74–75
Hindmarsh, Joseph, 26
Hinton, Edward, 56
An Historical and Critical Dictionary (tr. from Bayle's text), 112
The History of Barbados (Davies), 11
The History of England (Echard), 113
The History of England During the Reigns of the Royal House of Stuart (Oldmixon), 152, 167
The History of the League (Dryden), 21, 104
The History of the Most Renowned and Religious Princess, Elizabeth (Camden), 105
The History of Richard the Second (Tate), 98
Holborn, 1, 2, 3, 5, 6, 7, 8
Hollar, Wenceslaus, 120
Hollyport, 159

Pope, Alexander: works published by Tonson, 67, 68; publishes edition of Shakespeare, 68, 145; relations with Jacob junior, 68, 145, 165, 166; on Congreve, 69, 152; satirizes Tonson in "Sandys' Ghost," 124–125, and in manuscript version of *The Dunciad*, 140–141; on Maittaire, 140; on Chaucer, 148; on Dryden, 150; friendship with Tonson, 165–167, 174

Popish Plot, 97

"Popping, S." *See* Curll

Pordage, Samuel, 15

Porter, Edward, 151

Powell, Thomas, 167

Power, Thomas, 117

The Pretender. *See* James Francis Edward Stuart, Prince

Prideaux, Henry, 96–97, 113

Prior, Matthew: with Charles Montague writes *The Hind and the Panther Transvers'd*, 24–25, 45, 74–75; contributes to Miscellanies, 29, 76, 78, 110; expelled from Kit-Cat Club, 42, 59; votes for impeachment of Whig ministers, 45; early diplomatic career, 45; describes Tonson's manner of toasting, 49; composes verses for Kit-Cat Club, 55; reports on revival of *The Humours of Sir John Falstaff*, 56–57; "Mat's Peace," 63; Tonson spies on in Paris, 63–64; early life, 74; first poems, 74–76; works published by Tonson, 76 *seq.*, 111, 115, 134–137; pirated editions of, 78, 79–81, 135; on Spenser, 78, 147; end of diplomatic career, 81–82; fastidious supervision of 1718 edition, 134–135, 136–137

The Procession (Steele), 88, 91

Prologue Spoken at Court Before the Queen (Prior), 77

Prologue to the Duchess (Dryden), 20

Prologue to the Duke (Dryden), 20

Pulteney, Daniel, 110

Pulteney, William, afterwards Earl of Bath, 46, 173

Punch Club, 53

Purcell, Henry, 28

Rabutin, Roger de. *See* Bussy, comte de

Raby, Thomas Wentworth, Baron, later Earl of Strafford, 110

Racine, Jean Baptiste, 14, 150

Radcliffe, Alexander, 18

Radcliffe, Dr. John, 161

Ramillies, battle of, 77

The Reader (Steele), 91

The Reform'd Wife (Burnaby), 57

Regency Act, 60, 65

The Rehearsal (Buckingham), 35

Religio Laici (Dryden), 20, 22

Remarks on Several Parts of Italy (Addison), 84–85

Remarks upon Cato (Dennis), 151

A Report from the Committee of Secrecy, 113–114

Rialton, Lady. *See* Marlborough, Henrietta, Duchess of

Richardson, Jonathan, 167

Richardson, Samuel, 111

Richmond and Lennox, Charles Lennox, first Duke of, K. G., 46, 57, 59

Riversdale of Rathcormac, Colonel William (Hull) Tonson, first Baron, 8

Rogers, Samuel, 127

Rolij, Johannes, 110

The Roman History (Echard), 105, 113

Rosamond (Addison), 85

Roscommon, Wentworth Dillon, fourth Earl of, 22, 102

Round, James, 175

The Rover (Behn), 99

Rowe, Nicholas, 47, 56, 111, 112, 114, 125, 129–132, 145

Royal Society, 43, 44

Rymer, Thomas, 15, 17, 22, 29, 35, 127, 130

Sacheverell, Henry, 61–62, 113

Sackville, Lady Mary. *See* Beaufort, Duchess of

St. Albans, Diana de Vere, Duchess of, daughter of Aubrey de Vere, and wife of Charles Beauclerk, first Duke of St. Albans, 51

Jacob Tonson, Kit-Cat Publisher
has been cast on the Linotype in Caslon Old
Face with two-point spacing between the
lines. To preserve the continuity of design,
Monotype Caslon Old Style #337 was selected for display. The richness of kerned
swash italic characters in display (the typo-
phile will note that the printer has carefully
morticed the verso running heads) has permitted calligraphic embellishment from the
eighteenth-century source, *Calligraphia La-
tina.* The University of Tennessee Press is indebted to the Dover Publications, Inc., 1958
edition of *Calligraphy* by Johann Georg
Schwandner for these classic forms.

The book has been designed by Jim Bill-
ingsley; composed and printed by Heritage
Printers, Inc., Charlotte, North Carolina;
and bound by the Nicholstone Book Bindery,
Nashville, Tennessee.